# FISHING IN SOUTHERN CALIFORNIA

## THE COMPLETE GUIDE

Ken Albert

BOOKS

119 Richard
Aptos, CA 95003
(408) 688-7535

ISBN   0-934061-01-7

Cover Design:   Electric Art Studios
                Mountain View, CA


Printed By:   Delta Lithograph
              Van Nuys, CA

Carol,
Last book, in the dedication, I promised we'd
do something really important for a change . . .
I promised we'd fish more often.  This time
let's really do it!

Eat all day long . . . not possible.
Drink all day long . . . not good.
Sex all day long . . . not any more.
Fish all day long . . . why not!

## Acknowledgements

First and foremost, a special thanks to Carol, my wife and best friend. This book wouldn't exist without her. Thanks to all those good people in whole-saling, retailing and publishing for your support and encouragement. Thanks to Spiros at Electric Art Studios and Dan at Penaflor Litho Prep for a fine cover. Pat Arthur, thanks for your tireless proof reading. And finally, thanks to the many fishing experts who unselfishly shared their knowledge and insights.

## Two Great Fishing Books

Marketscope Books also publishes the best selling **Fishing in Northern California**, (8½x11, 228 pages), layed out just like the SoCal book. It includes How To Catch Sections on salmon, steelhead, sturgeon, shad, kokanee, lingcod, sharks, rockcrab and crawdads as well as sections on all major NorCal waters(19 lakes, San Francisco Bay, The Delta, many rivers and the ocean).

**Order Your Copy Today**

|  | Price | Sales Tax | Total Price | Qty | Total Amount |
|---|---|---|---|---|---|
| ☐ **Fishing in Southern California** | $13.95 | $ .90 | $14.85 | ____ | _____ |
| ☐ **Fishing in Northern California** | $12.95 | $ .85 | $13.80 | ____ | _____ |

Postage and Handling(1st book $1.25; each additional $ .50 . . . . . . . . . . . . . . _____

Check Enclosed . . . . _____

☐ **Special offer**(order **Fishing in Southern California** and **Fishing in Northern California** and we'll pay postage and handling).

Check Enclosed . . . . $28.65

Name _____

Address _____

_____

Send Your Order To: **Marketscope Books, Box 171, Aptos, CA 95001**

(Permission is granted to Xerox this page)

# Contents

Continued . . .

# Contents (continued)

# Great Fishing

Fishing is great in Southern California. There are thousands of lakes, streams and reservoirs, many very accessible to metropolitan areas. Then there are the big inland fisheries like the Salton Sea and Lake Havasu. And last but not least, there are the hundreds of miles of coastline, offshore islands and Baja waters. Anglers here are fortunate to have an immense variety of quality fishing opportunities;

- Rainbow, golden and brown trout in Sierra lakes and streams.

- Largemouth bass, trout, striper, catfish, crappie and bluegill in numerous lakes and reservoirs.

- Surfperch, bass, bonita, barracuda, halibut and croakers in coastal inshore waters.

- Yellowtail, albacore, rockfish, marlin and lingcod in the Pacific.

- Corvina, sargo and tilapia in the Salton Sea.

- Bass, stripers, trout, catfish and panfish in the Colorado River Lakes.

- Wahoo, dorado and other exotics in the Pacific off Baja.

And most of this great fishing is accessible, quite simple and requires only modestly priced tackle. An added benefit, fishing is a wonderful way to share the outdoor experience with the entire family.

But the immense variety of the Southern California fishing experience does raise many questions. Some major, others just puzzling;

- What size hook(or line) do I use for trout(or catfish)?
- Where are the bass hotspots at Casitas or Hodges?
- How do I catch striper in Havasu or Pyramid?
- If I catch a halibut(or catfish, or a . . .), how do I clean it?
- When is the hot halibut season in Santa Monica Bay?
- What is a spinnerbait?
- Can I fish for bass from shore at Lower Otay?
- Where are the best spots to fish at the Salton Sea?
- How do I clean and cook a corvina?

**Fishing in Southern California** answers all these questions and many, many more. For all of the types of fish and different locations, it tell **how** to fish, **where** to fish and **when** to fish. It tells what **equipment, tackle, rigs, bait** and **lures** to use, how to **clean** and **preserve** your catch and how to **cook** each fish.

A comprehensive SoCal fishing map is on the next page.

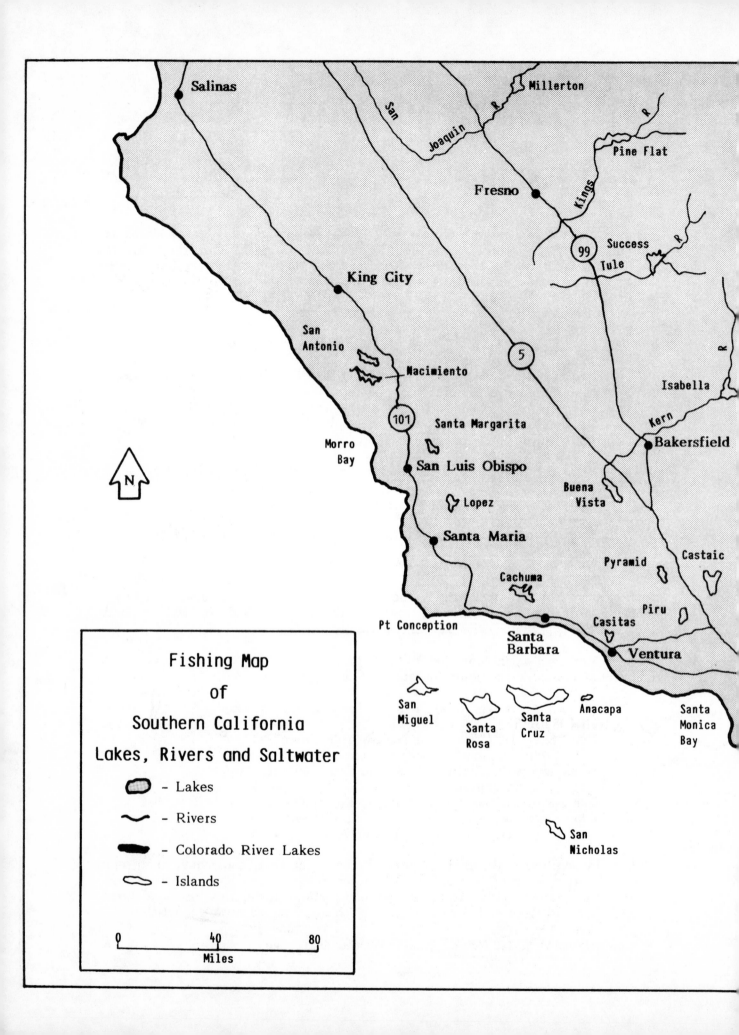

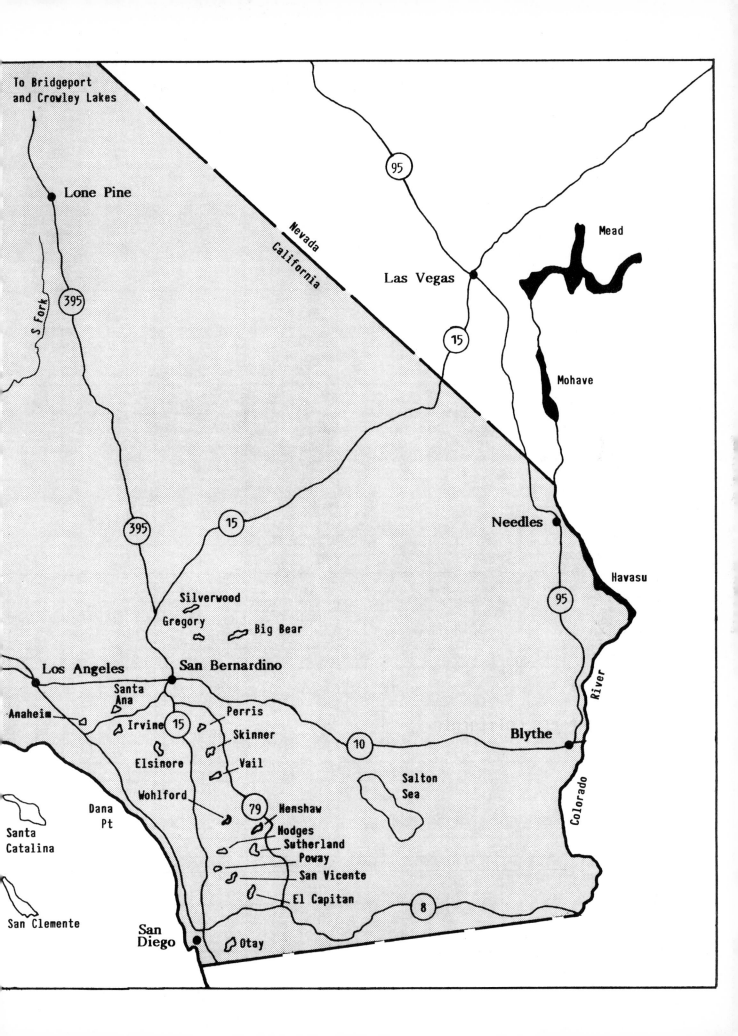

# Take a Kid Fishing—One Story

My thirteen year old son, Bruce, had been after me for months to go fishing with him in tiny Lake Freedom, about four miles from our home. He'd heard at school that kids had caught some nice bass there. So late one Saturday afternoon, we loaded our rowboat in the pick-up and drove to the lake.

I took my big, old metal tackle box. It had been my father's box. He had it packed with everything that was "state of the art" in the 1930's. He was killed in an industrial accident when I was a teenager. I inherited his love for fishing and his big, metal tackle box.

All the lures that my father used 40 and 50 years ago to entice the lunker bass are still in that metal box. But actually I hardly ever use any of his lures, since they're almost antiques and I don't want to lose them. Besides, I score most with spinnerbait and plastic worms. This is what Bruce and I were using at Lake Freedom and we were getting skunked. The sun had set and I was ready to go home for dinner.

For some reason Bruce looked into his grandfather's tackle box, spotted an old red bucktail with three small fish-shaped flashers that protected the hook. "Dad, why don't you try this? It's sort of like a spinnerbait, isn't it?" he asked.

"Yea, I guess it is," I responded, as I continued to work my worm.

"Come on, try it. Let's see how it swims."

"O.K., we'll give it a try."

I decided to humor him, so I put it on and pulled it beside the boat to watch the action. "It looks pretty good. Like a spinnerbait," I said. Bruce agreed.

My first cast with this well-built, old relic landed near some overhanging branches. When I began my retrieve, the line stiffened and my rod arched. "Damn, I've snagged an underwater branch," I said under my breath. I was upset. I didn't want to lose that lure. For some reason, I didn't want to lose anything from that old, metal box. But, then the snag began to "run" and take line against my drag. What do you know, I had a strike on the first cast of a lure that hadn't been in the water since before World War II.

We landed the bass. It was a beauty. Bruce couldn't resist the temptation to say, "See, Dad, I told you so. Those old lures are good."

"They sure are," I said, grinning.

Then we agreed that the fish should be released. Lake Freedom needed that bass, and we needed to know that it was alive and well. After all, it and that old lure performed 3 minor miracles. It was that old lure that gave Bruce and I a wonderful moment together. That old lure made me cherish my father's tackle box even more. And, it tied together a grandfather and grandson who never knew each other, except for a few moments at Lake Freedom.

Bruce switched to one of his grandfather's spinnerbait-like lures and we each made a few more casts into the twilight. Then Bruce said, "Dad, let's go home. I don't want to risk losing this lure. We can't see the overhanging branches." I nodded and we rowed to shore.

During the drive home, Bruce chattered about how to tell Mom our fishing story and how to convince her with no fish as proof. But, I was thinking about something else. I was thinking that someday Bruce would be a loving keeper of that big metal tackle box and those old lures.

# Fishing Tips

There is one element of fishing success that can't be taught or learned. Rather, it must be self-instilled. I'm talking about self-confidence. Often "how-to" fishing articles end with a pep talk on the importance of fishing with confidence - that old Positive Mental Attitude. You know it's corny, but somehow it works.

I personally feel so strongly about the need to have faith in your approach and your tackle, that I've reversed things and put this topic first. I love fishing even when I don't catch fish. But I love it even more when I do. Often the only difference between an angler who puts fish on the line and one who just wets his line, is attitude. So fish with confidence.

Confidence will make you more attentive and more aware. It keeps your mind in gear. But, most importantly, it will encourage you to experiment, to change baits, or lures, or depths, or location until you find fish. This book tells you all you need to know to catch any kind of fish in Southern California. Just add self-confidence. The positive effects of perseverence, confidence and variety of approach can't be over emphasized.

## When to Fish

There is no question that the time of year, the time of month and the time of day all impact on fishing success. More so, for some species, than others. All life moves in cycles. Fish are no different. For example, it's no coincidence, that most of California's fishing records were set in the spring months. March, April and May are probably the best months to fish. These are the spawning months. Simply stated, here are the best times to fish;

### Time of Year

Spring is best all around, followed by fall. Winter is surprisingly good. Summer, for many species is the worst. Yes, I know about summer vacations; the weather is beautiful and fishing seems to be a natural, warm weather sport, but often the fish don't know this. Or maybe they do! However, some fishing is good in summertime, especially if the proper approaches are followed. On the next page is a table that highlights the best time of year to fish for each species. It's easy to see why fishing is a four season sport in Southern California.

### Time of Day

For most types of fish, during most times of the year, there is little doubt

# Best Time to Fish

**Fishing Seasons** (+=good, -=fair)

| Species | J | F | M | A | M | J | J | A | S | O | N | D |
|---|---|---|---|---|---|---|---|---|---|---|---|---|
| Abalone | - |  | - | - | - | - | - | - | + | - | - | - |
| Albacore |  |  |  |  |  |  | - | + | + | - | - |  |
| Barracuda |  |  | - | - | + | + | + | - | - | - |  |  |
| Bass(largemouth) |  | - | + | + | + | - | - | - | - | + | - |  |
| Bluegill |  | - | + | + | + | - | - | - | - | - |  |  |
| Bonito | - |  | - | - | - | - | - | - | + | + | + | + |
| Calico Bass | - | - | - | - | + | + | + | + | - | - | - | - |
| Catfish |  | - | - | - | - | + | + | + | + | + | - |  |
| Crappie |  | - | + | + | + | - | - | - | - | - | - |  |
| Crawdads |  | - | - | - | - | - | - | - | - | - | - |  |
| Grunion |  |  | + |  |  | + | + | + |  |  |  |  |
| Halibut | - | - | + | + | + | + | + | + | + | - | - | - |
| Lingcod | + | + | - | - | - | - | - | - | - | - | + | + |
| Marlin(striped) |  |  |  |  |  |  |  | - | + | + | - |  |
| Rockfish | - | - | - | - | - | + | + | + | - | - | - | - |
| Striped Bass |  |  |  |  |  |  |  |  |  |  |  |  |
|   -Reservoirs | - | + | + | + | + | - | - | - | - | + | + | - |
|   -Col. R. Lakes |  | - | + | + | + | + | - | - | - | + | + |  |
| Trout |  |  |  |  |  |  |  |  |  |  |  |  |
|   -Streams |  |  |  | + | + | + | - | - | + | + | + |  |
|   -Lakes | + | + | + | + | - | - | - | - | - | - | + | + |
|   -Golden |  |  |  |  |  |  |  | + | + | - |  |  |
| White Sea Bass | - | + | + | + | - | - | - | - | - | - | - | - |
| Yellowtail |  |  | - | + | + | + | - | - | + | - |  |  |

that early morning(from first light until 8-9am) and late evening(the 2-3 hours before dark) are the best times of day to catch fish. These are the times of day when fish are active and feeding. For some situations night time is also good. For example, bass fishing after dark on warm summer nights, using noisy, dark surface plugs(in shallow water) can be good. Also, summertime catfishing can be good from 9-12pm and during the two hours before daybreak.

## Time of Month(The Tides)

Some would say that the phases of the moon have a great deal to do with fishing success, in any environment. This may or may not be true. But, there is no doubt that tides do impact fishing success in shallower tidal waters like bays. Surf, rock and pier anglers know how tide movements effect fishing. In tidal waters, it's always best to fish on days when there is a big change between high and low tide. Waters move faster, bait and bait fish get moved around, so game fish feed more actively.

The height of the tide varies according to the positions of the sun and moon in relation to the earth. These influences are illustrated below. The best fishing is during spring tide periods. Fish the hours before, through and after a high tide change for peak action.

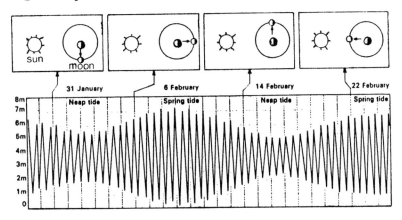

### More on the Moon

There is a school of fishing thought that says that the position of the moon(or some say the moon and the sun), on a daily basis, has an effect on the feeding and activity level of fish. These peak activity periods coincide with the moon's strongest gravitational pull which occurs twice each day when the moon is directly above or below a particular point on earth. When the moon is above, it's a major period, and when it's below it's a minor period, according to the theory. These activity periods are published in California outdoor newspapers and in magazines like "Field and Stream". Or a guide can be purchased to calculate major and minor acitvity periods each day. If nothing else, it's fun to see if the activity periods coincide with ones own fishing experience.

## Where to Fish

This book has tons of "where to fish" information in it. But there are three generalizations about "where to fish" that apply so universally, that they are worthy of special note.

### Fish on the Bottom!

To catch many varieties of Southern California fish you've got to fish on or near the bottom.  This is true for;

. Bass - even in deep water they're usually near structures.

. Catfish

. Halibut

. Lingcod

. Rockfish

. Striped bass(in shallow water)

. Trout - Stream trout will rise up for food, but then retreat to the
    bottom.  Trout near shore in lakes, are on the bottom.

I'd like to emphasize the truism, "fish on the bottom" with this analogy.  Most creatures that live on land, actually live on the bottom of a vast sea of atmosphere.  This atmosphere is about 100,000 feet deep, yet most creatures live right on the bottom of the atmosphere.  Of course, people and all fur bearing animals live on the bottom, but so do most birds and insects.  Birds and insects spend most of their time in and around the ground, plants and trees that are part of the atmospheres bottom structure.  Well, the same is true of most fish. Water is their atmosphere.  And the bottom of the water is their land.  It provides food, shelter and security.

**Fish at the Right Water Temperatures**

In some Southern California lakes and reservoirs, the key factor in finding fish during the summer months is water temperature.  Often lakes stratify into three distinct layers with the coming of summer and stay that way for extended periods.  The middle layer of water, called the thermocline, has a large concentration of dissolved oxygen, bait fish and therefore, trout and kokanee. The thermocline, which provides the right temperature for gamefish metabolism, is down from 10-80 feet, depending on season and lake characteristics.

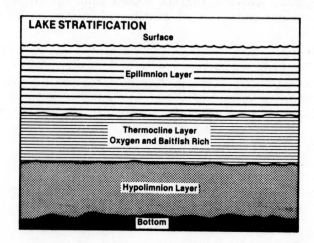

Gauges for measuring water temperatures at various depths are available for as little as $5-$10. Below is a chart showing the temperatures where you are likely to find fish;

| Species | Optimum Temperature | Temperature Range |
|---|---|---|
| Trout, brook and brown | 53° | 44-75° |
| Trout, rainbow | 56 | 44-75 |
| Bass, largemouth | 70-72 | - |
| Bass, striped | 70-72 | 60-78 |
| Panfish | 64-66 | - |
| Albacore | 64 | - |
| Yellowtail | 65 | - |

**Fish Don't Like Direct Light**

This is one reason why fishing drops off then the morning sun hits a lake. But, there are things you can do. For instance, if you're catching fish in a lake early in the day, try deeper down as the light increases. Or, if you're fishing a trout stream, work the shady side. This also applies to lake shores.

## Casting

Casting is an integral part of most fishing activities. This is true whether you bait fish with a sliding sinker rig for trout in a lake, or yellowtail live bait fish on a party boat. And it's also true that better, more accurate casts, catch more fish.

Casting with spinning or spincast equipment is quite straightforward, but accurate casting takes some practice. Freshwater or saltwater conventional reel rigs are more difficult to master because of backlash, but good equipment and practice will pay off here too. Novice anglers should read up on the subject at the library and observe more experienced casting whenever possible.

Flycasting is different. In spinning or baitcasting the weight that is cast is concentrated in the lure or bait. And it is the weight that pulls line off the reel. But in flycasting, the offering is virtually weightless, and it is the fly line that is the weight. Flycasting is probably the most difficult casting skill to develop. A good book on the subject is "Fly Fishing from the Beginning."

## Playing and Landing

A variety of fishing techniques are needed to entice a fish to bite or strike. Once this is accomplished, whether you've got a bass or an albacore on the other end of your line, there is a certain commonality in playing a larger fish. Here are the elements;

1. Pull the rod up and back forcefully to set the hook. Don't be tentative. Hold the reel handle firmly, so no line is given. After setting, adjust the drag, if necessary.

2. Hold the rod tip up when playing a fish. The rod butt should be held against the stomach area. Lower the rod tip and reel in, simultaneously. Pump the rod upwards to move the fish in. Then again reel in on the down stroke. This rod "pumping" allows you to reel in when tension on the line and terminal tackle is not at its maximum.

3. Never give a fish slack. If it charges, reel in fast. Try to guide fish away from your boat with rod tip high. But, if the fish does get under your boat, put the rod tip down into the water to prevent line abrasion or twisting around the outdrive.

4. If your fish runs, let him go against the drag. That's what it's for. Then, slowly bring him back by reeling in, or if necessary, using the pumping technique.

5. Keep the rod tip high while landing. This allows the rod to act as a shock absorber and prevents the chance of slack line. Net the fish from below and in front.

## Catch and Release

There is a growing awareness among anglers that the fish resource is limited. And some anglers now feel that the ultimate fishing experience is not to "take a limit" but to catch and release as many fish as possible. Of course, no one should keep more fish than they can use, or keep a fish that they don't enjoy eating.

Obviously, catch and release is a personal decision. It's also a practice that can be and should be exercised on a selective basis. Sometimes a fish shouldn't be released - for example, a badly hooked, bleeding fish, or a small rockfish that has been brought up from 50 fathoms, and is dead on arrival. For some reason, I personally don't like to take fish that are about to spawn. I know this is somewhat irrational since it's absolutely true that wherever in a fishes lifecycle, you take it, you're forever preventing that fish from spawning. But I guess I just feel that when a fish has made it through all the hurdles and survived all the predators and all the hazards, that it has a right to spawn without me interferring. On the other hand, I don't mind taking fish that are in abundant supply or even those that are planted regularly.

When you do want to release fish, there are several things you can do to improve the chances for the fish;

1. Use barbless hooks(or flatten down barbs with a pliers).

2. Avoid fishing with bait, if possible, and if you do use bait, don't use a sliding sinker rig. Hookings with sliding sinker rigs are often very deep.

3. Use a needlenose pliers to remove hooks.

4. Hold the unhooked fish in a swimming position in the water and quickly move it forward repeatedly, to force water through its gills. Do this until the fish revives enough to struggle and swim out of your hands.

## Rods and Reels

How-to-catch each of the major sport fishes in Southern California is described in detail in this book. There are 19 of them in all. Rod and reel recommendations are made in each section. But, not only are the most desirable rod and reel combinations noted, but so are alternatives that often work just as well. So happily, you don't need 19 rod and reel sets to enjoy all the fishing experiences in this book.

Often, one rod and reel is useful in several types of fishing. For example, a lightweight spinning outfit can be used to troll or cast for average striper(6-10 pounds). This same light spinning outfit can be used for trout(both lake and stream), bass casting and panfishing. In fact, an angler doesn't even need a fly rod and reel to fly fish, but don't tell avid fly anglers this. A casting bobber on spinning equipment will deliver a fly. See Catching Trout(in streams). And talking about stream trout fishing, one hot item now is the mini-spinning outfit - a 5 foot rod and tiny reel. It's fun to use, but spinners can also usually be delivered effectively using a 7 foot rod and normal sized reel filled with a 4 pound test line.

Saltwater equipment is usually more specialized. There are light(12-15 pound test line) and medium(20-25 pound test line)live bait rod and reel outfits. And then there are rods for jigging that are designed for 20-50 pound test line. Bottom fishing and surf casting equipment are also quite distinct. Try to purchase equipment that best suits the type of fishing you do most often. For many anglers a light or medium weight saltwater spinning outfit is a good choice. But make sure it has a strong, smooth drag mechanism and the capacity to hold 200 yards of 10-20 pound test line.

Fortunately, rods and reels of good quality(not goldplated, but good quality) are not that expensive. But, before considering a specialized rod and reel, first consider using what you've got on hand. Look at what others are using when you get to the water. I'm always surprised at the variety. Besides, the fish doesn't know what's on the other end of the line. Good line, tied well, a decent drag and know how will land most fish.

## Knots, Hooks and Line

A good fishing knot is one that stays tied and one that doesn't weaken the line too much. There are many knots that fit these criteria, but most veteran anglers use only one or two basic knots. The best overall knot is probably the improved clinch knot. It can be used to tie hooks to leaders, swivels to line, etc. There are two versions;

An often neglected item is the fishing hook. It's important to keep them sharp. Inexpensive little sharpeners are made just for this purpose. Both bait hooks and lure hooks get abused, in use, and in tackle boxes, so do sharpen them regularly.

The designation  system used in fishing hook sizing can be confusing for those who don't deal with it regularly;

- Large hooks(1/0 and up) increase in size as the number increases. (So a 4/0 is a larger hook than a 2/0).

- Small hooks(1 and down) decrease in size as the number increases. (So a 6 is a larger hook than a 10).

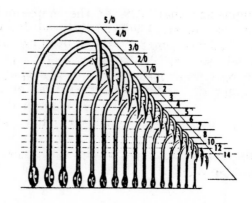

A leading hook manufacturer(Eagle Claw) makes the following hook size recommendations;

. Panfish:  Bluegill - 8 down to 12
            Crappie - 4

. Bass:     Smallmouth - 3/0 down to 4
            Largemouth - 8/0 down to 4
            Striped    - 3/0 up to 10/0

. Catfish:  up to 5#  - 4 down to 12
            large     - 4 up to 8/0

. Trout:    Rainbow   - 5 down to 14
            Brown     - 5 down to 14

Good quality fishing line is a wise investment.  Monofilament is appropriate for most fishing, and consider the flourescent feature.  It helps immensely in seeing where your bait and line is.

## Chart Recorder

A chart recording sonar(either paper or video) is the eyes and ears of any angler operating from a boat.  This device prints out a profile of the shape of the bottom and the shadows of bait schools and individual large fish.  Actually, the flasher-type depth sounder provides the same imformation, but this equipment requires more experience and judgment to use effectively.  Chart recorders are very helpful in saltwater fishing for rock cod and lingcod and for freshwater bass, striper and trout fishing.  There's little doubt that the proper use of a boat mounted chart recorder gives the angler an  edge - it allows him to "almost" see the fish.

## Maps

First, let me emphasize that none of the maps included in this book(or in any fishing book, for that matter) are to be used for navigational purposes.  Their only intent is to indicate where the fish can be found.  Navigational maps for coastal and bay waters are available at marine and boating stores.  These are published by the National Oceanic and Atmospheric Administration(U.S. Department of Commerce).

There are other good maps that are especially useful to anglers;

**U.S. Forest Service Maps** - especially useful in determining which land is publicly owned.

- **U.S. Geological Survey** - good for detailed topographical features and for locating out-of-the-way fishing spots.

- **U.S. Bureau of Land Management** - for streams and lakes in this agency's jurisdiction.

- **Park Scenic Maps** - both federal and state parks publish maps that can be quite helpful.

- **Recreational Lakes of California** - a book of lakes with maps and facilities.

- **Kym Guides** - publish about 40 different map guides for Southland waters.

- **Lake Topographical Maps** - when available, these are very helpful in locating likely fish holding areas.

# Regulations

Fishing regulations in California are simple and straightforward, but they are also detailed and specific. A Fish and Game Commission publication, "California Sport Fishing Regulations, A Summary" is available free at any location where fishing licenses are sold. This is a fact filled, well-organized brochure that has all you need to know about current regulations. Read it over and know the rules. I'm always bothered when I see a young child on a camping trip unknowingly violating regulations that are designed to protect the young fish. Parents should be aware of the regulations and supervise their children.

# Organizations and Publications

Some of the most active fishing organizations and some of the best publications for up-to-date Southern California fishing information are;

- California Angler
  Hare Publications
  6200 Yarrow Drive
  Carlsbad, CA 92008
  (619)438-2511

- Fishing and Hunting News
  Southern California Edition
  511 Eastlake Avenue E
  Seattle, WA 98109
  (206)624-2738

- Western Outdoor News
  3197-E Airport Loop Drive
  Costa Mesa, CA 92626
  (714)546-4370

- United Anglers of California
  1360 Neilsen Street
  Berkeley, CA 94702
  (415)526-4049

## California Angling Records

Athletes always say "records are made to be broken." Maybe that's **still** true of fishing records too. Sixty five percent(or 17 out of 26) of the records listed below were set in the 1970's and 1980's. Five were set since January 1980!

| Species | Weight (lb+oz) | Where Caught | Date |
|---|---|---|---|
| Barracuda | 15-15 | San Onofre | Aug 57 |
| Bass | | | |
|   -calico | 14-7 | San Clementi I. | Jul 58 |
|   -sand | 11-2 | Pt. Dume | Aug 74 |
|   -white sea | 17-4 | San Diego | Apr 50 |
| Bass(largemouth) | 21-3½ | Lake Casitas | Mar 80 |
| Bluegill | 2-10½ | Lake Los Serranos | May 76 |
| Bonito | 22-3 | Malibu Cove | Jul 78 |
| Catfish | | | |
|   -blue | 36-13 | Lake Jennings | Aug 77 |
|   -channel | 41 | Lake Casitas | Aug 72 |
|   -flathead | 55 | Colorado River | Apr 80 |
| Corvina | 36-8 | Salton Sea | May 80 |
| Crappie | | | |
|   -black | 4-1 | New Hogan Lake | Mar 75 |
|   -white | 4-8 | Clear Lake | Apr 71 |
| Halibut(California) | 53-8 | Santa Rosa I. | May 75 |
| Lingcod | 53 | Tinidad | 1969 |
| Rockfish(cabezon) | 23-4 | Los Angeles | Apr 58 |
| Sargo | 4-1 | Salton Sea | 1972 |
| Striped Bass | 65 | San Joaquin River | May 51 |
| Trout | | | |
|   -brook | 9-12 | Silver Lake | Sep 32 |
|   -brown | 26-5 | Lower Twin Lake | May 83 |
|   -golden | 9-8 | Virginia Lake | Aug 52 |
|   -rainbow | 27-4 | Smith River | Dec 76 |
| Tuna | | | |
|   -albacore | 73-8 | San Diego | Nov 82 |
|   -bluefin | 71-4 | San Diego | Sep 72 |
|   -yellowfin | 218 | San Diego | Sep 70 |
| Yellowtail | 62 | La Jolla | Jun 53 |

# Introduction to "How to Catch..."

Many fishing books are jam packed with interesting, colorful information. But they have one glaring shortcoming. They never answer the question "how". Our purpose in the next 19 sections is to remedy this problem. So if you want to know "how to catch . . ." just look in the appropriate section. The explanations are simple, straightforward, complete and understandable. And the fish are in alphabetical order for easy reference. And here they are . . .

Abalone
Albacore
Barracuda
Bass
Bluegill
Bonito
Calico Bass(and Sand Bass)
Catfish
Crappie
Grunion
Halibut
Marlin(Striped)
Rockfish
Striped Bass
Trout(in Streams)
Trout(in Lakes)
Trout(Golden)
White Sea Bass
Yellowtail

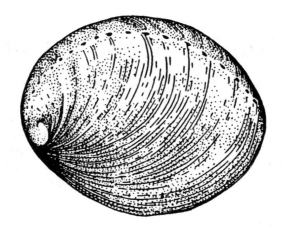

# How to Catch...Abalone

Abalone is a rock-clinging, single-shelled creature that inhabits shoreline waters (especially where there are concentrations of rocks and kelp) along the coast and islands of California. It has a large, fleshy foot and sensory projections on its underside. Most all seaside gift shop browsers have seen an eye-catching display of abalone shells. And those who have ordered them on restaurant menus know how delicious it is. But it's possible for anyone, with some insight and a little luck, to enjoy catching, preparing and eating abalone. That's what this section and each of the other "How To Catch" sections is all about.

## Fishing Techniques

There are three basic techniques for taking abalone;

1. Rockpicking - searching the rocky shore on foot.

2. Free Diving - diving near shore with a snorkel only(no aqualung).

3. Scuba Diving - diving with an aqualung.

North of Yankee Point(at Monterey), only rockpicking and free diving are allowed. But all three approaches are allowed and are practiced in Southern California waters. Although it is only fair to say that scuba divers probably are the most successful.

**Rockpickers** operate at low tides. Preferably a minus low tide and a calm ocean.

They start about an hour before the low tide and quit before the incoming tide threatens a soaking, or being stranded away from shore.

The basic technique is to comb an area looking for abalone attached to rocks. Often it is best to feel underwater in crevices and cracks that other rockpickers have missed.

**Free Divers** operate in the water. The wise ones in pairs, taking turns diving down to rocky bottoms in 5-30 feet of water. Abalone are pried off the rocks with a metal bar. Since this can fatally injure the abalone, it is best to be sure the abalone is of legal size before prying it off. Rockpickers must also make this judgment. To pry the abalone off the rock and avoid injuring it, slip the bar under the abalone. Then lift the handle end up, pushing the tip of the bar against the rock. This prevents injury to the abalone foot. If it is undersize, hold the abalone back on the spot where it was taken until it grabs hold itself.

Free diving lessons are available at selected locations along the coast. No one should attempt to free dive without proper instruction.

**Scuba divers** love abalone hunting, but investing the necessary time and money to learn to scuba dive just to catch abalone isn't worth it to most people. But exploring the undersea world with scuba equipment is a joy itself. Plus, scuba divers not only seek out abalone, but may also spear fish for lingcod, rockfish, halibut, etc. Since scuba divers have more time to judge the size of their quarry before removing it from the rocks, they should be extra careful not to disturb undersized abalone. Remember, everything looks bigger underwater than it really is.

## Tackle and Equipment

Equipment needed for rockpicking and free diving is listed below;

- . Abalone iron(of legal dimension)
- . Fixed caliper measuring gauge
- . State fishing license
- . Catch bag(at least a gunnysack)
- . Neoprene boots(optional)
- . Neoprene gloves(optional)

In addition, for free diving, you'll need a wet suit, hood, snorkel, mask, fins, knife(for escaping from kelp) and a weight belt. Scuba anglers obviously also need their tanks, regulators, etc.

## Where to Fish

Probably the most consistent producer of abalone are the Southern California islands. Excellent spots include San Miguel, Santa Rosa and Santa Cruz in the

Channel Islands chain. These are such good abalone hunting territories that party boats take divers out from such places as Camarillo, Oxnard and Ventura. Catalina Island is another good prospect. Along the coast itself, abalone can be found from Pt. Conception all the way south to San Diego, but the best areas are probably north of Santa Barbara and north of Palos Verdes Pt. towards Los Angeles. There are closed areas along the coast, so check current regulations. Check with dive shops for specific locales.

## Cleaning and Cooking

Cleaning abalone is different from most other sea food, but it is not actually difficult. Insert the abalone iron between the meat and the shell, at the pointed end of the abalone. Now, pop out the meat. Next, trim away the flanged edges and all the intestines. A pot scrubber can then be used to rub off the black skin. Scrape off the suction cups with a knife. Now it's time to tenderize the meat. Before slicing, pound it with a big mallet. Then slice it 1/8 to 1/4 inch thick. Use the mallet again for a final tenderizing. The end of a bottle may also be used for tenderizing.

Most people feel that the only way to prepare abalone is quick pan frying. Tenderized steaks are usually floured, or dipped in egg and sauteed over high heat for less than 1 minute on a side.

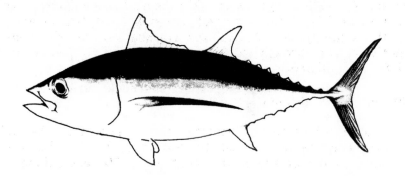

# How to Catch...Albacore

Albacore, or long-finned tuna, often take commercial fishing boats a couple hundred miles from shore.  Commercial boats stay out until their freezers are full.  Fortunately, there is a time each year when albacore come close enough to shore(35-50 miles usually), so that sport fishermen can get in on the fun.  These fish migrate continually throughout their lives, crossing the Pacific Ocean from Japan and up the coast of North America.  It's usually about early July when the smaller fish(10 to 15 pounds) appear in the San Diego area, as they move north.  Good fishing is sporadic, even after their arrival, probably because of anglers difficulties in locating the schools of fish that can move up to 50 miles per day.  But when it's hot, the fishing is fast and furious.  The bite can extend into early November.

There are years when albacore fishing gets hot as close as ten miles from shore.  These are the only times most sport fishermen consider albacore fishing in their own boats.  At other times it's proabaly best to venture out on a well-equipped, fast, large party boat especially rigged for albacore.  Typically the boats leave in the wee hours of the morning(about 1a.m.) and are back in port by 7p.m.  Cost ranges from $50 to $75.  There are also multi-day trips.

## Fishing Techniques

Trolling is the most popular technique for taking albacore. But, before we get into trolling specifics, a word about where to troll.  After all, it's a big ocean!  First, albacore congregate and feed in warmer water.  Most experts look for water in the 63-65°F range, with 60°F being the minimum. The second good fish finder is bird activity. Birds actively pursuing bait fish means that albacore may be doing the same thing. When birds are spotted, run the boat through the edge of the activity, not through the center. No need to chance scattering the bait fish and feeding albacore.

Albacore trolling is characterized by;

- Trolling close to the boat(the theory goes that the wake looks to the albacore like a bait fish feeding frenzy). Put the lure right in the white water wake of the boat, about 50 to 70 feet behind the stern.

- Fairly rapid boat speed(perhaps 7-10 knots) to move along the feathered or rubber-skirted jig at a good pace.

- Party boat captains usually troll in square grids of about 20 minutes per leg until fish are located. A zig-zag pattern is also a good approach.

The other method of albacore fishing is used on party boats and some private boats, after a school of fish is located by trolling. The boat is stopped, and scoops of bait fish(usually anchovies) are tossed into the water to raise the albacore up to the surface. This technique is called chumming. Fishermen drift live bait near the surface. Since albacore move in schools, it's always a good idea for even private boats to try drift fishing after a trolling hook-up is landed. Frozen anchovies often work, even without chumming. Casting out a Salas, Tady or similar jig can also work.

## Tackle and Equipment

Albacore are big, fast, open-ocean sport fish. One of the most sought after, or maybe the most sought after game fish in Southern California ocean waters. A good fish averages 15-30 pounds, with some ranging up to 40 pounds or more. The state record is 73 pounds, 8 ounces.

Essential equipment includes;

- Large, iced, fish storage box(or cooler, or a plastic trash container) and a good-sized gaff.

- A 6-6½ foot medium to heavy trolling rod(roller-tipped, a 4/0 to 6/0 size reel filled with at least 300 yards of 50-80 pounds monofilament line. This heavy equipment is needed to quickly land the first fish, so chumming and drift fishing can begin before the school disappears.

- For drift fishing, a light to medium action fast tapered rod mated to a conventional reel capable of holding 300 yards of 25-30 pound test line is suggested.

## Lures and Bait

The most productive albacore jigs;

        Description:    Chrome plated or abalone-pearl head and a natural feather or vinyl skirt.

        Colors:    Dark colors(like black, purple, green and yellow) during darker periods.  Light colors(like red and white, red and yellow) in bright periods.

        Size:    4-10 ounces.

The preferred bait is live anchovies.  The best are 3-4 inches long, green backed (they seem to be friskier), with no scale toss, or other signs of deterioration. For surface fishing, hook the anchovy through a gill cover.  For deeper action, nose hook the anchovies and use a 1 or 2 ounce rubber-core sinker about 30 inches up the line.

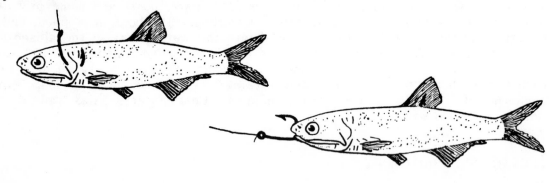

## Where to Fish

It varies.  Early season catches off San Diego come at the Dumping Grounds and 60-Mile Banks.  The San Clemente Islands, 43-Fathom Banks and the Channel Islands are usually the next to heat up.  By September-October the fishing extends up to Morro Bay.  See the Pacific Ocean Fishing Section of this book for more specifics.

## Bluefin Tuna

In the good old days of Southern California tuna fishing the bluefin was king. 200 pounders were not that uncommon.  Mostly due to the onslaught of commercial seiners, sport caught bluefins now average 10 to 25 pounds.  These are taken from late May through the summer near Catalina Island and Los Coronado Island. The best approach is drift fishing live, spunky anchovies.  Veteran anglers use 12-15 pound line, about a #8 hook and a long(about 7½-8 foot rod) to cast the offering away from the boat.  Bluefin, even of modest size, are fierce fighters.

## Yellowfin Tuna

Yellowfin tuna are usually caught on Baja trips.  But on occasion spotty runs of these fish develop off the San Diego area.  This is most likely to happen in late fall off the Coronado Islands, the 43-Fathom Banks and the 60-Mile Bank.  Yellowfins are caught with the same approach used on Albacore.  Trolling works. Chumming brings them to the boat.  But Yellowfin don't like water cooler than 72°.

## Cleaning and Cooking

Albacore is most often steaked.  Make sure the dark or red flesh is removed from each piece.

Albacore has a relatively high fat content.  The most popular way to prepare it is barbecuing.  The smoke seems to add to the flavor.  Poached albacore tastes like canned tuna, but even better.  Poached albacore may be stored in a refrigerator for several days, or frozen for a short time.  Since albacore and other tunas are strong tasting fish, they work well in recipes with spicy or tomato-based sauces.

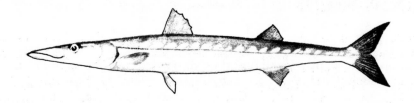

# How to Catch...Barracuda

Barracuda are torpedo shaped, hard-hitting and have a lethal set of teeth. The average keeper fish is now probably in the 3-5 pound range.

Barracuda frequent the offshore islands and close-in kelp beds and bays making them accessible to party boats, private fishing boats, skiff anglers and at times, pier and barge anglers.

Barracuda, as large as 8-12 pounds, were once commonplace from Pt. Conception south to the Cedros Islands area of Mexico. But overfishing, both sport and commercial, took its toll. Fortunately, a 28 inch minimum size limit, imposed in 1971, has helped restore this fishery. Be careful to check current regulations.

## Fishing Techniques

Barracuda are most commonly located by watching for sea birds working over schools of forage fish, like anchovies. The barracuda drive them up in a feeding frenzy. Anglers have two choices when this occurs. Either troll a feather or metal jig in the area, or just drift and cast to the breaking fish. After the first fish is caught, a few handfuls of live anchovies thrown into the water(this is called chumming) will bring them near the boat.

If the barracuda are near the surface a gill hooked live anchovy is in order. It should be offered without a sinker(called fly lining) or, if necessary, use a small rubber core sinker about a foot above the hook. Let the fish run with the anchovy for a few feet before setting the hook. Nose hooking, up through the lower lip and the nose, is called for when the barracuda are deeper. Also use a small sinker. Move the bait slowly and be ready to flip the reel into free spool or open the bail, to give the fish time to take the bait before setting the hook.

## Tackle and Equipment

Barracuda fishing, using live bait, is most fun on light spinning tackle - the same that is used most commonly for large trout or bass.  10-12 pound monofilament is more than adequate for most fish.  Some anglers even like to use fly fishing equipment.  When jig fishing, somewhat heavier tackle and about 20 pound line is recommended.  The Penn Jigmaster 500 is a typical reel choice.  Other things you'll need include needlenose pliers to remove the hooks(and avoid the sharp teeth), and a big rag to wipe your hands.  Barracuda are slimy creatures.

## Bait and Lures

Live anchovies are the bait of choice and account for most of the catch.  Use about a #4-#6 hook tied directly to your main line.  Gill hook(slip the hook under the bone behind the gill cover) for surface fishing and nose hook for deeper fishing.

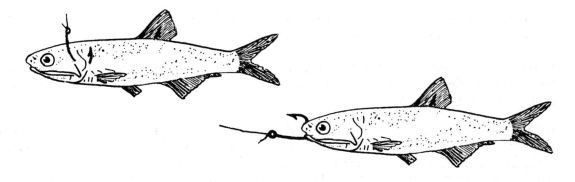

Barracuda are often suckers for both jigs and feathers, although feathers are not used as much as they once were.  Jigs have a built-in action, whereas feathers require the angler to provide the proper action.  The category of jigs called candy-bar shaped(e.g. Salsa, Straggler, Hacker) are most popular in all white, blue and white, and green and white.  The light weight size is most commonly used.

## Where to Fish

Good action can begin as early as February and March in places like Santa Monica Bay.  March and April are often good months near the Coronado Islands and La Jolla Kelp.  Oceanside, Dana Point, Huntington Beach Flats, Horseshoe Kelp, Rocky Point and Catalina Island are all productive in the May-June peak season.  Also, see the Ocean Fishing Section of this book.

## Cleaning and Cooking

Barracuda are most often filleted.  These moderate fat content fillets are good grilled or broiled.  It is very tasty when served with a full-flavored sauce.

**LARGEMOUTH BASS**

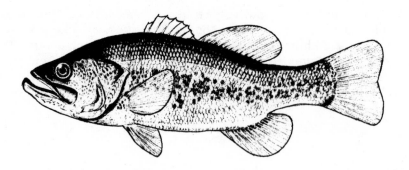

# How to Catch...Bass (Largemouth)

Largemouth bass are the most widely distributed and most pursued black bass. They inhabit many of the reservoirs and lakes in Southern California. The other black bass, the smallmouth, is found in only a few Southern California waters like Lake Cachuma, Lake San Antonio and Lake Nacimiento. Smallmouth prefer cooler water than largemouth, and are much smaller fish(a three pound small-mouth is almost a trophy).

There are two types of largemouth bass that are plentiful in Southern California. The first to be brought to California(no black bass are native) was the northern-strain largemouth, introduced before the turn of the century. It flourished and was the backbone of Southern California bass fishing until about 20 years ago. Around 1960, the Florida-strain largemouth bass was planted in some Southern California lakes. This was done because the Florida-strain grows faster(and thus bigger), spawn earlier and is considered more difficult to catch than the northern strains.

Now the northern-strain, Florida-strain and hybridized populations are found in Southern California lakes. Experts say that it is almost impossible to tell the strains of a caught fish since the young can exhibit the features of either parent strain. But you can tell by lake records. For example, the current California largemouth bass record, set in 1980 in Lake Casitas, is 21 pounds, 3½ ounces. That's a Florida-strain fish! Lakes that are northern-strain largemouth waters, usually have lake records in the 12 pound range. That's still quite a bass, and there's consolation in knowing that northern-strain fish come to the hook more readily.

# Fishing Techniques

Bass fishing is best during the spring and fall. But ironically, probably most people fish for bass in the warm summer months. Why not? Family vacations fit best when the kids are out of school. And the weather is comfortable "out on the lake." Don't get me wrong. Bass are caught in the summer. But it takes more effort, since the fish are usually down deeper.

The basic technique used in bass fishing is casting and retrieving a plug, a spoon, spinnerbait, a jig, a plastic worm or a live bait. Of course, the retrieve approach must match the lure. All types of casting equipment can and is used, including baitcasting, spinning, spincasting and flycasting. More on this in the Tackle and Equipment section.

Successful bass fishing centers around the answer to three questions. Where to cast? How to cast? What to cast? Here are some guidelines;

- Bass are almost always on or near the bottom, or near underwater cover like a fallen tree. The "bottom" could be near shore(say in the spring) in 2 feet of water, or it might be in 40 feet of water on the slope of a sunken island.

- Largemouth prefer to be near structures, whether it be a rocky fall-off, a sunken log, a weedbed, standing timber, a rocky point, etc.

- Largemouth bass prefer a water temperature of about 70°F. This means that in the spring and fall, bass are likely to be nearer shore, in shallow seventyish water. When the surface temperature is well above 70°, bass hold out deeper, but do make feeding forays into shallower water, primarily at night.

- If you(or someone else) catches a bass at a particular spot, and the lake temperature conditions don't change, the spot will probably produce more bass.

- At an unfamiliar lake, seek information about "good spots" from other anglers, bait shops, marinas, etc.

- Cast your offering so it lands near structures, or will be retrieved near structures. For example, put it next to a pile of boulders that are partially submerged, or right by a fallen tree. Retrieve parallel to a submerged log, not across it. Try inlets where streams flow into lakes.

- Retrieve slowly. Seventy to eighty percent of the time, a slow retrieve is best. But, if it's not working, don't hesitate to try a rapid retrieve. A combination may be in order also. For example, a few quick turns of the reel handle just after the offering lands(to get the bass's attention), followed by a slow retrieve.

. Retrieve everything, except surface plugs, near or on the bottom. Since the bass are on the bottom, you've got to put your offering on the bottom. Afterall, we live and eat on the "bottom" of the atmosphere, so doesn't it seem natural for some fish(particularly bass) to live and eat on the bottom of their "atmosphere."

. With plastic worms and jigs, "feel" the bottom during your retrieve. No doubt this practice will result in some lost rigs, but it will also result in more bass. Using snagless, or near snagless, offerings as described later, will minimize loss.

. Cast quietly. In fact, fish quietly. Minimize engine noise, oar lock noise, "scraping tackle box along the floor of the boat" noise, and so on. Bass fishing is akin to stalking.

. Catchable-sized bass feed mostly on smaller fish(like shad, minnows, bluegill, etc.), crawdads and worms. This means that offerings that are successful look and act like swimming fish, moving crawdads or worms.

. At times, bass strike out of reflex action. Sometimes they attack an offering the instant it hits the water. At these times, you could be casting anything and it would work.

. Many professional bass anglers feel that bigger bass come on bigger bait.

## Lures and Bait

Many an otherwise sane person is driven absolutely crazy by the immense selection of bass plugs, jigs, spoons, spinnerbaits, plastic worms. etc. And professional bass-tournament fishermen seem to own at least one of everything, based on the size of the tackle boxes in their boats!

But, don't despair. You don't need one of everything to take bass. Largemouth bass offerings fall into 7 categories;

1. Crankbaits          5. Jigs

2. Surface Plugs       6. Plastic Worms

3. Spinnerbaits        7. Live Bait

4. Spoon Jigs

It's probably a good idea for a serious bass angler to have a sampling of the basic offerings in each category, but that isn't even necessary. For example, some bass fishing experts say that one or two types account for more bass than all the others combined. These two are plastic worms and spinnerbaits.

## Crankbaits

Crankbaits are a broad category of lures, mostly plugs, that get their name because the reeling speed determines how much the lure dives, vibrates and wobbles. Most of these lures have plastic, fish-shaped bodies. They also have a plastic tip, the size, shape and angle of which imparts action to the reeled lure. Many have 2 sets of treble hooks which provide a good chance to hook a striking bass. But this also increases the chance of snags, so crankbaits are best used in open water. Crankbaits work, to one degree or another, almost all year long in such structures as sloping points, along shorelines, in shallow flats, etc.

Crankbaits either float at rest, sink slowly or sink rapidly. The most common way to fish these lures is to first jig it for a moment before beginning the return. Then reel fast to get the lure to the bottom. Now slow down enough to either drag the lure along the sloping bottom or bump it along, or return steadily right over the bottom. Crankbaits are designed to be fished parallel to the shoreline so you can keep the lure near the bass, and at the prescribed depth for the longest time.

Popular bass crankbaits include Bomber Model A's, Rapala Fat Rap and Storm Wiggle Wart. Shad and crawdad styles are popular.

## Surface Plugs(and Stickbaits)

Surface plugs are top-water lures that simulate a sick or injured baitfish, frog or other creature. They float both when still and when retrieved. Most surface plugs have an action designed into them using blunt ends, propellers, dished-faces, etc. The proper retrieve for most of these is slow, erratic and stop-and-go. But before retrieving, many anglers will just let it sit in the target area for up to a minute or two, just twitching it, to send out vibrations and small ripples around it. Popular surface plugs include Devil's Horses, Rebels and Rapalas.

There is another class of surface plugs called stickbaits that are unique because they don't have any action built into them. Probably the most famous of these is the Zara Spook. The action needed to make a stickbait work must come from the skill of the angler. This takes several hours of practice to develop. Articles and bass books can be found at your local library to show you how to do it. The reading and the practice may be worth it because stickbaits have one profound advantage over other surface plugs. They can be kept in the target area longer because very little forward motion is required to give them the action needed. So a stickbait in skilled hands may catch more fish than other surface plugs.

The prime season for surface plugs is in the springtime spawning season when bass are in shallow water, especially in early mornings and late evenings. They are also good in summertime, in shallow water, after dark.

## Spinnerbaits

Spinnerbaits are one of the most productive of all bass catching lures and are simple to cast and retrieve. They are good all year, especially in water up to 10 feet deep. Use them along brushy structures, in flooded trees or fallen trees. Most spinnerbait designs are semi-weedless so hangups are not a constant concern. Veteran anglers vary the return to change depth and action, but in most cases the slower the retrieve the better.

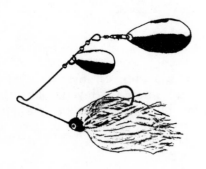
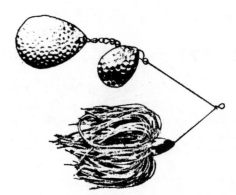

Here are some tips. The best, all around colors are probably white or chartreuse (yellowish). Spinnerbaits with two easily rotating blades seem to produce better. Spinnerbaits can be hopped along the bottom like a jig. In this style of fishing, blades that flutter freely on the downfall bring strikes. The size of spinnerbaits should approximate the length of the bait fish in the area. Skirts can be trimmed to accomplish this.

Now, the best tip of all. Add a plastic worm or pork rind on the hook of the spinnerbait. It produces more strikes from bigger bass. Probably because it keeps the lure up in the water, even with a slower retrieve.

## Spooning

Jigging a spoon is a little-practiced largemouth technique, that is easy and effective. It's a great method to take bass from late autumn through early spring. That's when largemouths seek warm water down deep in Southern California reservoirs. It can also work in mid summer when bass go deep to find water cooler than surface temperatures.

A wobbling spoon is dropped down over the side of the boat, and then raised up and fluttered down at whatever depth the bass are at. The more flutter the better on the down drift. Work the jig in about a 3-5 foot, up and down range. Hopkin's 75 and Haddock Structure Spoons in about the 1/2-3/4 ounce range are about right. Fish can be taken in depths between 30-60 feet with this approach.

## Jigging

Jigging, typically with a skirted leadhead jig, is somewhat more complicated than spoon-jigging, but it is a very productive technique. The jig is cast out or flipped out(more on this later) and then allowed to drop to the bottom. The most common retrieve is to skip the jig along the bottom in short, sharp jerks. Imagine you're dragging the jig along the bottom from a drifting or steadily trolled boat. That's about how you want your jig to act. Most strikes occur on the initial drop or on the ensuing flutter downs. Garland Spider Jigs and Haddock Kreepy Crawlers are popular.

Weedless Jig(with pork rind)

Non-weedless Jig

The most famous jig rig in Southern California bass waters is the "pig-n-jig." It's a 3/8 to 1/2 ounce, skirted jig(usually dark colored, like brown) with a weedless hook. A pork rind(or plastic trailer) is put on the hook. The rind makes it look more like a crawdad and also slows the rigs descent. When you move the pig-n-jig off the bottom, don't just let it drop, let it down and be alert for a take. Keep slack out of your line to feel the strike and watch your line for unnatural movement.

## Plastic Worms

Some people claim that each year more largemouth bass are taken on plastic worms than on all other artificial lures combined. This could well be true. Plastic worms do have several special advantages over other lures;

1. They can be fished at all depths of water.
2. They have outstanding action at different retrieve speeds.
3. Weedless rigging is a snap.
4. They're inexpensive, so anglers don't mind risking them in heavy cover.
5. They can be rigged in different ways for different situations. For example, in shallow spring spawning waters, they can be fished weightless. They can also be rigged with a dropper or a sliding sinker.

Here are three popular rigging styles;

**Texas Style Rig**

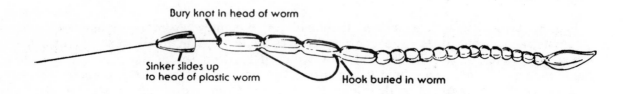

**Carolina Style Rig**

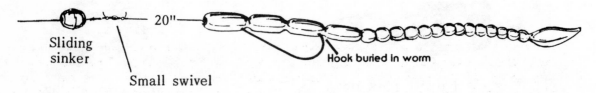

**Dropper/Dual Weedless Hook Rig**

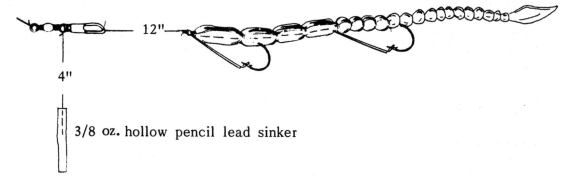

12"

4"

3/8 oz. hollow pencil lead sinker

Plastic worms(from 4-6" long) are worked along the bottom, much the same as in jigging. Work them slowly and erratically, like a night crawler twisting and drifting in the current. Dark colors, like purple and brown are most productive. Plastic worms can also be used for vertical jigging, like spooning.

## Live Bait

Live bait bass fishing isn't all that common anymore. That's strange, in a way, because live bait was the only way bass were caught before plugs, spinnerbaits and all the other artificials came along. For instance, I have several live frog harnesses in my collectables. It holds the little guy in a swimming posture and would be great for casting and retrieving a frog without putting a hook through it. I've never even thought of using it.

But, other live bait are a different matter. Especially live crawdads. These critters are the way to go it you want to catch a really big largemouth bass. Here's one way to rig them;

18"

Some anglers prefer to just put some splitshot up the line about a foot or two from the hook. Others use no sinker at all. Use a #6, 8 or 10 sized bait hook, depending on the size of the crawdad. Cast them out gently. Let them sink and slowly crawl them along the bottom. When you see a twitch, that is the largemouth picking up the crawdad. As the fish moves off with the bait, the belly will come out of your line.  Let the bass run a few feet and then set the hook hard.  Don't allow any slack in your line when playing the bass.  Fish rocky points, dropoffs and ledges.  Spring is the best time to catch the lunkers on live crawdads.

## Casting and Flipping

Accuracy is the measure of a good cast.  Consistently accurate bass casters will hook more fish.  Besides the traditional overhand cast, often a sidearm or even a underhand cast is called for to reach the target(when casting under an overhanging branch, for example) and to gently put the offering on the water.  The three keys to accurate casting are practice, practice and practice.

Flipping(or Flippin') is a specialized casting technique.  It's used to delicately put a jig or plastic worm on the water, especially near or in heavy cover. Springtime shallow water bassing is prime flipping time.  In elementary terms, the standing angler strips line off the reel, much like a fly angler, as the offering swings from the rod tip like a pendulum.  On a forward swing the jig is flipped out and gently "put" on the water.  Accuracy is critical as is an almost ripple-free landing.  Weedless offerings are a rule.  And in order to fight the bass in close and keep it out of cover, heavy equipment is used.  Specialized flipping rod(about $7\frac{1}{2}$ feet) are matched with 15-25 pound test line.

## Tackle and Equipment

Today, many bass anglers use what is known in the trade as a bass boat.  These boats were popularized in Bass Derbys.  They are about 16-20 feet long, with pedestal seats, large outboard motors, an electric trolling motor(used for maneuvering, not trolling), several depth finders, a fish box, flashy-sparkling finish and on and on.

These boats are fun and functional, but the good news is that you don't need one to catch your share of bass.  The bad news is that successful bass fishing probably does require some kind of boat that can be manuevered along an irregular shoreline.  Many kinds of boats will do, from an inflatable to a canoe, to a dingy, to a row boat, to an aluminum boat, to a small stern-drive cruiser. Shore fishing for bass is possible.  And some lakes, like Lower Otay offer good shore bass angling.  But, covering very much promising structures at most lakes, on foot, is difficult.

To find promising bass territory, during all seasons, you'd best be equipped with maps of the lake, a thermometer that works well under water and a depth sounder.  A flasher type will do, but a graph recorder is preferred.

Now for the tackle itself.  Here, there is a great deal of lattitude.  The possibilities include;

- Spinning equipment – 6-7 foot, light to medium action spinning rod. Open-faced reel with 10-12 pound monofilament line.

- Spincasting equipment – 5-6 foot pistol-grip, light to medium rod. Closed-faced spinning reel with 10-12 pound monofilament line.

- Baitcasting equipment – 5-6 foot pistol-grip, light to medium rod(can be used with spincasting reel). Baitcasting reel(some have magnetic anti-backlash mechanisms) with level-wind feature, star drag and 10-12 pound monofilament line.

What lures to use with these rods and reels? Beginners and once-in-a-while anglers should probably have a good selection of spinnerbaits, crankbaits and a surface plug or two. These are the easiest to retrieve with good action, and catch a lot of fish. A few wobbly spoons for spoon jigging in deep water are also handy. More experienced anglers wouldn't be without a good selection of plastic worms and leadhead jigs.

Professional bass anglers often put scent formulas on all their lures. It adds attracting odors and covers up human odors. Next to vibration, bass probably respond most to odor. This is an inexpensive way to improve your chances. Tests indicate that the color of ones lure is also important in producing strikes, depending on the water clarity. There's a new electronic instrument called a Color-C-Lector on the market that tells anglers which color offerings to use at a given depth in a particular water clarity. Results have been promising. It's worth looking into.

## Cleaning and Cooking

Bass can be scaled, gutted and beheaded. But, many prefer to fillet them. This is the easiest way to remove the scales and skin. Any muddy flavor is in the skin.

Bass is mild and flaky. It can be cooked in a variety of ways including sauteing, broiling, poaching, baking and frying. But, in any case, do remove the skin before cooking.

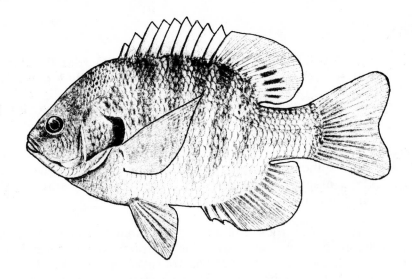

# How to Catch...Bluegill

Bluegills are the most abundant panfish in California waters. They're in virtually all warm water lakes in Southern California. These fish are fun to catch and are very enjoyable eating. And in many locations, they are abundant, so there is no need to feel guilty about taking them. They reproduce with great success and heavy populations can crowd out large sportfish.

Bluegill angling is easy and relaxing fishing. And it is especially enjoyable for youngsters. Give them a rod and reel, a can of worms and a little dock and they're set for hours of fun and adventure.

## Finding Bluegills in a Lake

The easiest time to find bluegills is when they spawn in shallow water in spring (March-April-May). They'll be in 4-6 feet of water over sand or gravel bottoms. Be careful not to spook them if the water is clear.

In summer, bluegills behave like bass, moving to submerged channels, under docks, over bars, to weed-beds or drop-offs. It's at these times that it may be necessary to fish 10-20 feet down. A drifting, rowed or trolled boat with baits suspended at various depths can often find them. Bluegills are always in schools, so when you find one, you've found a bunch.

## Bait Fishing

This is probably the most popular approach especially for kids. Some of the best baits are redworms, cricketts and small grasshoppers. Commercial dough-type baits also work. A bobber is most often used, to keep the bait off the bottom and to signal a bite. From boat, shore, or dock you can use a bobber rig;

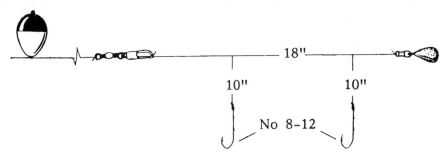

From a boat or dock you can use the same bobber rig or take it off and fish straight below the pole or rod tip.

Still fishing, or bait fishing for bluegills might be somewhat of a misnomer. Most experts agree that a slight movement of your bait is desirable. With any rig, flick the rod tip frequently to move your bait. Another principle is to change depths, if action is slow. Frequently, large bluegills are down deeper than most bobber anglers suspect.

## Fly Fishing

Flycasting for bluegills is enjoyable and productive. A medium action, $7\frac{1}{2}$-$8\frac{1}{2}$ foot rod is suggested, but any will do. A wide variety of offerings will produce depending on the lake, the time of year and the time of day;

- . Panfish poppers - swim them slowly along in a stop and go fashion.

- . Rubber or plastic-legged spiders.

- . Mosquitos, Ants, Wooly Worms, Black Gnats(in size 10 or 12).

- . Bucktail streamers, size 8.

- . Nymphs(black and white, white, brown, etc.).

- . Indiana spinners(2 blades, #8 hook).

A casting bobber is a small bobber, usually made of clear plastic that is attached to monofilament line. Because of its weight(some allow you to let in water to make it even heavier) it allows anglers to cast poppers, flies, etc., using spinning, spincasting or baitcasting equipment. So you can enjoy "fly fishing" without having to use a flyrod and reel.

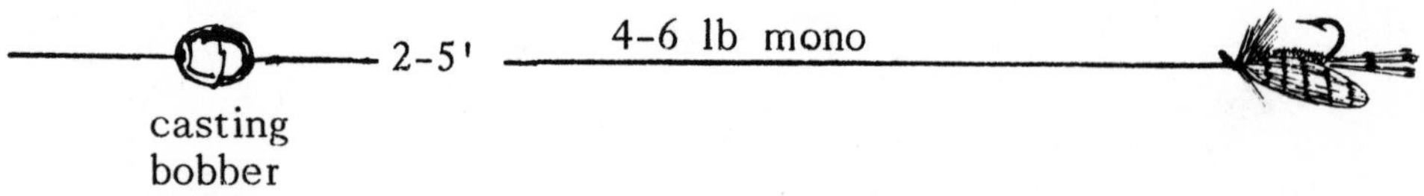

casting
bobber

2-5'

4-6 lb mono

## Where to Fish

Bluegills can be found in just about any waters holding bass or other warm-water species. See the Lake Fishing Section of this book.

## Cleaning and Cooking

Since bluegills are small, most people clean them in the traditional way. Scale them by rubbing a knife or scaling tool from the tail of the fish towards the head. Next, cut open the belly, starting from the anus, and remove the guts. Finally, cut off the head. Rinse them off and they're ready for the pan.

An alternative is to fillet them. This yields small fillets, but eliminates skin and bones in the cooked fish. See instructions on filleting in the Fish Cleaning Section of this book.

Sauteing the whole fish or individual fillets is most popular. See Crappie Section for an excellent recipe.

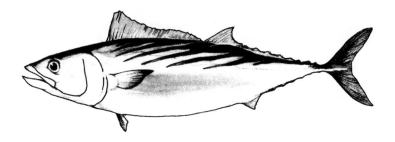

# How to Catch...**Bonito**

Bonito are one of the finest sport fishing opportunities for inshore ocean anglers. They are caught from breakwaters, piers, barges, small skiffs, private boats and party boats. Bonito can range in size from a pound or two up to 12 pounds. The average catch is about 6 pounds. And some say that for their size Bonito are the best fighting fish caught in Southern California ocean waters. Bonito, which are related to the bluefin tuna, fight just as hard as many tuna.

## Fishing Techniques

The first order is to find the fish. Shore anglers should keep up on local reports of fishing activity. Party boat anglers count on the skipper to take them to the right spot, and on the deck hand who attracts fish with generous helpings of live anchovies tossed overboard. This approach, called chumming, is also practiced by private boat anglers. Bird activity can also be a tip-off of bonito feeding action near the surface. Boaters sometimes also use a "Bonito Splasher." Dragging it through the water, trailing a feather jig on a leader, causes a surface commotion that hungry bonito can't resist. After the feather-jig hooked fish is landed, chumming, live bait fishing or lure casting can begin for the rest of the school.

The vast majority of bonito are caught on collar hooked(slipping the hook under the bone behind the gill cover) live anchovies. This applies to shore anglers, private boat anglers and party boat anglers. But cast lures are also used successfully.

When large schools of bonito are migrating offshore, trolling is a good method for taking them. Trollers used 20-30 pound test line on live bait outfits. Most successful lures are small albacore feathers(from 4-6 inches) and chrome-headed bonito feathers. All white, all black, and blue or red mixed with white are good. Troll the lure close to the boat(like albacore trolling) at about 5-8 knots.

## Tackle and Equipment

Heavy freshwater or light saltwater tackle is the way to go for bonito angling. For example, some anglers use a largemouth bass rod with 10 pound test line and an adjustable drag reel. An average fish will put up an exciting 10 minute fight on this equipment. Fly-rodders also get in on the bonito action. Whatever tackle you use, make sure it holds adequate line for the bonito's long surface runs. 100 yards of line is a minimum.

## Bait and Lures

Live anchovies are the bait of choice. Collar hook them(see Barracuda Section of this book) and don't use any sinker, if possible. A #2 to #6 hook is tied directly to the main line. If you need to go deeper, nose hook the anchovy and use a small rubber core sinker. Small(1/4-3/8 ounce) feather jigs, spoons, plugs and spinners(like Rooster Tails) often work when cast. Noisy largemouth bass surface plugs are also a good bet. Bonito like the commotion.

## Where to Fish

One place where bonito congregate year around in Southern California is King's Harbor in Redondo Beach. They like the warm water flowing out of the Southern California Edison power plant. Besides water inflows, bonito are also found along kelp beds and at the islands. Also see the Ocean Fishing Section of this book for more boat locations and shore locations.

## Cleaning and Cooking

Bonito are usually filleted although they can be steaked. Be sure to remove all the dark lateral meat and the skin. Many anglers are not that excited about the taste of bonito, but they are good smoked, or barbecued. Fresh bonito should be bled when caught and eaten that same day, unless its headed for the smoker. Bonito are bled by cutting the fleshy portion under the head, where the gill covers come together. Some suggest that bonito make fine garden fertilizer. But if you're not going to eat it, why not release it.

CALICO BASS

# How to Catch...Calico Bass (and Sand Bass)

This is the third of three popular inshore fish. The first two are barracuda and bonito. Calico bass are often called kelp bass, and are considered one of the best eating fish in local waters. They are found over reefs, around rocks, jetties and breakwaters, in kelp beds and off islands like Catalina. Calico bass are most often caught in the 2-4 pound range, but a few reach 12 pounds or more.

Sand bass are closely related to calico bass. They are often found in schools on sand flats and along breakwaters. Sand bass are almost as good eating as calico bass, and are caught in about the same size range.

## Fishing Techniques, Lures and Bait

These two fish combined, represent the largest sport catch of ocean going surface game fish in Southern California. This may be true because there are so many successful ways and places to catch these voracious feeders. Shore, private boat and party boat anglers all share in the fun.

Calico bass in kelp beds go for both bait and lures. Favorite baits include squid, anchovies and mackerel. They will strike Clouts, Scampi and Haddock Structure spoons. When fishing breakwaters, put a small sliding sinker on your line and then tie on a 2/0 to 4/0 sized bait hook. Load it up with a piece of squid and pull it along and around the rocks and kelp.

Chumming(live anchovies thrown overboard) works great for attracting larger bass in kelp beds. And, when available, the best bait for calico and sand bass is live squid. Frozen squid also work. A sliding sinker above a 2/0 to 4/0 hook or a comparable-sized leadhead hook jig is the best way to rig squid. Set the hook as soon as a sharp hit is felt. See the Yellowtail Section of this book for a diagram of the squid rig. Calico and sand bass also go wild over the twister-tail type plastic leadhead jigs. However, sand bass are less likely to take lures than calico bass.

## Tackle and Equipment

You don't need heavy tackle for these fish. On party boats, where anchovies are chummed and used as bait, skippers recommend a #500 reel, 15-25 pound test line on a 6-7 foot saltwater rod, with a fairly light tip. You'll want to cast or flip your offering over to the kelp line. For breakwater or bay fishing a heavy freshwater bass outfit with about 15 pound line is fine, as is a light saltwater outfit.

## Where to Fish

Many good spots, both from shore and boat, are discussed in the Ocean Fishing Section of this book. Early morning and late evening are the best fishing times.

## Cleaning and Cooking

These fish are almost always filleted. They make delicious eating, no matter how they are prepared.

**WHITE CATFISH**

**CHANNEL CATFISH**

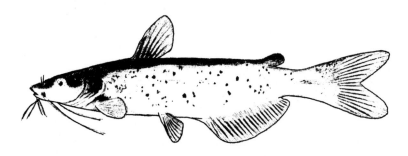

# How to Catch...Catfish

Catfish are widespread and abundant in Southern California lakes and rivers. And despite their unappetizing appearance, and somewhat negative image, catfish are very good eating(catfish are not as difficult to clean as one might suspect, either). The delicious meals provided by catfish are attested to by the existence of hundreds of catfish farms, primarily in the southeastern U.S., where these fish are raised and sold to restaurants and foodstores.

## Fishing Techniques

Catfishing means still fishing. And catfishing means warm weather fishing since these critters like warm water and are most active when lakes, ponds and rivers warm up in the late spring, summer and early fall. Boats are not needed for catfishing. Simply find a spot on shore where you have enough room to cast out your weighted rig. Let it sink to the bottom. Snug up the line. And wait for the prowling whiskerfish to find your offering. A bank, a dock or a pier where you can sit on a comfortable chair, makes things perfect.

The best catfishing and the largest catfish(they can go up to 5, 10, or 20 pounds or more) are caught after dark. From dark to midnight and the several hours before sun-up are particularly good. But many catfish, including big ones, are caught on lazy summer afternoons.

Bring several baits along. If one doesn't produce, try something else. Often, this single maneuver can make all the difference.

## Tackle and Equipment

Any rod and reel combination that can cast out a rig with a 1/2 - 6 ounce sinker will do just fine.  These include specialized bass fishing tackle, light to medium spinning equipment and surf casting equipment.  In some situations, you'll probably be better off with a longer rod(say 7-8 feet), so longer casts are possible.

Use monofilament line, at least 10 pound test.  But heavier line is no problem, say 15-20 pound test.

## Bait and Rigging

Catfish will eat almost anything.  And they feed by both sight and by smell. Their smell sensors are on their whiskers.  In fact, some catfish baits are often referred to as stink baits, because at times, it seems that catfish prefer smelly offerings such as beef liver, coagulated blood, chicken entrails, etc.

But in Southern California, some of the most successful baits are less repulsive. These include;

- Cut pieces of mackerel.
- Nightcrawlers.
- Fresh clams(keep them on ice, pry them open with a knife, thread hook through hard outer edge).
- Anchovies.
- Redworms.
- Sardine chunks.
- Crayfish tails.
- Chicken livers.

The most common catfish rig is shown below;

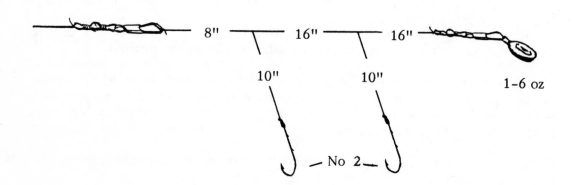

8" — 16" — 16"     1-6 oz

10"     10"

— No 2 —

Use enough weight to get the casting distance you want and to hold the rig on the bottom, if there is a current. Some anglers prefer a dipsey sinker. It has a flat metal rim around the edge which makes it flutter up on a quick retrieve, so it's less likely to get caught in rock crevices and roots. Another alternative that some use is a sliding sinker rig. Instead of attaching the weight at the end of the rig, its slid on the main line before the snap swivel is tied on. This is the same approach as is used in bait fishing for trout in lakes.

## Where to Fish

Some of the best spots are at the lakes and reservoirs included in this book. The Colorado River Lakes are also good. Actually, almost all Southern California impoundments are inhabited by at least one variety of catfish.

## Cleaning and Cooking

The first step in catfish cleaning is skin removal. To skin a catfish, cut through the skin all around the fish, just below the gill cover. Then, using a pliers, pull the skin down the fish, while holding the fishes gills. Be careful not to be poked by the sharp pectoral and dorsal fin spines. Some people nip these off with wire cutters. For larger fish, it is suggested that the fish be nailed(through the head) to a tree trunk or fence post, using an adequate sized spike. The skinned catfish can then be filleted or steaked. See Fish Cleaning Section of this book.

Catfish meat is flaky, mild with a moist texture. It is good sauteed, fried or poached.

52

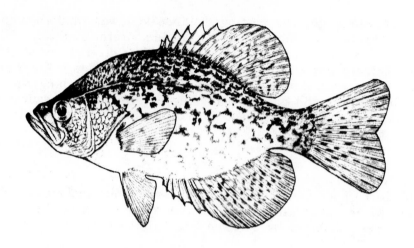

# How to Catch...Crappie

Crappies(pronounced krŏp'-i) are the king of the panfish.  Both black crappies and white crappies can grow quite large(the state records are black crappie-4 pounds, 1 ounce and white crappie-4 pounds, 8 ounces).  Most crappies average a pound or even less.  A 2-pounder is bragging size.  Crappies provide fun and relaxed fishing on light tackle and are excellent eating fish.

Black crappies are the most wide spread of the two types, and do best in clearer water.  Adult crappies are fish eaters, so they need an abundant supply of forage, like shad, to do well.  Surprising to some, crappies also need a good deal of fishing pressure, otherwise they overpopulate their lake and all are stunted.  So enjoy catching and eating crappies, it's good for the fish and good for the angler.

## Finding Crappies in a Lake

The key to successful crappie fishing is finding them.  These are school fish that cluster in different parts of a lake depending on season, water temperature, reproductive cycles, underwater contours, etc.

Crappies are easiest to find, and to catch, when they move into shallow water to spawn.  This happens when the water temperature reaches about 60-65°.  March, April and May are the likely months.  These fish like heavy cover to accompany the shallow water.  Look for water 3-8 feet deep with sunken trees, tule beds, cattails, lily pads and undercut rocky banks.  This is much like the cover used by largemouth bass.  Shore anglers do well in spring, as the fish move in close.

In summer and winter, crappies are harder to find, so stringers get skimpier, or empty. But they are still there and eating. Here's some ways to find them. Look in deeper water. They're usually down from 10-20 feet, in water that deep, or deeper. They like underwater islands, underwater stream beds, ledges, etc. Often they are in deeper water just adjacent to where they were in the spring. One way is to troll a jig or minnow across likely spots with lines of various depths. Mark the spot and depth when you get a hit. Troll slowly with oars or electric motor, or drift. Graph recorders also will do the job, for those who have them.

Fall crappies are not quite as deep as in the summer. Say 8-16 feet. And early and late in the day, crappies, like bass, move into shallower water to feed. So, even in summer, the first angler on the lake, or the last to call it a day, may fill a stringer with crappies in shallow water.

## Jig Fishing

This is, by far, the most popular method of taking crappies - all year long. A word of caution before getting into the technique of this approach. It's easy to spook schools of crappies(especially in shallow water) so fish quietly and keep a low profile. And don't, for example, slide an anchor or tackle box along the bottom of your boat. Approach likely spots slowly and carefully.

Crappie jigs, or mini-jigs, are in the 1/32 to 1/8 ounce size range. Most are little leadhead jigs with a bright colored feather covering the hook end. Eyes are often painted on the head end. Some, like Sassy Shad Jigs have rubber bodies that imitate swimming shad.

Tie these jigs directly on about a 4 or even 2 pound test line. Light line gives the jig better action. Short, accurate casts are called for, from boat or shore. But since you'll be casting into cover, expect snags and expect to lose some jigs. Allow the jig to sink to the desired depth and then retrieve either smoothly and slowly, or impart a twitching action with the rod tip.

A small, clear casting bobber can be added up the line from the jig, if it's too light to cast the desired distance. The bobber will also permit the jig from going deeper than it is set below the bobber. See Fly Fishing for Bluegill for illustration of casting bobber. Boat anglers, when directly over a school of crappie, can drop a jig straight down, and then twitch it around.

Crappie jigs come in many colors. Here are some guidelines. Light colors, like white, work well on clear days in clear water. Yellow is better on overcast days and at dawn and dusk. In off-colored water try dark colors like brown and blacks. Experiment with different styles and color. These jigs are inexpensive. Some times color doesn't even seem to matter.

## Bait Fishing

Crappies love minnows, so if you prefer live minnow fishing, this is the way to go. Bait can be fished from shore, dock, or boat. Most anglers use a bobber. A typical rig is shown below;

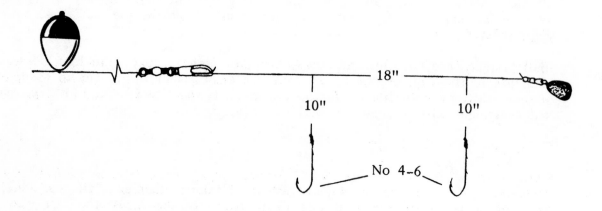

Minnows are best hooked up through both lips;

Most experts agree that a slight movement of your bait is desirable. Flick the rod tip frequently to move your bait. Another basic principle is to change depths, if the action is slow. Frequently larger crappies are deeper down than most bobber anglers suspect.

## Tackle and Equipment

Just about any light freshwater tackle will do, from light spinning, to spincasting, to bamboo poles, to long fly rods. Actually the lighter the tackle the better, since it will help cast out the light jigs and baits. Ultra-light spinning tackle is popular. The only other thing you'll need is a stringer.

## Where To Fish

Crappies are found in abundant supply in many Southern California lakes. See Lake Fishing Section of this book. Some of the lakes that are known for fine crappie fishing are Henshaw, Vail, Isabella, Silverwood, Casitas and El Capitan.

## Cleaning and Cooking

Many people clean crappie in the traditional way. Scale them by rubbing a knife or scaling tool from the tail of the fish to the head. Cut open the belly and remove the guts. Finally, cut off the head. Rinse them off and they're ready for the pan.

An alternative, for good-sized fish, is to fillet them. This yields a little less meat, but eliminates skin and bone in the cooked fish. See instructions on filleting in the Fish Cleaning Section of this book.

Sauteing the whole fish or individual fillets is most popular. Dip them into sifted flour and sprinkle with salt, pepper and parsley and lemon flakes(if desired). Melt butter in a hot skillet, toss in the fish and turn until golden brown. Here's another recipe: Pieces cut from fillets can be battered and deep fried, and are also delicious.

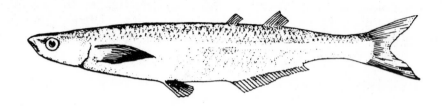

# How to Catch...Grunion

Grunion catching, or watching other people catch grunion, or watching other people try to catch grunion, or all three, is a special treat that all anglers and their families should experience at least once in their lifetimes.

Grunion catching is done on the beaches in Southern California. You see, these fish spawn by the light of the moon, not in the water, but right on the beach. Why should we be so surprised. Some people do the same thing. In fact, maybe the grunion learned it from us.

Grunion spawn only 3 or 4 nights after the highest tide associated with a full moon, or new moon, in the spring and summer. A run lasts from one to three hours. Females bury themselves in the sand up to their pectoral fins before dispeling their eggs which are eagerly fertilized by males surrounding her. Both males and females then return to the sea. Falling tides cover over the eggs. They incubate for about 2 weeks and then hatch after being exposed by ensuing rising tides. These newborn little grunion then swim into the sea. Isn't nature marvelous?

## Fishing Techniques

Full size grunion are about 5 to 6 inches long. The first sign of a run occurs when a smattering of male grunion show up on a beach. If all looks right(anglers should stay back and be quiet at this point) hoards of male and female grunion will soon follow. This in turn prompts grunion seekers to run onto the beach with pail and flashlights. They pick them up as best they can - using bare hands. It's best to grab the front half of the fish to prevent them from wiggling away

It's hard not to get a lot of fish during a good run. But don't take more than you can eat, or freeze, for future eating. They're also good for bait.

## Tackle and Equipment

The Department of Fish and Game regulations are simple. No tackle or equipment can be used to catch grunion. Only bare hands. No bucket scooping, either. It's illegal. Bring a flashlight to see the grunion and a bucket to hold them.

## When to Fish

Forecasts are made to predict summer grunion runs. In some areas these are broadcast or printed in local papers. Ocean-oriented bait and tackle stores can be helpful. Most of the predicted runs are around midnight.

## Where to Fish

The best beaches are gently sloping and have fine sand. If there are crowds of people on the beach(not spawning, but watching for grunion) move to the end of the beach (grunion don't like people to watch). Some of the top Southern California beaches for grunion are;

- Santa Barbara
- Santa Monica
- Venice
- Hermosa
- Cabrillo
- Long Beach
- Malibu
- Huntington
- Newport
- Corona Del Mar
- La Jolla
- Mission Beach
- Coronado Strand
- Catalina Island

## Cleaning and Cooking

Scale, gut, behead and wash before cooking. A popular way to prepare these little guys is to roll them in a mixture of cornmeal, flour, salt and pepper. Then fry briefly in hot oil.

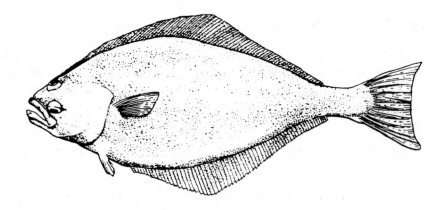

# How to Catch...Halibut

Growing up in the Midwest, as we did, halibut was one of the few store-bought fish that our family enjoyed.  As a boy, I didn't know where halibut came from (except from the ocean), what they looked like(I had no idea halibut had both eyes on the same side of their head), or how to catch them.  But, the firm, flaky white meat was sure a treat on our table.  Everybody in Southern California is lucky to live so close to some fine halibut fishing grounds.

California halibut is a flatfish and can range in size up to 50-75 pounds.  The typical keeper is from 10-20 pounds.  The minimum legal fish of 22" will weigh about 3-4 pounds.  Adult halibut move into shallower water in the late spring and summer to spawn.  Young fish swim upright, but during their first year, one eye migrates to the other side of the head and they begin to swim in a horizontal position.  Also, the side with the two eyes(the top) turns dark, or sand-colored, while the bottom-side turns light.

Halibut live right on the sandy bottom.  A ruffling of fins and tail kicks up a cloud of sand, that settle back on the fish, hiding it from both its predators and its prey.  Only its two eyes are noticeable above the sand.  They don't look for food, rather wait in hiding for it to come to them.  So, successful anglers, in one way or another, keep their offering moving along sandy bottoms.

## Fishing Techniques

California halibut fishing is primarily shallow water fishing.  Because of this situation, it is possible to catch halibut from piers, by surf fishing on beaches, or from a boat.  In all these cases, the basic idea is the same, get your offering down on the sandy bottom and keep it moving.

Pier anglers should cast out, let their offering sink to the bottom, and then retrieve.  Move along the pier, putting special attention on casts just at the surf line.

Surf anglers have much more latitude.  They can move along the beach, but can't reach as far out as pier casters.  For specifics on pier and surf fishing for halibut, see the Pier Fishing and Surf Fishing Sections of this book.

Fishing for halibut from a boat can be done by either trolling or drift fishing.  Drift fishing here means to fish, using bait, from a boat drifting over productive areas.  This is the dominate method for taking halibut in Southern California waters.

Waters of bays like Santa Monica and San Diego are popular halibut grounds.  Most action takes place in depths of 6-60 feet.  Some anglers seek out bottoms that are a combination rocky-sandy area, a good habitat for forage fish.  In bays like San Diego, drifts across a channel are a good bet.  Fishing is often best the few hours before and after high tide.  In the protected bay waters, large boats are not necessary.  Bass boats, tri-hull, ski-boats and aluminum cartoppers are all used successfully, as are 40 foot yachts.

Drift anglers lower their baited rig until they feel bottom.  Let out some line (maybe 30 yards) to begin the drift.  Then they either set the drag just enough to prevent more line from going out, or release the bail or spool, and hold the line between their fingers.  When a halibut picks up the bait most anglers give it line immediately.  Some count to 20 or 30 before setting the hook!  Others give the halibut "time to eat" before setting the hook.  There is much controversy on "when to set the hook" when halibut fishing.  Whatever you do, don't set the hook too hard.  Many halibut are lip-hooked.  It's best to error on the gentle side.

## Tackle and Equipment

Either spinning or conventional reels can be used for drift fishing.  Since there is little or no casting involved a conventional reel, with a spool release and star-drag, won't give backlash headaches.  A medium to heavy spinning reel that will hold 150-200 pounds of 10-12 pound test line is a good alternative.  Use a rod of 6-7 feet with a sensative tip.  You'll also need a gaff, a large landing net and a fish billy.  A sharp blow midway down the body is recommended.  Use a needlenose pliers to remove the hooks, and watch out for the sharp teeth.

The most popular bait is live anchovies. These and other bait are nose hooked. Speaking of other baits, there is a group of them. These are usually referred to as brown baits. Brown baits include tomcod, kingfish, herring and smelt. More and more anglers are finding success with these offerings. Some are bigger and tougher than anchovies.

Two types of rigs and two types of hooks are used by halibut anglers. One rig uses a dropper for the sinker and the other uses a sliding sinker. Some prefer a treble hook(#8 or #10) while others prefer a single hook(#4 or #6). Either hook can be used with either rig;

**Dropper Rig**

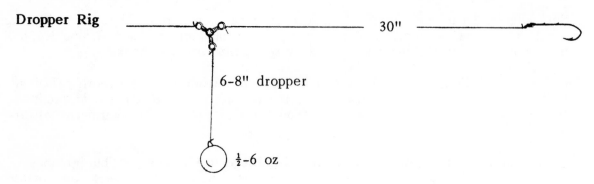

**Sliding Sinker Rig**

## Where to Fish

Santa Monica Bay and San Diego Bay are well known halibut grounds. For other boat spots, and shore fishing opportunities, see the Ocean Fishing Section.

## Cleaning and Cooking

Smaller halibut can be filleted. Larger ones are steaked. Even when filleting, the tail section can be steaked. When filleting, first make a vertical cut(the fish is laying flat) along the lateral line down to the spine. This allows you to "lift off" two manageable-sized fillets from each side of the fish. Halibut is dense, mild, somewhat sweet and low in fat. Popular cooking methods include broiling, barbecuing, poaching, frying and baking. The fillets can be sauteed.

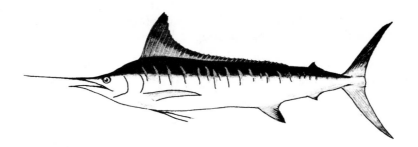

# How to Catch...Marlin (Striped)

Striped marlin are one of the truly exotic sport fish that is available in the Pacific off Southern California. They are spectacular, strong, big fish. Some caught in local waters, exceed 200 pounds. And they often make spectacular leaps when hooked.

Striped marlin, at times, make their first appearance in Southern California waters as early as July. But the best fishing months are usually September and October. Some striped marlin can still be around in November or even early December. In Baja, they are available year around.

Striped marlin are not generally considered good eating fish, although there is a big commercial market in Japan. But, they do make spectacular trophies. And many anglers catch these fish for the sport of it and release them to be caught again some other day.

## Fishing Techniques

Striped marlin are sometimes seen before they are hooked. They seem to live most of their lives near the surface and jump spontaneously. Often when sighted they are swimming lazily at the surface with their dorsal fin and upper half of their tail fin sticking up out of the water. Anglers who sneak up on these schools of "sleeping" fish often get a strike by casting live Spanish or green mackerel or sardines.

But most striped marlin are caught by trolling. Anglers troll near sighted fish and also take fish that suddenly surface to hit a lure. When a hook-up occurs it's a good idea to use the boat to help set the hook in the marlin's tough mouth(even with the sharpest of hooks). Accelerate the boat for a short burst and let the fish take line against a snugged-down reel drag.

## Tackle and Equipment

Some party boats will incidentally hook-up with a striped marlin when trolling for albacore, but they generally do not actively pursue marlin. This fact, plus the fact that striped marlin are a true blue water fish means that anglers need an open ocean boat to pursue marlin. Or they need a friend or relative that has one.

A heavy trolling rod with roller tip and a 4/0 to 6/0 sized reel with 30-40 pound test monofilament line is also a must. Outriggers are also helpful.

## Lures

The most popular striped marlin trolling lures go by such names as Clones, Koneheads, etc.

Size: about 10-12 inches with a size 7/0 to 10/0 hook.

Color: very bright psychedelic colors.

Desc: Clear plastic head with multi-colored skirt trailer.

## Where to Fish

The best Southern California area is a strip of water which ranges from the east end of Santa Catalina Island offshore to about San Clemente Island and south, in the direction of Los Coronados Islands, to the Mexican boundary.

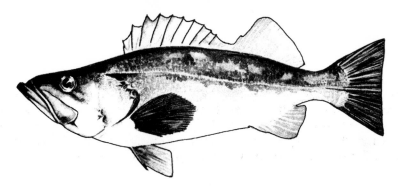

# How to Catch...Rockfish

Rockfish, often called rock cod, are a group of about 50 different bottom dwellers. They congregate around bottom structures like reefs and canyons all along the Southern California coast. Rockfish are fun to catch and among the best eating fish found in our ocean. Some of the most common rockfish names are salmon grouper, vermillion, olive, chili pepper and cow cod. In general, rockfish are bass-like in appearance with a compact body and large mouth. These bottom and kelp bed dwellers run up to 10 pounds or more but the average catch is 1-4 pounds.

## Fishing Techniques

Rockfishing for most anglers means drift fishing from a boat. It can be done as close in as ½ mile from shore to as far out as 25 miles or more, where the reefs and banks are 600 feet down.

The technique is quite simple. With the use of a depth sounder, locate the boat over a rocky bottom. Often the best location is one where a depth is changing, either on the upslope of a canyon or on the changing slope of a reef.

Now just lower your rig over the side until you feel the weight hit the bottom. Put the reel into gear, and crank up a foot or two. Check for the bottom, by lowering your line frequently, to avoid drifting into snags, or letting your bait move too far from the bottom. Jigging(moving your offering up and down a few feet) is always a good idea. The motion catches the eye of the rockfish.

Sometimes rockfish, usually smaller ones, are also caught alongside kelp beds in the shallows near shore. Again, fish near the bottom and reel in fast to keep the fish from snagging in the kelp.

## Tackle and Equipment

The heft or weight of the tackle needed for rockfishing depends primarily on the depth of water you're fishing in. See next page for details.

|  | 50-100 Feet | 300-600 Feet |
|---|---|---|
| Rod: | | |
| -length | 6-7 feet | 6-7 feet with rail board |
| -stiffness | med-med. heavy | med. heavy-heavy |
| -guide | roller tip helpful | roller |
| Reel: | med. ocean baitcasting | Penn Senator 114 6/0 |
| Line: | 25-40 lb. mono | 50-80 lb. mono or dacron |
| Sinker: | 4 oz.-1 lb. | ½-3 lb. |

At the end of your line, fasten a heavy swivel snap. To this, attach a rock cod rig or shrimp fly rig with 6/0 size hooks. I prefer the shrimp fly rig since they have feathers that add to the attractiveness of the offering. Shrimp fly rigs can be purchased in most ocean fishing-oriented bait and tackle shops for less than a dollar each. They typically have 3 or more hooks and a snap swivel at the end to attach the sinker.

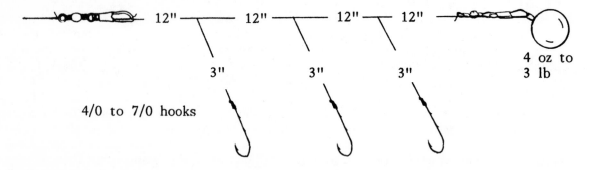

## Bait and Jigs

The most common baits for rockfishing are cut-up anchovy and squid pieces. Cut the pieces large enough to cover the hook. Other common baits are pieces of small rockfish. At times fish can be hooked using bare shrimp fly rigs. But bait adds an odor that is often helpful in enticing a bite. Chrome hex bar jigs(in the 4-16 ounce range) are also good producers.

## Where to Fish

See Pacific Ocean Fishing maps.

## Cleaning and Cooking

Rockfish are almost always filleted. Since almost all varieties of rockfish have very large heads, the yield of fillets can be as low as 20-30% of fish weight. Rock cod meat is lean, has low fat content and is mild tasting. These fillets lend themselves to the cooking method of choice including sauteing, broiling, poaching, frying or baking. Rockfish are also excellent when baked whole.

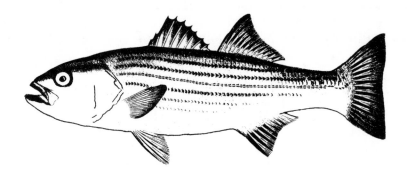

# How to Catch...Striped Bass

Striped bass represent a marvelous, relatively new freshwater fishing opportunity for Southern California anglers. And they are just about everything one could want in a sport fish:

- . Stripers are relatively easy to hook because they are voracious feeders.

- . These are tough and spunky fish, so expect a good fight.

- . Stripers are big fish. It's quite possible that when you catch your first striper, it will be the biggest fish of your life. Twenty pound fish are common!

- . They are excellent tablefare.

Striped bass are native to the Atlantic coast. They were first introduced to California, in the San Francisco Bay, in 1879. Striper are naturally anadromous fish, which simply means they breed in freshwater and live much of their lives in saltwater. Salmon are the most famous of this class of fish, but are not related to striped bass. Striped bass have flourished in the San Francisco area over the last 100 years, migrating back and forth from the ocean to the freshwater Sacramento and San Joaquin Delta system.

Then starting in the 1960's the Department of Fish and Game experimented with plants of striped bass in landlocked freshwater in Southern California. And guess what? The stripers don't seem to miss their time in the ocean at all. In fact, they're thriving in places like Lake Havasu, Lake Mead, Pyramid Lake, Lake Nacimiento and other Southland waters. The Southern California record fresh-water striper is in the 60 pound class! By the way, stripers have populated some Southern California lakes by the migration of small fish through the Aquaduct System.

The best fishing technique for catching striped bass depends on many things, including the nature of the waters being fished, the season, etc. In this section the basics of each of the most successful approaches is covered. If you want to know more about which works best, where and when, refer to the part of this book that deals with lakes and other Southland waters. For example, if you want to know what works at Havasu, look in the Lake Havasu Section of this book.

## Trolling

Trolling(pulling a lure through the water behind a boat) is one of the most popular techniques. It allows the angler to cover a wide area, if you're not sure where the fish are. Once a striper that hits a trolled line is landed, some anglers shift to one of the other techniques like casting, jigging or bait fishing. They do this because striper are often in schools, so if you've got one there are probably others in the vicinity. Of course, trolling through the area where the first hook-up occurred is another option.

Most striper trolling is done by tying the lure directly to the main line, or a snap swivel may be used. Big(5-7 inches) minnow-shaped plugs, like Rebel, Rapala, Bomber, Cordell Redfin and Storm Big Mac are the choice of most trollers. These lures come in differing depth configurations, such as shallow running(4-10 ft.), deep diving(8-10 ft.) and extra deep diving(15-30 ft.). Try several configurations on different rods to locate the right depth.

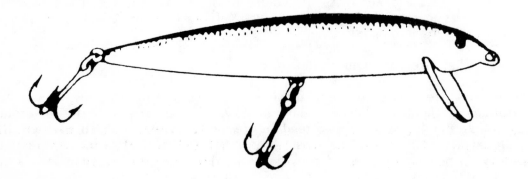

Once a rig is in the water, check the tip of your rod. It should be twitching constantly. This is the action from your lure. Adjust the boat speed to get this effect. Set the drag on your reel just firm enough to prevent line from being taken out. Set the clicker in the "on" position. A singing clicker means a strike. The forward motion of the lure will usually set the hook. Tighten down slightly on the drag before playing the fish.

Sometimes stripers are down deeper than simple trolled lures can reach. If you're equipped, lead core line or downriggers can be used to troll at the depth that the stripers are lurking. The same type of lures or Kastmaster or Hopkins type spoons can be used. More information on deep trolling is in the Trout(Lakes) Section of this book.

## Graph Recorders

The wide spread use of graph recorders has provided another way of finding stripers, besides trolling. Both paper and video depth recorders are great for locating schools of stripers that are over underwater dropoffs and points, or just suspended. Knowledge of the stripers location and depth make them easier to catch. This is especially true when using bait fishing or jigging techniques. Let's take a look at bait fishing first.

## Bait Fishing

Bait fishing can be done from a boat or from shore. Boat anglers usually anchor. A large hook(about 2/0 to 4/0) can be used since stripers are not hook shy. The most common rig used is a small rubbercore sinker, with the hook held directly to 12 to 20 pound line.

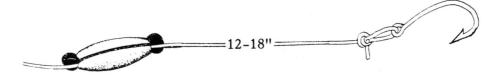

Sometimes, especially if lighter line is used, it's possible to eliminate the sinker all together. This allows the bait to free fall and flutter on its way down below the boat. This approach is the same as used on saltwater party boats.

Shore anglers, or shallow water bait anglers are more likely to use a sliding sinker rig. This is much like a trout bait rig, but on a larger scale. When the striper takes the bait, play out 5-10 feet of line, When it hits hard, set the hook. Some anglers prefer a catfish type rig for striper(see Catfish Section of this book.

**Sliding Sinker Rig**

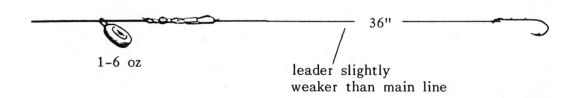

1-6 oz

36"

leader slightly
weaker than main line

The most popular striped bass bait is probably frozen anchovies.  Other baits that are used with success include nightcrawlers, mudsuckers and threadfin shad.

Local bait shops will know which are most effective depending on location and season of the year.  Live bait fish are hooked just below the dorsal fin, with the hook entering on one side and exiting on the other side of the fish.  Or you can hook them through the lips.  Once a live bait fish dies, the hook may be put in more securely, often with the leader secured to the tail by a half-hitch knot.

## Jigging

Once striped bass are located, especially if they're found down deep below a boat, the vertical jigging approach has proven to be dynamite.  Here's how it works.  Drop a spoon-type lure(tied to the line, or attached with a snap swivel) over the side and let it flutter down to the depth where the fish are feeding. If it's not taken instantly a yo-yo action is used to bring on a strike.  When the striper are on the bottom, flick the rod tip to raise the spoon up off the bottom, and then let it flutter back down.  Strikes seem to occur most often on the fluttering fall.  Kastmaster and Hopkins(say a Shorty 75) are popular.

## Casting

Sometimes striper anglers are lucky enough or cunning enough to be there when stripers are surface feeding on shad.  The tip off is bird activity and/or a noticeable "boiling" of shad forage fish on the surface.  This is one of the occasions when casting is the way to go.  First, approach the boil carefully and slowly. And move slowly to within casting range.  You don't want to drive the frenzied striper back down.  Some of the best casting lures are Pencil Poppers, Zara Spooks, ½ ounce Krocodiles or Kastmasters.

Another casting approach that works on stripers, especially when they're feeding in shallow water, is structure casting; casting near dams, rocky shorelines, shore cover, bridge columns, etc.  It's the same as largemouth bass casting.  The approach is the same and the same types of lures often seem to work.

## Tackle and Equipment

Striper fishing can be done with a wide variety of tackle. Light weight black bass tackle can be used. Medium weight spinning equipment, or free spool/star drag conventional reel–light action rods are used for trolling. Light spinning equipment can also be used for trolling. Some feel this is the most exciting way to take stripers in the 4–12 pound range. Rods in the 6–7½ foot range are about right. Live bait saltwater equipment is also widely used.

## Cleaning and Cooking

Small stripers are usually filleted. Large ones(above say 10 pounds) can be steaked.

Striped bass fillets or steaks are white, mild in flavor, low in fat and especially good eating. Barbecuing, broiling, poaching, baking and frying are all good approaches.

**RAINBOW TROUT**

# How to Catch... Trout (in Streams)

We are blessed by the numerous, fine trout streams in Southern California(many of these are described in the Mountain Trout Fishing Section of this book). Stream trout fishing is appealing because it can be the type of experience you personally want it to be. It can be accessible or remote, challenging or relaxing, simple or complicated.

Many people have a stereotype in their minds of the typical trout angler. It includes a flyrod, hip-high waders, a vest decorated with multicolored flys, a hat with more multicolored flys, a landing net hanging from the waist, all topped off with a Norman Rockwell-like wicker creel. This, of course, exactly describes some trout fishermen. But, forget this stereotype. Stream trout fishing can be productive and enjoyable, not only for the avid, well-equipped fly fisherman, but for everyone. You don't even need to use a flyrod, if you don't want to.

The purpose of this section is to describe, in detail, several of the basic ways to catch stream trout, regardless of the type of fishing you prefer and the type of tackle you have.

There are several different types of trout in Southern California streams. The most common are rainbow. Most are planted, but some are native. Others include the German brown trout, the brook trout and the golden trout(see the How to Catch Golden Trout Section of this book).

## Some Fundamentals

Stream trout fishing, no matter what equipment is used, focuses on casting a fly, spinner, spoon or bait into a likely place in the stream and then retrieving it in as natural a manner as possible.

Other fundamentals;

- Trout always face upstream, watching for food to be delivered to them by the moving water. So your offering should be presented in the same manner - moving from upstream to downstream.

- Trout are very leary and easily spooked. Since they're facing upstream and smelling the water that comes from upstream, always move upstream as you fish. This way, you're less likely to be detected. Move quietly and stay out of the line of sight of likely trout hangouts. Keep your shadow off the water.

- In the same vane, fish on the shady side of the stream, especially in the hours just after sunrise and just before sunset.

- Casts in an upstream direction or up and across the stream are preferred over downstream casts. Downstream casts require a retrieve that is against the current and therefore, unnatural in appearances.

- Trout stay near the bottom of the stream. So your offering must move along near the bottom. The exception to this rule is when dry fly fishing. Dry flies(floating flies) imitate floating insects being carried along by the current. Trout will rise up to take these flies. Dry fly fishing is evening fishing.

- As with most fishing, early morning and evening are best fishing periods. But, trout can be caught at any time of the day.

- Keep hooks sharp. Banging rocks and pebbles can dull them quickly.

- If you're not succeeding in whatever approach you're using flies, spinners, bait), try other offerings until you find the one that works.

- Trout hang out behind boulders that break the current, in deep holes, in slower water near the undercut edge of a stream(especially in shaded areas), and at the head and tail of pools. Concentrate your efforts on these areas.

- When you spot an obviously expert trout angler, watch where he or she casts from, where he or she put the offering and how it is retrieved.

Often the best places to cast from are in the water.  Don't let that
stop you.  Just be careful and carry a wading staff to probe the bottom and improve balance.

# Fly Fishing

Flies,both dry(floating) and wet(sinking) are very small and light.  Too light to
cast any distance.  In fly fishing this difficulty is overcome by using flyline that
has enough weight so it can be cast.  The fly, connected by a light leader to
the end of the flyline "just goes along for a ride" as the line is played out and
finally set on its final trajectory.  The purpose of the fly reel is simply to store
line that is not being used, at the moment, and to retrieve line when necessary.

Fly fishing is an art and a science.  Some say it is the ultimate fishing experience.  Some people **only** fly fish.  Many whole volumes have been written on
fly fishing.  In our limited space here we cannot compete.  But here are the insights that produce fish in Southern California;

- If you're having trouble handling fly fishing equipment and making a
  good cast, consider a fly fishing class, watch others do it, read up on
  the subject in specialized books, and practice, practice, practice.

- Dry flies must float.  Floating solution, leader sinking solution, tapered
  leaders and generally good floating fly line make this possible.

- As the old truism goes, "match the hatch."  Dry flies must imitate
  nature.  Good Southern California dry flies include California mosquito,
  light Cahill and the Adams.  Size #14 and #16 are best.

- Present the dry fly above the suspected feeding fish and let it float
  naturally through that feeding area.

- Dry fly fishing is an evening affair.  The several hours before dark
  are best.

- Wet flies imitate underwater creatures such as the larva or pupa state
  of aquatic insects, nymphs, grubs, etc.

- Successful wet flies in Southern California include #6 and #8 Mayfly
  nymphs, Woolly Worms, and Zug Bug and light tan caddis larvae flies.

- As the fly drifts back to you, take in excessive line.  Then you'll
  be ready to strike.

- Watch the tip of your floating fly line.  If it hesitates or pauses, set
  the hook.

. Standard streamers(which immitate bait fish) are the matuka(in olive), the marabou streamer and the muddler minnow.

. Many wet fly devotees use two different flies at a time.

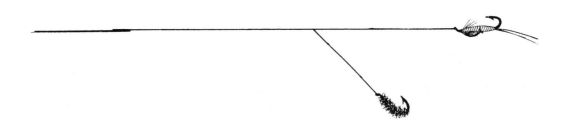

There is a great deal of variety in fly fishing equipment. One can spend hundreds of dollars or you can buy a rod/reel combination that is quite decent for less than $50.00. For starters, a 7½-8½ foot rod matched with #6 line is good. An automatic reel costs a few dollors more, but makes taking up excessive line so much easier.

## Spinning

Spinning fishing means stream trout fishing using spinning or even spincasting equipment. The most popular set-ups include light spinning tackle and ultra-light spinning tackle. Ultra-light tackle is the easiest to handle and probably the most appropriate. It's capable of casting even small offerings, to sufficient distances with a 4 pound test line. Here are the fundamentals of stream trout fishing with spinning tackle;

. The most common lures are very small spinners, probably never larger than a #2. Since retrieves are with the current(you're still casting upstream), a spinner whose blade rotates freely with little more motion than current speed is more desirable. These spinners imitate swimming bait fish. A popular example of a spinner of this caliber is the Panther Marten #2, 1/16 ounce black bodied spinner. Gold blades are good for low light or overcast periods, chrome blades are recommended for sunny periods, and copper is good for not-so-clear water. Try several.

. Besides spinners, spoons are also good, like the Super Duper. Retrieval speed is critical for the success of both spinners and spoons. Test both in quiet pools. Both types put out a vibration that can be sensed in the motion at the tip of the rod. Watch for this and adjust retrieval speed accordingly. Also, frequently change return speed to give offerings a more natural swimming pattern.

. Spinners need to be worked near the bottom. Adjust your retrieval speed to achieve this.  You'll hang up some spinners, but you'll catch more fish.

. Some lures are best tied directly to the main line.  Others may twist the line if a small snap swivel is not used.  Experiment, but if using a swivel, make sure it is in good working order and has a rounded connector at the lure end.  This will insure proper action in the water.

## Bait Fishing for Trout

Stream trout fishing with bait is the most flexible of all approaches.  It's flexible because of the wide choice of baits that produce fish.  And it's flexible because it can be done with either fly fishing equipment or spinning equipment.  Some devotees even combine the two by using monofilament line on a fly rod and reel.  All these possibilities are fine.  Here are the fundamentals of trout stream bait fishing;

. Redworms are probably the most popular bait followed by bottled salmon eggs.  Cheese and marshmallows are also popular.  Then, there is a whole category of natural, live baits including crickets, beetles, grubs, larvae and pupae.  Some anglers collect bait right out of the stream by using a fine mesh screen to trap bait dislodged by moving large rocks in the streambeds.

. If you're using live bait, it should be alive.  So, store and transport them carefully and hook them so as not to inflict fatal damage(at least not instant fatal damage).

. A short shank #8 or #10 hook is good.  Try to conceal the entire hook into the bait.

. You want the bait to drift along with the current near the bottom of the stream.  Unweighted drifting is best.  If you need weight to get near the bottom, use as little split shot as possible, about 8-10 inches from the hook.

. Since your bait is under water and drifting, it's not all that easy to detect bites.  It helps to keep slack out of the line(while still allowing drift) and to set the hook on any sign of hesitation or pause in drift.

## Using Casting Bobber for Trout

Purest fly fishermen may cringe at this approach, but here goes anyway.  Some people would like to be able to cast flies or small baits without mastering a fly rod.  And some can't afford fly fishing equipment.  For this group a casting bobber is the answer.

A casting bobber is a small, clear plastic float that adds enough weight to a fly or a small bait to allow casting with a spinning or spincasting reel and monofilament line.

casting
bobber

Casting bobbers are available in several sizes and configurations  Some even allow you to vary weight by allowing water inside the bobber.

Fish a casting bobber rig just as you would a dry fly.  If you use a wet fly or bait, allow enough distance between the bobber and the hook so your offering gets down to near the bottom.  In rapidly flowing water, some split shot about 8 inches from the hook may be added.

## Tackle and Equipment

Besides your choice of rod, reel, line and enticements to put at the end of it, trout anglers need several other items.  Essential are both a creel(canvas ones can be purchased for as little as $5.00) or a fishing vest and an inexpensive landing net.  A needle-nose pliers or other hook removing device is also essential.  Small trout should be released, with as little hook damage as possible.   In fact, some trout fishermen flatten the barbs on all their hooks to facilitate catch and release.  Releasing large trout is possibly even more important.  It takes large ones to produce small ones.

Optional equipment for trout fishing includes polarized sun glasses, waders and a wading staff.  The sun glasses help take the glare off the water and improve underwater visibility.  The use of waders depends on air temperature, water temperature, the number of stepping stones in a stream and ones desire to stay dry. Wading staffs(just a light tree limb) are great to help maintain balance.

## Cleaning and Cooking

Small trout(pan size) are generally just gutted and gilled(field cleaned).  Larger trout are often filleted.  Trout is mild, lean and sweet.  It is suitable for just about any cooking approach.  Sauteing is probably the most popular. The flesh of trout is tender, delicately flavored and can range in color from white to a pinkish we associate with salmon.

**BROWN TROUT**

# How to Catch... Trout (in Lakes)

Fishing for trout in lakes is very different from stream trout fishing. This is true because the lake environment changes the behavior of trout. Stream trout are always facing upstream, confined to shallow waters, on or near the bottom, and near or behind structures like boulders, undercuts, etc. The stream determines the location and habits of trout.

Trout in lakes have different ground rules dictating their lives. Food doesn't necessarily "flow" to them, they must find it. Lake water temperatures vary by season and depth, so trout will change depth to find oxygen rich water of a comfortable temperature for them. At times they may be near the surface, and at other times they may be down 80 feet or more.

A few Southern California trout lakes also have king or silver salmon planted in them. Salmon and trout in lakes behave and are caught using the same techniques, lures and bait. Usually, anglers pursuing trout will catch an occassional salmon.

If you're catching trout in a lake, especially in the summertime, and you'd like some salmon, it sometimes helps to fish a little deeper. Research has shown that rainbow and brown trout favor water temperatures of between 55° and 60°. But, the same research determined that king and silver salmon favor 55° water, which will be down deeper.

## Reading a Lake

The specifics of a lake says a lot about the location of trout. And, as many anglers have discovered, you've got to find them before you can catch them. As a matter of fact, catching trout in lakes is quite easy, once they are located. Here are the fundamentals;

.   Trout, even in lakes, relate to structures. Trout use structures to shelter themselves from predators and to keep out of direct sun. Depending on the time of year, overhanging trees, cliff areas, submerged points, coves and submerged river channels are good starting points.

.   Trout move to locate food and oxygen. The primary inlet to a lake is always a prime location. It washes in food and cool, oxygen-rich water. In cooler months, shoreline weedbeds may also provide insects and bait fish. The windward shoreline is also a good possibility. Drifting food will concentrate here. Finally, newly planted trout usually hang around the planting site for several days or more.

.   A depth sounder can be an important tool. It not only will locate struture-like underwater islands and submerged drop-offs, but it will also locate schools of bait fish and the trout themselves.

.   Trout are found down deeper in lakes in the summer months. Some Southern California lakes stratify(or divide) into three layers during the warming months and can remain in this condition until fall. The top layer is too warm and too low in oxygen for trout and salmon. They concentrate near the top of the second layer, or thermocline. In this layer there is plenty of oxygen and forage fish. This layer may be from 15-50 feet down depending on lake depth and size. Water temperature will be in the 55-60° range. A depth sounder, underwater temperature gauge or locals can all help you to determine the proper depth to fish.

LAKE STRATIFICATION
Surface
Epilimnion Layer
Thermocline Layer
Oxygen and Baitfish Rich
Hypolimnion Layer
Bottom

## Fishing Techniques

There are three primary methods of catching trout in lakes;

1. Trolling - In one form or another, this is probably the most productive method of catching trout in lakes.

2. Bait Fishing - A very good method, especially for shore fishing. Can also be done from a boat, for example, at a stream inlet of the lake.

3. Casting - Also a very productive shore fishing method. Can also be done from a boat.

It is also possible to catch trout in lakes by fly fishing. But, even avid fly fishermen will admit it is difficult. Dry flies will only work, for example, when an insect hatch is taking place. Even then, they may not work because they don't move with the current as they do in streams. Wet flies, streamers, etc., can be used in lakes, and can produce at times, if you're either very skillful or very lucky. Remote, high altitude mountain lakes, when there are hungry trout and little angling pressure, are the best candidates for lake fly fishing success. If you're interested in more information on lake fly fishing, check out several fly fishing books from you local public library.

## Trolling for Trout

Trolling is simply pulling an offering at the end of your line, through the water, using a boat. It can and is done with boats ranging from a canoe, to a rowboat, to an inboard/outboard.

There are actually two separate and distinct aspects of trolling for trout. The first is the trolling rig itself, and the second is the tackle/equipment combinations used to troll the rig at a prescribed depth. Let's look at each separately;

**Trolling rig** - A trolling rig is made up of these components(in order of placement on line);

1. Rudder - A blade to prevent line twist.

2. Flasher - An attractant which imitates a school of bait fish.

3. Swivel - Prevents twist.

4. Snubber - Absorbs shock of a strike. Use is optional, but recommended.

5. Leader - About 18 inches of monofilament.

6. Offering - Spoon, plug or baited hook.

The flasher and rudder are usually sold in a packaged unit. Use larger units for murky water or deep trolling. Then you just attach on the snubber, tie on a leader and attach your offering. See diagram below;

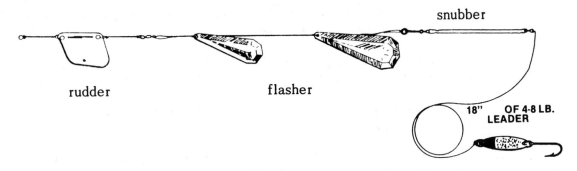

snubber

rudder                    flasher

18" OF 4-8 LB. LEADER

**Trolling Tackle/Equipment** – Unlike the trolling rig, which is quite standard, trolling tackle/equipment provides several options and alternatives.

In the cold months of the year when trout are found near the surface, trolling rigs can be handled with light spinning or baitcasting tackle and about 10-12 pound monofilament line. This is especially true if a flasher is not used. Weight can be added to the rudder(using tied line) to troll 2-10 feet down below the surface.

Unfortunately, many of us do most of our lake trout fishing in the summer when the trout are down deep in the lake. To get a trolling rig down to 30, 60, or more feet you have these choices;

. Use leadcore trolling line on a good sized conventional reel. Medium Penn freshwater reels with levelwind are popular(e.g. 210 series). With slow trolling speed, leadcore line sinks at about 45°, so, for example, 50 feet of line, will produce a 25 foot trolling depth.

. Use a downrigger – This is by far the most desirable approach, especially if you need to go down more than 40 feet. A downrigger will take your trolling rig down to a known depth(they're equipped with depth counters) and allow you to play and land the fish on light tackle. See the next page for illustration.

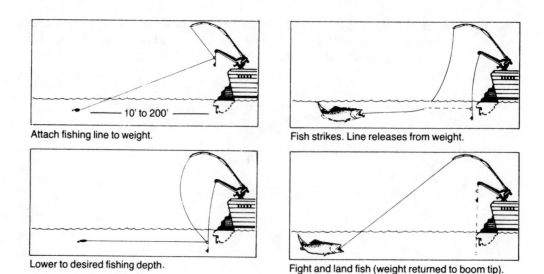

Attach fishing line to weight.

Fish strikes. Line releases from weight.

Lower to desired fishing depth.

Fight and land fish (weight returned to boom tip).

**Trolling Tips** - No matter what depth you're trolling or what equipment you're using, these tips will help produce fish;

.   Troll slowly.  The best trolling is slow trolling.  Some highly success- ful trollers, for example, use only oar power.

.   Change trolling speed often.  Every minute or two isn't too frequent. Sometimes it even helps to speed up for just a few seconds and then slow down.  This gives added up-and-down action to the flasher and lure.

.   Change depth.  If you're not sure of the depth you're trolling at(it can vary depending on boat speed and amount of line out, for all approaches except downrigging) or the depth the trout are at, vary depth until you get a strike.  Then stick there.

.   Troll an "S" Pattern.  Trolling experts suggest this approach, 1)because it covers more territory than straight line trolling and, 2)because it causes speed, direction and depth changes to occur in the flasher and lure.  These movements and resulting vibrations attract trout.

## Bait Fishing for Trout

Bait fishing can be done from shore or boat.  The most common tackle is light spinning equipment.

Despite all the variety in trout bait fishing, the most productive technique is probably the sliding sinker rig.  It is most often used from shore, but also is well suited to anchored boat fishing in coves and inlets;

sliding
sinker

baitholder No 6-12
or, treble No 16

The purpose of the sliding sinker rig is to allow the bait to move freely when a trout picks it up. With a fixed sinker rig, the trout would notice the drag on the offering and drop it.

The process begins by casting out the baited rig to a likely spot. Let it sink all the way to the bottom and then slowly crank in any slack. Now, sit down, get comfortable and open the bail on your spinning reel. Personally, I don't believe in putting a rod down or propping it up on a stick. I believe in holding the rod. Then you can feel the slightest tug on your bait. In fact, I like to have my line, in front of the reel, go between the thumb and index finger of my non-reeling hand. This puts my senses directly in touch with my bait.

When the trout picks up the bait, play off line from the spool, so no resistance is felt by the fish. A pause may be detected after the first movement of line. Wait until it starts moving out again(this means the trout has swallowed the bait, literally swallowed the bait). Close the bail and set the hook. You've got yourself a fish.

A wide variety of baits are used. Salmon eggs, cheese, minnows, shad, worms crickets. A combination of baits is also popular. Some use a small marshmallow/salmon egg/nightcrawler combination. The egg provides visual attraction and the marshmallow provides buoyancy so the whole offering floats slightly off the bottom. Another way to accomplish this buoyant effect using nightcrawlers is to inflate them with air. Crawler inflaters are available to accomplish this task. Many large trout are caught on both combination baits and inflated nightcrawlers.

Bobber fishing can also be quite effective for trout. This is an especially effective method in winter and early spring when lake surface temperatures are cool and trout are often feeding near the surface. Simply tie your hook to the line, put a split shot a foot or so up from the hook, and snap on a bobber up the line. Six feet is a good distance to try first. Cast it out and watch your bobber closely.

## Casting for Trout

Casting for trout is a popular shore fishing option, especially among younger anglers. And it can be effective. The most popular tackle is again light spinning or spincasting.

Lures can be tied directly to the end of the main line or attached with a snap swivel. I prefer the snap swivel. It prevents any line twist and provides a way to change lures easily. Most trout lures imitate small bait fish. Silver and gold colors are good in 1/8 to 3/8 ounce sizes;

- Kastmasters

- Roostertails

- Phoebes

- Mepps Spinners

Cast out as far as possible, let lure settle to the desired retrieve depth and return at the speed that provides the most natural action. Slower is probably better. And vary the pace of your retrieve. The small bait you're trying to duplicate don't swim fast and they don't swim at a steady pace. Sometimes it's best to let the lure sink for sometime before starting your retrieve. A problem with this approach is the frequent snags(on sunken branches, etc.) and lost lures. Some anglers minimize this difficulty by replacing the original treble hook with a weedless hook.

## Cleaning and Cooking

See Trout(in Streams) for cleaning instructions.

Smaller trout are best when sauteed or oven fried, or when baked, either plain or with a light sauce. The larger, whole trout are excellent when baked or poached. Trout is at its best when prepared simply.

**GOLDEN TROUT**

# How to Catch... Trout (Golden)

Are you ready for a completely different kind of fishing experience?  Well that's what fishing for our state fish, the golden trout, will provide.  Goldens are considered by many to be the most beautiful fish in California, or anywhere, for that matter.  They appear almost luminescent when contrasted to the blue and green hues of their high, clean, mountain water habitat.

Goldens were first discovered around the turn of the century in waters of the Kern River system, where they then inhabited about 300 miles of streams.  Golden trout are native to no other waters.  Later, rainbow trout were planted in tributaries of the Kern River, resulting in widespread hybridization with goldens.  Introduction of brown trout also displaced the golden from many of their ancestral streams.  By the 1950's  these actions combined to squeeze the pure golden trout into about 20% of its original territory.

Fortunately due to man's positive actions, golden trout are much better off today.  Six lakes in the Cottonwood Lake System are used to protect golden trout brood stock and supply hundreds of thousands of eggs to California hatcheries each year.  These eggs are taken down from the lakes by pack mules.  Now the list of golden trout lakes and streams is 5 pages long(single-spaced, 2 columns per paper).  Most of these waters are in the Southern Sierra.

But golden trout fishing is not for everyone.  You can't park on the shores of golden trout streams or lakes.  To catch golden trout, and enjoy the magnificent mountain scenery  you must be prepared to backpack or ride a horse to the high-country. Many good spots are at an elevation of 8,000 feet or more. Here the air is thin and the effort is great, but the goldens make it all worthwhile.

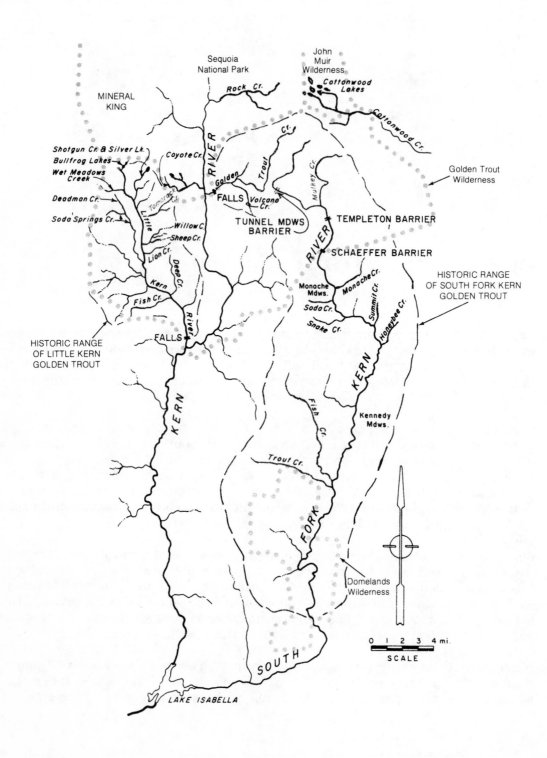

## Where to Fish and What to Take

The California Department of Fish and Game publishes a list entitled, "Where to find California's Golden Trout." It is available if you write them at Resource's Building, 1416 Ninth St., Sacramento, CA 95814. As mentioned earlier, this is a long, 5 page list, so there are many opportunities. Interestingly, many spots on the list are high mountain, alpine lakes where the golden trout have been planted. None of these lakes contained trout prior to this, and contrary to popular belief, golden trout never occurred naturally in lakes. For more information on golden trout locales, see the Bakersfield Trout Section of the Mountain Trout chapter of this book.

Backpack anglers obviously need light gear and equipment, like sleeping bags, tents, cooking gear, freeze-dried food, etc. Good hiking boots are also a must. For those interested in horse packing, seek out a guide or outfitter. They advertise in outdoor papers and magazines and are also listed in the local yellow pages for a given area.

## Tackle and Lures

Rod and reels that are especially designed for backpacking are the equipment of choice. For example, pack rods come in about 4 sections of 15 or 16 inches each and ultralight spinning reels weigh about $\frac{1}{2}$ pound. But most 2 piece spinning or fly rods and reels aren't that bulky or heavy, so they will do nicely.

Spin anglers should bring a good assortment of small spinners and wobbling spoons. Red and whites are good colors. Also take some casting bobbers to use with flies. Flyrodders can take a wide selection of favorite dry flies, wet flies and nymphs.

## Catching Golden Trout

Golden trout are on-again, off-again biters. This makes catching them as easy as tossing something into the water one day and getting skunked the next day. Maybe this just makes them like any other fish. Of course, only artificial lures with single hooks(except in the mainstream of the Kern River) are allowed in the Golden Trout Wilderness Area.

The best advice for catching golden trout is to be persistent. Experiment with different offerings. Try something, and then try something else. And when you do catch golden trout, consider releasing many of them. But the few you keep, you'll enjoy eating. They are delicious. See Trout Cleaning and Cooking in the Trout(Streams) Section of this book, for specific instructions.

# How to Catch...White Sea Bass

The white sea bass is a highly prized sport fish in Southern California waters, not because of its fighting ability, but because it is outstanding on the table. Unfortunately, its numbers and size have declined over the years. There are season, size and limit regulations on this fish, so be aware of current regulations.

White sea bass are not bass, but members of the croaker family, along with corvina and white croaker(or kingfish). They can be caught in Southern California waters almost any month of the year, but February through June are probably the best months. The average catch is in the 10 to 25 pound range, but lunkers exceeding 60 pounds are also caught.

## Fishing Techniques

White sea bass respond best to live squids. Sandy bottom areas are usually most productive, and these bass are generally taken nearer to the bottom than to the surface. Most often a single hook, 2/0 to 4/0, tied directly to 25-40 pound test line is the rig of choice. A small rubber core sinker or sliding sinker rig is put ahead of the hook to help take the squid down. The rig is illustrated in the Yellowtail Section of this book.

Gently(hooks in squid's tails can tear out) toss the baited hook into the water and give line off the spool as it sinks. The bass often take it on the way down. If not, use a hesitating retrieve on the way up. When the squid is taken, give about 3-5 feet of line(if you're on the way up, you must release the spool) before setting the hook.

Other white sea bass baits that are good, when available, are sardines and green mackerel. Or, if the bass are really on a hit, they will take vertically worked jigs. White colors and candy-bar styles are best.

## Tackle and Equipment

Often the prime time to take white sea bass is at night, in spring, when the squid are mating. But many white sea bass are caught in daylight hours. Heavy, conventional saltwater rod and reel are used for white sea bass. They don't fight long, but do put up a tenacious, deep battle, and, at times, use the kelp to get tangled and escape.

## Where to Fish

Some of the best places are the Coronado Islands(in winter), Catalina Island, Santa Cruz Island, off Carpenteria and Rocky Point near Redondo Beach. But white sea bass are taken all along the Southland coast, some in bays and shallow inland waters. See the Ocean Fishing Section of this book.

## Cleaning and Cooking

White sea bass are filleted or the bigger fish are steaked. The preparation method of choice will result in a delicious meal.

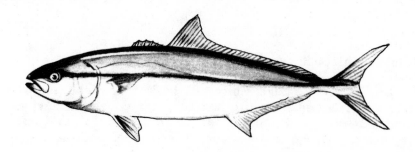

# How to Catch...Yellowtail

Yellowtails, or "yellows" or "tails" are one of the premier sport fish in Southern California waters. These close relatives of the amberjack have earned this reputation because it is a vicious striker, a hard and cunning fighter and more prevalent and accessible than many other fish in Southern California waters. Besides all this, it is good eating. Some fish are caught from shore, but the bulk are caught from rented skiffs, private boats and party boats. The average yellowtail catch is in the 5-20 pound range, but some exceed 40 pounds.

Yellowtail fishing in Southland waters can begin as early as March, but late spring is usually the peak season. Summer can be good and then there is usually an upsurge in the fall. Yellowtails like a water temperature of 67-69°. Once hooked, yellowtails have the unnerving ability to head for the nearest object that will help them break loose. This could be kelp, rocks, boat propellers or anchor lines. Maximum drag tension short of breaking the line is needed in this instance to prevent the fish from reaching these objects.

Although yellowtail will often take a variety of baits and jigs, at times they are finicky eaters. It's at these times when sly anglers go down in line and hook size. Live squid, mackerel and anchovies all work for yellowtail, as do several types of jigs. Let's look at each approach.

## Live Squid Fishing

Live squid is the "bait of choice" for yellowtail, as well as for white sea bass, large calico bass, rockfish, and large halibut.  If an angler has live squid in his or her bait tank, the chances of yellowtail success rises sharply.  Squid are seasonal, but when they are available, they are worth going after.  In the spring(the squid spawning months) boat anglers sometimes fish for the squid, before fishing for the sport fish.  There are two approaches.  At night squid are attracted by light.  Bright lights from the boat are shined into the water and when the squid arrive, they are corraled in a net.

Hook and line are necessary to catch squid at times.  A 3-3½ inch squid jig is used.  Two or three jigs are placed about 1 foot apart and are taken down to the bottom with a 1-6 ounce sinker.  The jigs have two sets of bristled metal rings at the bottom.  Squid attach themselves to the jigs and are reeled up.  A little shaking puts them in the bait tank.  Veteran squidders like spots at about the 18 fathom mark.  Good squid concentrations are south of Catalina Island, the Channel Islands and the La Jolla Beds.

Fresh dead or frozen whole squid are also used, if live squid aren't available.  Squid are hooked through the tail on a single 3/0 to 5/0 hook with a 1-2 ounce sliding sinker riding right at the hook.  Lead head hooks can be substituted for the sliding sinker.  No sinker is used if the fish are near enough to the surface to be seen.

There is a technique to hooking squid.  It's best to hold the squid so that its head(and sharp beak and tennacles) are in the palm of one hand with its tail stretching out between your thumb and index finger.  Now just take the hook in the other hand and run it through the pointed tail.

Cast the hooked squid out gently and allow it to sink to the bottom, thumbing the spool as line goes out.  Strikes often occur on the way down.  Give line and count to 6 or 8 before setting the hook.  If the squid makes it to the bottom unmolested, retrieve it with a pumping, stop and go motion.  You'll need to throw the reel out of gear when a hit occurs.  Give the yellowtail about 4-5 feet of line and then put the reel back in gear and set the hook.  25-30 pound test line is good for live squid angling.

## Live Mackerel Fishing

Both Spanish and greenback mackerel are used.  But the smaller Spanish variety is more desirable.  They are also good for large calico bass and white sea bass angling.  They are sometimes available from bait sellers, and can be caught quite easily on multihook rigs like Lucky Joes or Shrimp fly rigs.  At times its difficult not to catch a mackerel.

Mackerel are most often fished on a hook tied directly to a 1/0 to 4/0 hook, depending on the size of the bait.  25-30 pound test line is recommended. Many anglers prefer to hook the mackerel across the nose.  Others prefer to hook them through the anus to make them swim deeper.

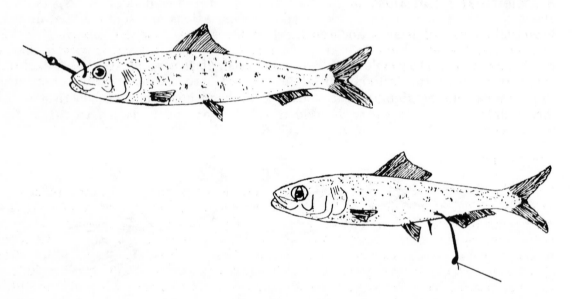

Since mackerel have a rather tough head, a stiff rod is helpful in setting the hook.  Allow the yellowtail to swallow the large bait before the set.

## Live Anchovy Fishing

Anchovies are small and more fragile than mackerel and squid.  So live anchovy angling requires lighter line to get a good swimming effect in the water.  20 pound line or even 15 pound line is needed.  The problem with this situation is that this light line might not be enough to prevent wise yellowtails from running for the kelp, rocks or whatever.  But if squid or mackerel aren't available, and the fish are leary of heavier line, anchovies on 15 pound line is worth the gamble.  Hook the anchovies through the nose or gill cover on about a #4 hook. See the Barracuda Section of this book for illustrations.

## Jig Fishing

There are several jig approaches that work, at times, on yellowtail. The most popular is called "yo-yo" jigging. A 4-12 inch "candy-bar" type, or C-Strike jig is used on about 40 pound line. Begin by dropping the jig straight down all the way to the bottom. Sharply lift and crank the jig up 4-5 feet. Drop it down and repeat it a time or two. If no strike occurs, retrieve the jig as fast as possible. Party boat captains tell customers to "crank like crazy" all the way up to the surface. Yellowtail, that aren't otherwise interested in feeding, will often strike a fast moving jig.

## Tackle and Equipment

Most yellowtail anglers use conventional reels. Popular models are the Penn Jig-master and Newell equivalent size. Spinning reels are not recommended because of the need for relatively heavy line and tough drag systems to keep yellowtails out of obstacles. Rods like the Sabre 660, 665 and 670 are good matches. For live anchovy angling, 15 pound line and something like a Sabre 870 is more appropriate.

## Where to Fish

Yellowtail are always on the move, but they do hang out in selected places. Some of the best are rock pinnacles, floating kelp patches or even sunken wrecks. Anchoring near these types of structures rather than drifting is recommended. Birds working the surface are always a tip off. Good fishing spots are detailed in the Ocean Fishing Section of this book. The North Island, South Kelp, Middle Ground and Rockpile are good in the Coronados. Southland hot spots include the Channel Islands, reefs near Santa Barbara, kelp at San Pedro, La Jolla and Pt. Loma, Santa Catalina Island and San Clemente Island.

## Cleaning and Cooking

Yellowtail are most often filleted, but large ones can be steaked. The fish is moderately fatty and nearly as rich as tuna in flavor and texture. Freshly caught fish is good barbecued, smoked or canned.

# Surf Fishing

I always think of William Conrad, casting into the surf at sunset on a beautiful Pacific beach, when I think of surf fishing. He started his outdoor program on T.V. with this scene, year after year. And why not? Surf fishing is man and nature at its best. It's just you, the roaring breakers, the sea birds, and salt spray and hopefully the fish.

For those who demand more than sea birds and salt spray, there are practical reasons why so many people enjoy surf fishing;

- There are miles and miles of accessible beaches to fish.

- It can be done year around.

- The necessary equipment is inexpensive.

- Bait is often free.

- Fish can be caught without a great deal of skill.

## Fishing Techniques

Later in this section some of the best surf fishing spots are listed. But exactly where on a beach to fish is important. It's best, if possible, to scout a beach at low tide. Steeply sloping beach areas are best. Look for holes and channels where the surf is not breaking. When the tide floods in, these become the feeding grounds for fish. The rising tide, up to high tide and an hour or two after are usually the best times to fish.

Southern California anglers catch a good variety of fish, including California halibut, spotfin and yellowfin croaker, California corbina, barred surf perch and walleye surf perch. The basic approach for taking all these fish is the same. Anglers cast out a rig consisting of a 2-6 ounce pyramid sinker at the end of a leader that has 2 or 3 baited hooks on it. They then set the rod in a sandspike rodholder and wait for the bite. If nothing happens in a few minutes, slowly move the rig in about 3-5 feet and try this new location. Some novices are tempted to run back from the beach, especially when a large fish is hooked. This is not a good idea. Rather reel the fish in steadily, and move back only if the fish is charging faster than you can take in line. When a large fish is near shore, time your retrieve with the surf so the momemtum of a breaker will skid the fish up on the sand. Run and grab him under a gill cover and quickly move back to higher ground.

## Tackle and Equipment

As mentioned earlier, tackle and equipment requirements are quite minimal. All you need are;

Rod:     10-12 foot surf spinning rod with 2-handed grip.

Reel:    Saltwater spinning reels are most popular. It should hold 200-250 yards of 15-20 pound monofilament line.

Other:   Pyramid sinker(assorted 2 to 6 ounce - use the smallest that tide and wave conditions will allow), surf leaders(available at most tackle counters), hooks(#2, #6), sand spike rodholder, and a big pail(for bait and your catch).

**Bait and rigging:**

The basic rig is straightforward;

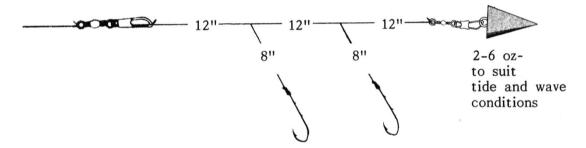

The hook size depends on the fish;

| Fish | Typical Catch(pounds) | Hook Size |
|------|-----------------------|-----------|
| California halibut | 4-8 | #2 |
| Spotfin croaker | 3-6 | #2 |
| California Corbina | 3-4 | #2 |
| Barred surfperch | 1 | #6 |
| Walleye surfperch | $\frac{1}{4}$ | #6 |

Most anglers prefer frozen anchovies when fishing for halibut. Some surf anglers like to use one of the two rigs shown in the Halibut Section of this book, and slowly and continuously retrieve through holes and slopes. Perch, both barred and walleye, are suckers for bloodworms and sandcrabs. Bloodworms are natives of Maine and are available from bait shops. Soft-shelled sandcrabs and another free bait - mussels, are gathered by anglers themselves. Hook the sandcrab up through the tail end, with the hook tip barely showing. Hook the mussel through the tough grissle-like edge. Croaker also hit bloodworms, sandcrabs and mussels, as do corbina. If possible, it's probably best to be prepared to toss out several of these baits, and let the fish decide. Cut pieces of frozen squid is another good alternative. These strips stay on the hook very well.

## Where to Fish

Actually any accessible surf has the potential of being a good surf fishing location. But some locations are more accessible and have developed a reputation as productive fishing stretches. Working south along the coast, here are some of the best;

- San Luis Obispo County: Hearst Memorial and Pismo State Beaches (both for perch and jacksmelt).

- Santa Barbara County: Jamala Beach County Park(perch), Gaviota State Park(halibut in spring and summer), El Capitan State Beach(perch), Carpenteria State Beach(perch).

- Ventura County: San Buenaventura and Point Mugu State Beach(both for perch, halibut and croakers).

- Santa Monica Bay Area: Zuma Beach County Park(perch, halibut, croakers), Dockweiler State Beach, Manhatten State Beach, Hermosa Beach, Redondo Beach(all offer perch, corbina and some halibut).

- Orange County: Bolsa Chica and Huntington State Beaches and Balboa Peninsula beaches(perch and crobina).

- San Diego County: San Onofre State Beach(croaker); Carlsbad State Beach(corbina and croaker); Leucadia, Torrey Pines and La Jolla State Beaches(corbina); Silver Strand State Beach(corbina, croaker).

# Pier and Barge Fishing

Pier and barge fishing is a special way to fish the Pacific Ocean.  Often there is a fellowship and spirit among these anglers that you don't find in other situations.  Maybe that's because a number of people share the same experience and the same piece of ocean.  Or maybe it's just because there are so many regulars.  One fun way to get to know more about this type of fishing is to stroll out onto a pier and ovserve for an hour or two.  You'll see all ages and types of people enjoying pier fishing.  And don't hesitate to strike up a conversation or two, especially with anglers who look like regulars.  A hint - look for older people with more equipment and more skill.  Many anglers are happy to talk.  It's part of the whole scene.  Slip in the questions that come to mind between their fish stories.

Pier and barge anglers do quite well depending on season, locale and conditions.  Among the species caught are halibut, croaker, rockfish, mackerel, surfperch, bonito and yellowtail.  Often the fish caught are quite large.

## Piers

There are a number of fishing piers along the Southland coast.  A list is included later in this section and there is additional information in the Ocean Fishing Section of this book.  One of the pleasant surprises about pier fishing is that many of them are public.  At these facilities, fishing is free and no fishing license is required.  Piers offer good facilities including benches, bait(some have live bait), beverages and food, washrooms, fish cleaning tables, etc.

Fishing techniques vary depending on the species being sought.  Many times anglers cast out a baited rig(like a surf fishing rig) and wait for a bite.  Fishing straight down from the rod tip is also popular.  Perch which frequent the pilings are taken this way.  Halibut anglers know that they must keep their offerings moving, so they cast out a halibut rig or jig and slowly retrieve it through likely spots, like depressions.  Bonito, and some other species, can be caught using a bobber and hooked anchovy.  Specific questions aimed at seasoned pier anglers are a great way to learn.

## Barges

Unfortunatly there aren't as many fishing barges as there once was.  A fishing barge is a giant fishing platform anchored permanently over a good fishing area, like a reef or underwater canyon.  In a lot of respects it's like an anchored party boat.  And the fishing techniques are the same as described in the "How To Catch" sections of this book.  For example, bottom rockfishing from a barge is the same as from a party boat. And barges(and piers) are nice because they are less likely to cause sea sickness.

The barges still operating in the Southland are unique and special. They are safe, have bait and snack shops, and their shore boats operate on a regular schedule. Depending on the season, barge anglers can catch barracuda, yellow-tail, calico bass, sand bass, rockfish, as well as inshore species. Southland fishing barges are at Redondo Beach, Seal Beach, Belmont Pier and Santa Monica Pier.

## Tackle and Equipment

Any type of rod and reel made has been used by pier anglers but since we're talking good-sized fish, tackle should be hefty enough for the fish being sought. For good-sized fish(like bonito, yellowtail or halibut) use a heavy freshwater or light-medium saltwater rod(6-8 feet), a reel capable of holding at least 100 yards of 10-25 pound line that has a decent drag system(either spinning or conventional). For bottom fishing you can use a rockfish rig or a striper rig(see these sections for details). Bobbers are also used to drift bait. Popular baits include anchovies, squid, clams, pileworms and bloodworms.

Other things you'll need are a big pail(for your catch), a long piece of clothes-line, and a crab net. The net is used to raise-up good-sized fish from the water line to the pier level. Have a fellow angler operate the net and be sure the fish is tired-out before netting and raising it.

## When and Where to Fish

Timing is all important to successful pier and barge fishing. Since we can't take the pier or barge to the fish, we've got to go to the pier when the fish are there. And, most fish are not there most of the time. They come and go, often in as little as several days or several weeks. This is where local, timely information is essential. Keep in frequent telephone contact with local bait shops, piers and barges. When fish are there, go after them.

At many piers, tide movements can also effect the bite. A large swing in tides (a large difference between high and low tide) marks a good day to fish and just before, during and after high tide is a good time. A morning incoming tide is good. But, this isn't always so. Some days the fish are just there and biting no matter what, especially if the bait fish are near the pier.

Some of the most popular fishing piers are listed on the next page;

### Santa Barbara Area

Gaviota Beach
Goleta Beach
Santa Barbara Harbor

### Ventura Area

Ventura Pier
Channel Islands Harbor
Hueneme Pier

### Santa Monica Area

Paradise Cove
Malibu
Santa Monica
Venice
Manhatten Beach
Hermosa Beach
Redondo Harbor

### Los Angeles Area

Cabrillo Beach
Belmont Pier
Seal Beach
Newport Beach
Balboa Pier
Aliso Beach

### Solano Beach to Dana Point

Dana Harbor
San Clemente Pier
Oceanside Pier

### San Diego Area

Pacific Beach
Ocean Beach
Shelter Island
Imperial Beach

# Rock, Jetty and Breakwater Fishing

There are some things rock anglers know before they even begin fishing. They know they'll catch some fish. They know they'll get wet, sooner or later. And they know the experience at the margins of land and sea will be special. But there are some things they don't know. For instance, they don't know what kinds of fish they will catch and they don't know how many hooks, sinkers, jigs and fish they will lose because of snags and hangups on the rocks. Fortunately the best bait is free, sinkers and hooks are cheap and a dry change of clothing just takes some forethought. So the good side of rockfishing surely outweighs the bad.

But a word of caution is necessary. People die every year walking along slippery, moss-covered ocean front rocks and cliffs. So do exercise caution and wear shoes that provide good traction.

## Fishing Techniques

Rockfishing is one of the first ways man took food from the sea. But today rock anglers work both natural rock formations as well as jetties and breakwaters.

Rockfish(over a dozen varieties), calico bass, sand bass, cabizon, opaleye and croaker are just some of the fish that are caught. It's not unusual to catch a half dozen varieties on one outing. And the nice thing is that only one basic approach is needed.

Most say that rockfishing is at its best on an incoming morning tide. Anglers sometimes like to arrive before sunrise to gather mussels(for bait) and scout the rock formations before the water covers them over. Fishing is often good up to one hour past high tide. By the way, calico bass, a delicious and highly prized catch, often only bite in the first hour of daylight.

Good spots to fish include deep slots or passageways between rocks and pockets where there is some wave action and surging. Quiet water is usually not productive. Another tip. You usually don't need to cast long distances to find fish. The best spot is often right below where you are standing. The fish you're after have moved in with the tide to feed in and about the rocks. Sometimes anglers drop a jig straight down in water 5 or 10 feet deep.

Another key to successful rockfishing is to keep moving. Try a good looking spot for only a short time and then move to another. If the fish are there they'll hit right away. Speaking of hits. Fish in this habitat are aggressive eaters. They hit hard and then shoot for cover, so set the hook immediately and don't give any line. Keep the fish moving in slowly and steadily. Abrupt yanks can tear out the hook.

Landing a hooked fish is often a challenge. Smaller ones can be lifted out of the water. If you're lucky, there will be a good miniature bay or shallow where you can guide your catch. Another good approach is to use a surge of water to bring the fish up on a flat that will be aground when the water recedes.

Casting is the basic technique used in rockfishing. A baited hook or jig is cast out to a likely spot and then retrieved. The slowest possible retrieve is usually best. Keep the line taut on the retrieve, always being alert for bites and snags. Maneuvering or speeding up a retrieve for a brief moment will often prevent a snag. If the pool is open, allow the offering to settle a little before retrieving. If you're fortunate enough to be fishing straight down, yo-yo your offering up and down. In some situations, a bobber can be used to help catch fish. Put it about 2 feet above the hook. Now you can bait fish in spots where a sinking rig would result in snags. Kelp-covered areas are one possibility.

## Tackle and Equipment

Most rock anglers use light tackle. A 6-7 foot medium spinning outfit loaded with 10-15 pound test line is popular. Baitcasting equipment is also used. Heavier rods and reels are used by some. Accurate casts are a must, so use equipment that allows you to accomplish this.

A backpack is good for carrying hooks, sinkers, bobbers, pliers, knife, towel, snacks and maybe a second pair of tennis or jogging shoes. A gunny sack is fine for holding your catch. Keep it wet and in the shade, when possible. Some anglers use tidepools, safely above the swells, as a good spot to put fish, once on a stringer.

## Bait, Lures and Rigging

The most popular rockfishing bait is probably mussels. Pry them off the rocks and open them with a knife. Now use the knife to cut out the strong portion in the middle along with the adjoining more delicate portion. Thread the hook through the tougher section and you're set to fish. Don't forget to check your bait frequently.

Other baits that work include cut pieces of frozen squid and anchovy. Surprisingly moss is a good bait for opaleye and blue runners(half-moon), but mussels also work. Anglers twist the moss into a rope and then weave it onto the hook until it's secure.

Rigging for rockfishing is best when kept simple. This prevents lots of snags. Most anglers use a single hook, often tied directly to the main line. Weight is provided by a sinker up about a foot above the hook. Split shot, rubber core sinkers or clinch-on sinkers are all used. An egg shaped sliding sinker, put on the line before the hook is tied on, is also a workable rig. The cardinal rule for all of these is to use as little weight as possible. Use just enough to make the cast. Then your offering will settle slower, a slower retrieve will be possible and less snags and hang-ups will result.

Bait holder hooks in the #1 to #6 size range are best. The bigger hooks(like #1) are best for cabizon, rockfish and calico bass. Small hooks(like #6) are good for fish like opaleye. Speaking of hooks, they're the cause of most hang-ups. It often helps to use a pliers to turn in the tip of the hook(toward the shank) a little ways.

If you're willing to take the risk of loosing more expensive offerings, leadhead jigs are very effective rockfishing lures. Jigs like Scampi, Clouts, and Scrounger are popular, and often deadly on calico bass, for example. Twin tail and curly tail models are both good.

## Where to Fish

There are many good places to fish rocks and jetties. There are many listed in the Ocean Fishing Section of this book. Here's another list of good places;

### Los Angeles County

Leo Carillo State Beach
Escondido Beach
Corral Beach State Park
Santa Monica State Park
Ballona Lagoon, Venice
Marina Del Rey(No. & So. Jetties)
Ballona Creek(So. Jetty)
Kings Harbor Breakwater & Jetty
   (Redondo Beach)
Palos Verdes Estates
Pt. Vicente County Park
Abalone Cove County Park
Royal Palms State Beach
Pt. Fermin Park
San Pedro Breakwater
Long Beach Basin Breakwater
Mouth of LA River
Alamitos Bay West Jetty

### Orange County

San Gabriel River(So. Jetty)
Newport Bay(No. & So. Jetty)
Corona Del Mar State Beach
Laguna Beach
Aliso Beach
Niguel Park
Dana Pt. Harbor Breakwater
South Dana Pt. Harbor Jetty

### San Diego County

South Oceanside Harbor Jetty
San Luis Rey River Jetty
Goldfish Pt. South
La Jolla Hermosa Park
Palisades Park
Pt. Medanos Jetty
Sunset Cliffs
Pt. Loma Naval Reservation
Cabrillo National Monument

# Party Boat Fishing

Well over a half million anglers enjoy ocean fishing on a party boat, or sport fishing boat, each year in Southern California. To say the least, this is a popular and relatively inexpensive way to pursue saltwater fish.

Most party boats take reservations from individuals and operate on a daily schedule. Charter boats are also available for group rental. Party boat anglers range from regulars who go out every week to vacationers from Peoria who've never even seen the ocean, let alone fished it. One appeal to newcomers is that no equipment or prior knowledge is needed. Rod and reels can be rented(for about $3-5.00 a day). Burlap sacks, to hold the catch are sold for less than a dollar. Bait is included in the price of the trip and fish filleting services are available at dockside at a modest cost. And there are plenty of helpful people around to explain the best way to catch fish. Observing those that are most successful help the newcomers with the finer points.

Party boats are large, safe, well-equipped fishing machines. They have galleys, washrooms, lounges and other amenities. But no matter what the season and the shore weather, it's best to bring along warm clothing. It gets cool out on the water. Dress in layers. Then you can build-up or strip down depending on conditions.

Spring and summer trips most often concentrate on the exciting live bait bite for calico bass, barracuda, bonito and yellowtail. Late summer and early fall trips are scheduled for albacore. Winter runs focus on bottom fishing for rockfish. The techniques used for all these fish are described in the "How To Catch" Section of this book.

## Party Boat Particulars

It's always best to make a reservation in advance. There are several types of trips including half-day(either morning or afternoon), three-quarter day and full-day. Call for specifics. Many anglers bring along their own rod, reel, hooks, jigs and so on. Most boats prohibit ice chests and no alcohoic beverages may be brought onboard. Beer is available in most galleys.

Costs of trips vary, of course, but are quite reasonable. For example a half-day trip is less than $20.00. All party boats are equipped with a live bait tank and chumming(attracting sport fish to the bait by tossing scoops of bait fish into the water) is a big feature of most fishing trips. While baiting your hook, be sure to select a good, lively fish from the bait tank. The most active bait usually get the strike. And don't hesitate to change bait often. Some skippers suggest changing bait as often as every 30 seconds. Live bait fishing is done for bass, barracuda, bonito, yellowfin and albacore(after a school is found by trolling).  Live bait rods have a sensative tip and stiff butt.  About 20 pound monofilament on a conventional(level-wind is a little easier to handle) or heavy duty spinning reel completes the live bait rig.

On an anchored boat anglers often prefer a stern(aft) fishing position.  To make it fair to all anglers, many skippers rotate anglers on a pre-announced schedule.  But some anglers catch fish more regularly than others, no matter what position they are in.  These are the people to watch and learn from.

## Where to Fish

Party boats, or sport fishing boats, operate out of over a dozen locations(or landings) along the Southern California coast.  Specific operators are listed in the telephone book.  Here are the landings, from north to south;

- Morro Bay
- Avila Beach
- Goleta
- Santa Barbara
- Ventura
- Oxnard
- Port Hueneme
- Paradise Cove
- Malibu
- Santa Monica
- Redondo Beach
- San Pedro
- Long Beach
- Seal Beach
- Newport Harbor
- Dana Harbor
- Oceanside
- Mission Bay
- San Diego

# Introduction to Lake Fishing

People who don't know Southern California would be surprised by the number and variety of outstanding fishing lakes and reservoirs. The purpose of this section is to profile a cross section of these waters. The lakes in this book range from small to very large, from metropolitan to up-in-the-mountains and from "fishing only" to full-use facilities. The one thing they have in common is the fine fishing opportunities they offer. In alphabetical order . . .

| | |
|---|---|
| Anaheim | Nacimiento |
| Big Bear | Otay |
| Bridgeport | Perris |
| Buena Vista | Piru |
| Cachuma | Poway |
| Casitas | Pyramid |
| Castaic | San Antonio |
| Crowley | San Vicente |
| El Capitan | Santa Ana River |
| Gregory | Santa Margarita |
| Henshaw | Silverwood |
| Hodges | Skinner |
| Irvine | Success |
| Isabella | Sutherland |
| Lopez | Wohlford |

## Anaheim Lake

Anaheim Lake is a very convenient place to catch better-than-average sized rainbow trout in a pleasant urban setting. This 100 acre lake(2½ miles of shoreline; maximum depth of 50 feet) is located several miles north of Interstate 91 (Riverside Freeway). Take the Tustin Avenue exit, right in the city of Anaheim. The lake is actually a percolation pond for the Orange County Water District. It is filled with water in the fall and then planted(twice weekly) with trout. The average catch size is about one pound. The fishing season here extends from October to early July. Facilities at Anaheim include a paved launch ramp, large picnic area, cafe, bait and tackle shop and a paved road encircling the entire lake for easy access. No fishing license is required but there is a moderate per person fishing fee at this private lake.

**Fishing Seasons**  (+=good, -=fair)

| Species | J | F | M | A | M | J | J | A | S | O | N | D |
|---|---|---|---|---|---|---|---|---|---|---|---|---|
| Trout | + | + | + | + | + | – | | | | – | + | + |

**Fishing Tips**

The number of fish in the lake is kept high enough so it's not difficult to catch your limit. All basic methods can be productive. Bait anglers use a #16 treble hook(baited with nightcrawler/marshmallow combination) about 3 feet down from a sliding sinker(1/8 oz.). This can be fished on the bottom or below a bobber, using light line(4 pound or even 2 pound test). In the fall(when water is cold a good fishing depth is about 8 feet). Lures seem to work best in the morning hours(from opening time of 7am to about 10am). Popular choices include light colored sonic Roostertails, gold or silver Kastmasters, gold Phoebes and size 4 Panther Martens. Trollers find good results(around islands and along shore) at about 15 feet down, using the same lures.

**Information/Bait/Tackle**

Anaheim Lake - 3451 Miraloma Ave., Anaheim, CA, (714)524-7100.

| Boating Facilities | Launching | Dockage | Fuel | Boat Rental |
|---|---|---|---|---|
| Anaheim Lake Marina | Yes | Yes | Yes | Yes |

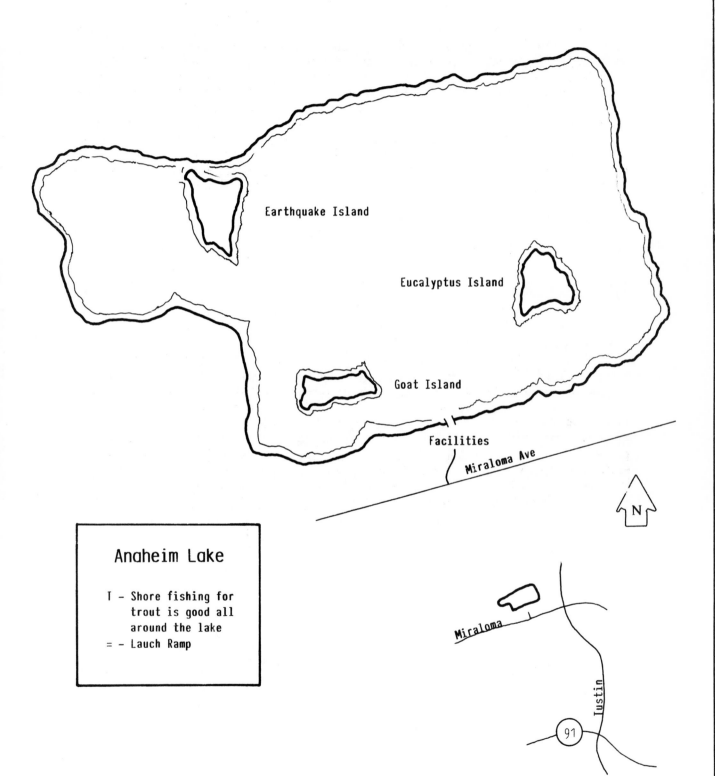

Earthquake Island

Eucalyptus Island

Goat Island

Facilities

Miraloma Ave

N

**Anaheim Lake**

T – Shore fishing for
    trout is good all
    around the lake
= – Lauch Ramp

Miraloma

Iustin

91

# Big Bear Lake

Big Bear Lake is an excellent mountain(6750 foot elevation) fishing lake, offering trout(rainbow and brown), silver salmon, bass, catfish and bluegill opportunities. It is 7½ miles long and up to 1½ miles wide, with about 22 miles of shoreline. Maximum depth is about 70 feet. Big Bear is located about 90 miles east of Los Angeles in the San Bernadino National Forest. A wide variety of facilities are available, including marinas, campgrounds, restaurants and motels, at this popular resort area. The Big Bear area is only about a 2 hour drive from most places in the Los Angeles basin. It's popular with both vacationers and weekenders.

**Fishing Seasons**   (+=good, -=fair)

| Species | J | F | M | A | M | J | J | A | S | O | N | D |
|---------|---|---|---|---|---|---|---|---|---|---|---|---|
| Trout   |   | - | + | + | - | - | - | + | + | - |   |   |
| Salmon  |   | - | + | + | - | - | - | + | + | - |   |   |
| Bass    |   |   |   | + | + | - | - | - | + | - |   |   |
| Catfish |   |   | - | - | - | - | - | - | - | - |   |   |
| Panfish |   |   | - | - | - | - | - | - | - | - |   |   |

## Fishing Tips

As is true in many mountain lakes, trolling is the most productive trout and salmon catching approach. Spring trolling depths are 5-10 feet in the morning to 10-15 feet in the afternoon. Summer trollers go down 6 to 8 colors of lead core line. Big Bear trollers use flashers in front of nightcrawlers, Kastmasters, Phoebes and Rapalas. Trollers concentrate on the triangular area between Boulder Bay, Gray's Boat Landing and Papoose Bay. This is the circular trolling pattern shown on the map. Springtime bass fishing is done primarily in the east end of the lake, along the north shore and Eagle Point. The bays are good bass areas later in the season. Plastic worms(purple,brown, black) with a weedless rig, spinnerbaits and shad imitations are all productive. Weed growth in the east end of the lake during summer, moves both the fish and the anglers to the west end of the lake. Underwater springs in this area help keep the water cold.

## Information/Bait/Tackle

There are numerous sources for fishing information, bait and tackle at Big Bear. Resorts and marinas are anxious to provide information and supplies. The Big Bear Chamber of Commerce can be reached at(714)866-5652.

## Boating Facilities

Big Bear Lake has about a dozen marinas and launch ramps. There is a free public launch ramp about 2 miles from the dam along the north shore.

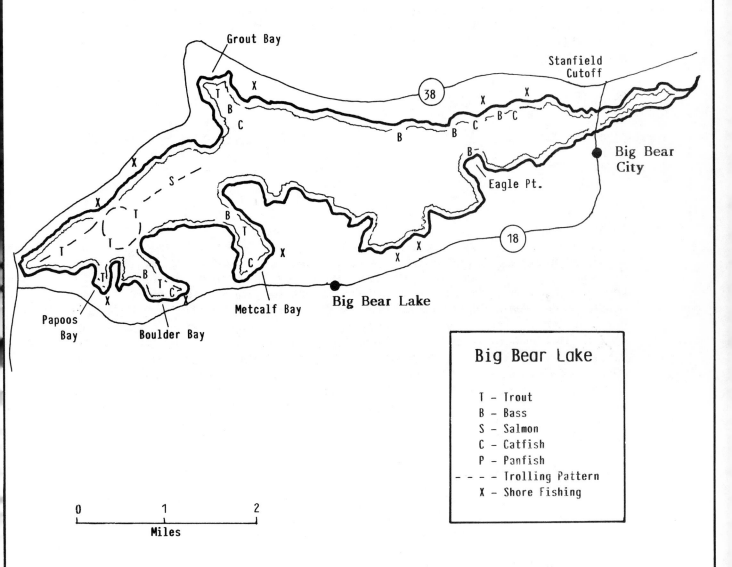

Grout Bay

Stanfield
Cutoff

N

38

X

X         X

B   C    B   C

B      B   C

X

B

B

Eagle Pt.

Big Bear
City

S

X

X

T

B

T

C

X

18

T

T

X         X

T

C

T

B

T   C

X

T   C

X

Metcalf Bay

Big Bear Lake

Papoos
Bay

Boulder Bay

0          1          2

Miles

Big Bear Lake

T – Trout
B – Bass
S – Salmon
C – Catfish
P – Panfish
– – – – Trolling Pattern
X – Shore Fishing

## Bridgeport Reservoir

Bridgeport Reservoir is probably the most consistent producer of trout in the Bridgeport area. Both rainbows and browns are caught here, and they are good-sized(1-4 pounds). Planted fish grow fast here because of the abundance of food. The reservoir is about 5½ miles long and covers almost 4,500 acres. But Bridgeport is not deep, so the water warms up in the summer months. This contributes to moss and algae growth, and affects fishing techniques and hot spots. There are complete boating facilities at the lake. And the town of Bridgeport and surrounding area provide a full range of resort and camping facilities. There is also a bow-shooting derby for Carp in Bridgeport Reservoir. Bridgeport Reservoir is located in the eastern Sierra, via Rte 395, from the Los Angeles area.

**Fishing Seasons**   (+=good, -=fair)

| Species | J | F | M | A | M | J | J | A | S | O | N | D |
|---------|---|---|---|---|---|---|---|---|---|---|---|---|
| Trout   |   |   |   | + | + | + | - |   | - |   | - |   |
| Carp    |   | - |   | - |   | - | - |   | - |   | - |   |

### Fishing Tips

In the springtime, trolling worms behind flashers, is the most popular and productive technique. Shore fishing, especially with nightcrawlers, is also productive at this time, since the trout are still in shallow water, near shore. Concentrate on stream inlets and near the dam. Casting gold Phoebes and Kastmasters(about ¼ ounce size) and Rapala style lures can be good. These can also be trolled. In the warmer months most trout are taken by boat in the deepest part of the lake by stillfishermen. They use inflated nightcrawlers and other baits that float up off the bottom. Fly anglers can also do well at stream inlets in the cooler months.

### Information/Bait/Tackle

Falling Rock Marina - (619)932-7001.
Ken's Sporting Goods, Bridgeport - (619)932-7707.
Bridgeport Chamber of Commerce - (619)932-7500.
Toiyabe National Forest - (619)932-7070.

### Boating Facilities

There are several full service marinas and launch ramps on Bridgeport Reservoir. All are located off Hwy 183, along the east shore of the lake.

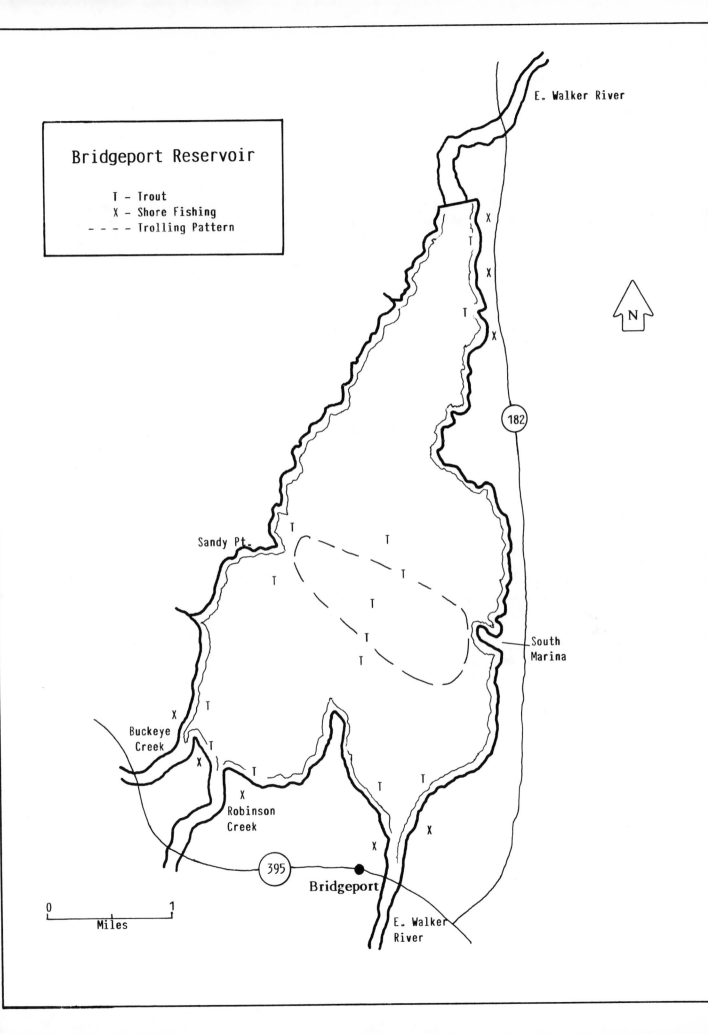

## Buena Vista Lake

Buena Vista Lake combines fine year around fishing with a modern, complete 1600 acre recreational facility. Lake Evans, the smaller(86 acres) of the two Buena Vista Lakes is dedicated to angling. Its main attraction is the trout plant(nothing less than 3/4 pounds) that runs from November to early April. Lake Webb is much larger(873 acres) and provides excellent bass fishing(both largemouth and striped) as well as sailing and waterskiing. Webb Lake is one of several lakes along the California Aquaduct that is known for its fine striped bass fishing. Facilities at Buena Vista include over 100 developed campsites, bait and tackle shops, picnic areas, snack bar, grocery store, and laundromat. Each lake has paved launch ramps. Buena Vista Lakes(formally called the Buena Vista Aquatic Recreation Area) is 23 miles southwest of Bakersfield and about 115 miles north of Los Angeles.

**Fishing Seasons**  (+=good, -=fair)

| Species | J | F | M | A | M | J | J | A | S | O | N | D |
|---|---|---|---|---|---|---|---|---|---|---|---|---|
| Trout | + | + | + | + | - | | | | | | - | + |
| Bass | | - | + | + | + | - | - | - | - | - | - | |
| Striped Bass | - | + | + | + | + | - | - | - | - | + | + | - |
| Catfish | - | - | - | - | + | + | + | + | + | - | | |
| Panfish | | - | + | + | + | - | - | - | - | - | - | |

**Fishing Tips**

Striped bass are the biggest prize in these waters. Average stripers are in the 7 to 10 pound range with lunkers running over 30 pounds. Live shad(netted from the lake) is an excellent bait. Fish in deep holes in Webb(its average depth is about 10 feet). Anchovies are also used. Artificials that work include Pencil Poppers and Cordel Spots. Largemouth fishing is often good at the west end of Webb where the most underwater structures are located. Trout fishing in Evans can be very productive from shore. When water temperature is low fish are caught only 4 to 5 feet down. Good baits are cheese, salmon eggs and nightcrawler/ marshmallow combos. Casters use Rooster Tails and Panther Martens. Crappies, abundant in both lakes, go for yellow or white mini-jigs.

**Information/Bait/Tackle**

Kern County Parks Dept., 1110 Golden State, Bakersfield, CA, 93301,
    (805)861-2345.

| Boating Facilities | Launching | Dockage | Fuel | Boat Rental |
|---|---|---|---|---|
| Evans | 2 Lanes | Yes | Yes | Yes |
| Webb | 4 Lanes | Yes | Yes | Yes |

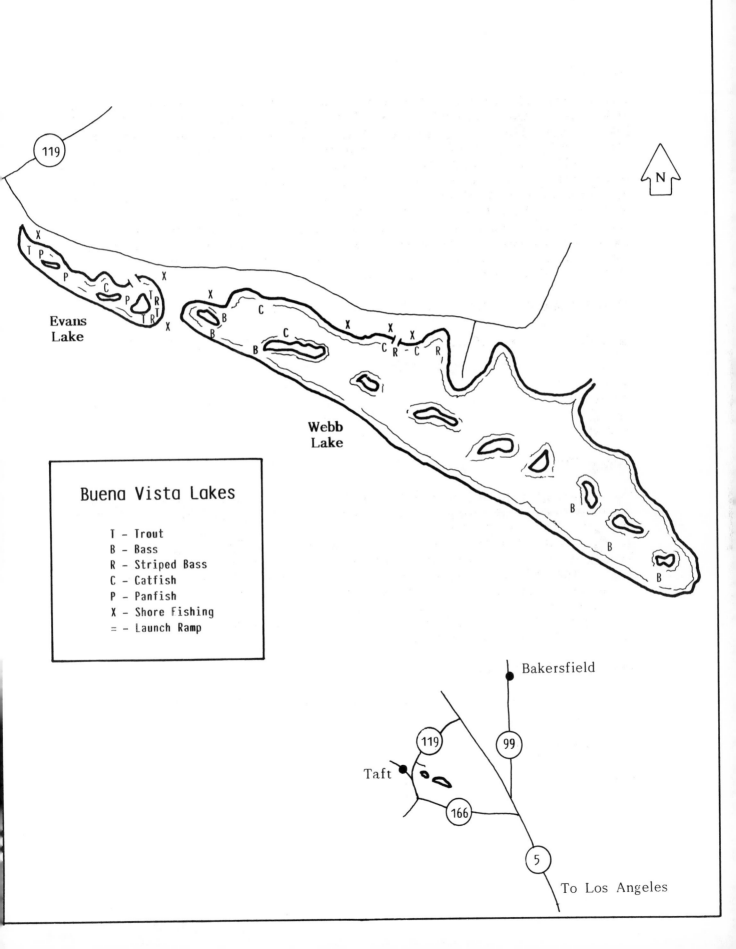

119

N

Evans
Lake

Webb
Lake

**Buena Vista Lakes**

T – Trout
B – Bass
R – Striped Bass
C – Catfish
P – Panfish
X – Shore Fishing
= – Launch Ramp

Bakersfield

119

99

Taft

166

5

To Los Angeles

## Cachuma Lake

Lake Cachuma is an excellent fishing lake in a beautiful setting. The lake it-self is about 7 miles long, one mile wide, and covers just about 3200 surface acres. Rainbow trout are planted from October to March, and catches are typically in the one-to-two pound range. But six pound trout are caught at times. This is also an outstanding bass lake because of its rocky drop offs, shallow areas and weedbeds. Cachuma offers both bragging-size largemouths and smallmouths. Catfishing, peaking in August and September, is also excel-lent, as is the panfishing(redear sunfish, crappies and bluegill). There is no swimming or waterskiing at Cachuma, so life is a little more pleasant for the summertime angler. Adding to this tranquil, oak covered hills setting is the abundance of wildlife including dear, bobcat and quail. Lake Cachuma is loca-ted 25 miles north of Santa Barbara, and has more than 400 campsites. They are close to the lake, and some have hookups.

**Fishing Seasons**   (+=good, -=fair)

| Species | J | F | M | A | M | J | J | A | S | O | N | D |
|---------|---|---|---|---|---|---|---|---|---|---|---|---|
| Trout | + | + | + | - | - | - | - | - | - | - | + | + |
| Bass | - | - | + | + | + | + | - | - | - | + | - | - |
| Catfish | - | - | - | - | - | - | + | + | - | | | |
| Panfish | - | + | + | + | - | - | - | - | - | | | |

**Fishing tips**

Trout can be caught near the surface(from shore or boat) in the cooler months. But deep trolling out in the lake(from the mouth of Cachuma Bay to the dam, east side of Chalk Cliffs to Santa Cruz Point and from the Cistern to the bar-rel line at the dam) is necessary in summer. Leadcore line trollers go out as many as nine colors in August. No.2 Needlefish, Kastmasters and Phoebes are most popular. Summer trout bait anglers fish as deep as 60 feet off the Cis-tern, at the entrance to Cachuma Bay, Santa Cruz Bay and their inflows. Plas-tic worms(in dark colors) are productive for largemouths in the warmer months. Crankbaits and jigs dominate the spring bass scene. Shrimp, mackerel and night-crawlers are best for catfish, using a sliding sinker rig at dawn or dusk. Crap-pies fall to 1/16 and 1/32 ounce mini-jigs in white or yellow. Anchor near sub-merged trees and fish from 10-25 feet down. Bluegills go for mealworms and redworms on No. 6 or No. 8 hooks. When you find a school, stay put.

**Information/Bait/Tackle**

Lake Cachuma Boat Rental - Box 287, Solvang, CA 93463, (805)688-4040.
Cachuma Lake, Star Route, Santa Barbara, CA 93105, (805)688-4658.

| Boating Facilities | Launching | Dockage | Fuel | Boat Rental |
|--------------------|-----------|---------|------|-------------|
| Lake Cachuma Marina | 5 Lanes | Yes | Yes | Yes |

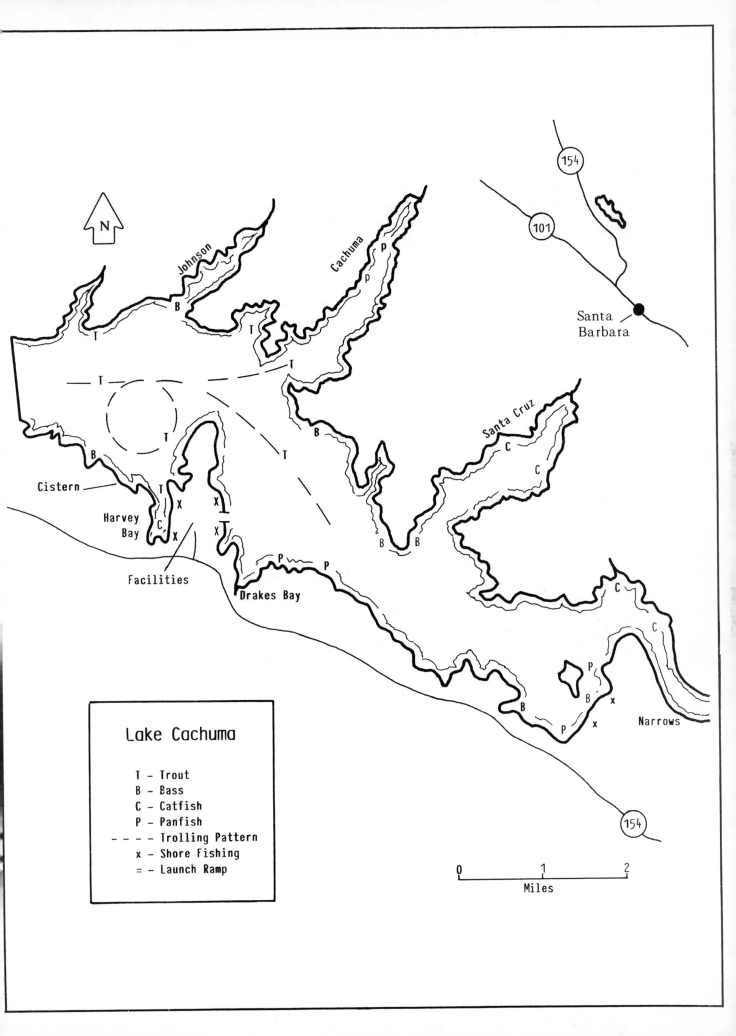

## Casitas Lake

Lake Casitas is a famous Southern California fishing lake, not only because it provides excellent fishing, but because three state record fish were caught here in recent years. They are; largemouth bass - 21 pound, 3½ ounces, March 1980; channel catfish - 41 pounds, August, 1972; redear sunfish - 3 pounds, 7 ounces, August 1976. Casitas has both largemouth bass and the Florida - strain largemouth that grows big and fast. Rainbow trout are stocked in Casitas from October to May. Nightcrawlers, trolled or stillfished, are a favorite bait for trout. Catfishing is good in the heat of the summer, or whenever it rains. Cut mackerel is a favorite bait. Casitas has 32 miles of shoreline, around its 2700 acres of water. Facilities at Casitas are complete. There are 480 developed campsites. No bodily contact with the water is allowed. Lake Casitas is located 78 miles from Los Angeles; 12 miles north of Ventura.

**Fishing Seasons**  (+=good, -=fair)

| Species | J | F | M | A | M | J | J | A | S | O | N | D |
|---|---|---|---|---|---|---|---|---|---|---|---|---|
| Trout | + | + | + | + | + | - | - | - | - | + | + | + |
| Bass | | + | + | + | - | - | - | - | - | + | + | |
| Catfish | | - | - | - | - | - | + | + | + | - | - | - |
| Panfish | | - | + | + | + | - | - | - | - | - | - | - |

**Fishing Tips**

Large bass can be caught anywhere in the lake. The entire shore is lined with small coves. But a favorite spot is just outside the marina in the Santa Ana Creek Channel. Live crawdads are the most popular bait for super-big bass. And surprisingly, bass in the 10-15 pound range are not unusual at Casitas. Here's the basics of big bass fishing at Casitas. Casitas waters are unusually clear, so monofilament in the 6-10 pound range is called for. Use a 6, 8 or 10 sized bait hook, depending on the size of the crawdads. Some anglers put a little split shot up the line, to help keep the crawdad near the bottom. Crawdads are worked along the bottom just like you would fish a plastic worm. Crawl them slowly along the bottom. When you see a twitch, that is the bass picking up your offering. As he moves off with the bait the belly will come out of your line. Let the bass run a few feet and then set the hook hard. Don't allow any slack in your line when playing the fish. Fish the rocky points, dropoffs and ledges. Bassing starts in the north end of the lake in early spring and then opens up all over the lake as the water warms. Some anglers will work a good spot from an anchored boat for hours. Lead head jigs and plastic worms are also productive at Casitas, as are popular lures like Rapalas, Rebels, Lucky 13's, Jitterbugs and Devil's Horses.

**Information/Bait/Tackle**

Casitas Recreation Area - 11311 Santa Ana Rd., Ventura, CA 93001
    (805)649-2233.

| Boating Facilities | Launching | Dockage | Fuel | Boat Rental |
|---|---|---|---|---|
| Casitas Marina | 2 Ramps | Yes | Yes | Yes |

boat rental - (805)649-2043
5:30 a.m → 8 p.m.
6 hrs   $24.50
1 day   $33.00

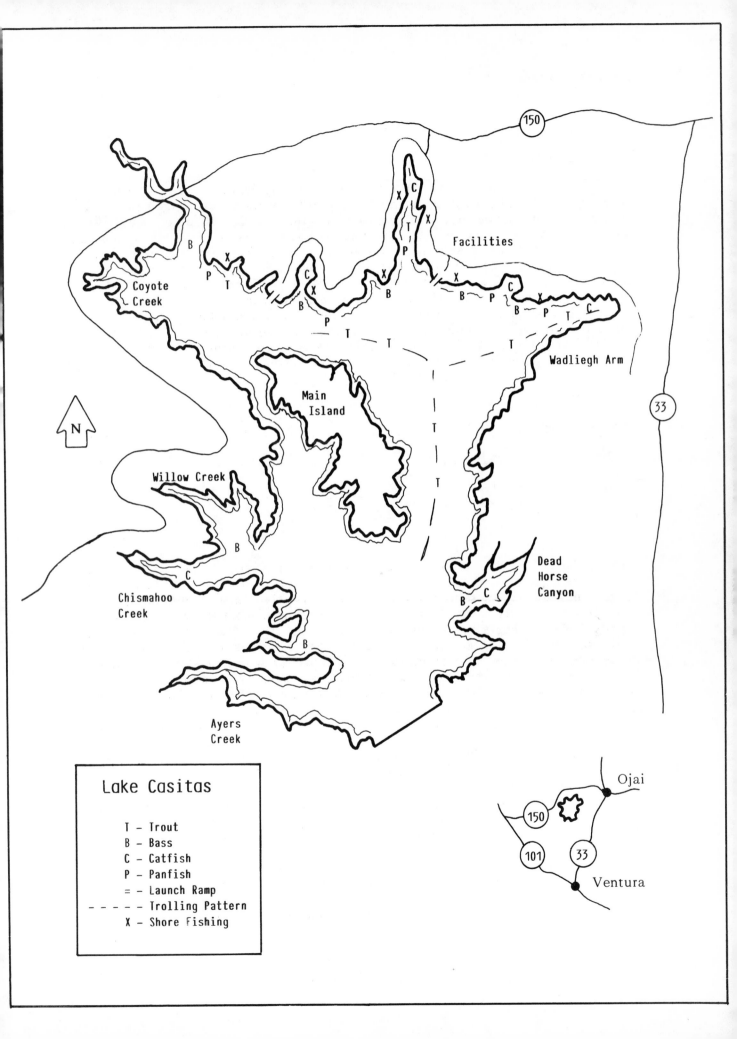

## Castaic Lake

Castaic Lake and its afterbay, are excellent fishing waters, located 45 miles north of Los Angeles via Interstate 5. The Florida strain of largemouth bass are numerous here; and it's common to catch them in the 10 pound class. Bigger fish are taken, on occasion. Castaic is also a good trout fishery because of Department of Fish and Game plantings nearly nine months of the year. The largest rainbow is over 10 pounds. Fishing is good in both the main lake and in the afterbay. Only daylight fishing is allowed in Castaic but 24 hour fishing is permitted in the afterbay. Although all four species are in both waters, the afterbay is known for turning out big catfish. Only non-power boats may use the afterbay. It is 180 acres, while the lake itself is about 2,500 acres. Castaic is located in a recreation area of over 9,000 acres, but there are no public camping facilities. There are picnicking, snack bar, marina, bait and tackle facilities, and camping nearby. Take the Hughes Exit off I-5.

### Fishing Seasons  (+=good, -=fair)

| Species | J | F | M | A | M | J | J | A | S | O | N | D |
|---|---|---|---|---|---|---|---|---|---|---|---|---|
| Trout | + | + | + | + | - | - | - | - | - | + | + | + |
| Bass | + | + | + | + | + | - | - | - | - | + | + | |
| Catfish | - | - | - | - | - | + | + | + | - | - | | |
| Panfish | - | + | + | + | - | - | - | - | - | - | | |

### Fishing Tips

Castaic has a long shoreline(35 miles) that is dotted with points and coves. These are the places to find Castaic bass. The best months are January thru May. Since ski boats aren't out in force during the cooler months, anglers work both arms of the main lake. Plastic worms, crawdads and pig-n-jigs are all productive. The lake record, as of this writing, is 18 pounds! Catfish get large here, also. Fish in the 15 pound range are not uncommon. Mackerel is a good bait to try. The lake coves and afterbay, especially after dark, are good producers. Rainbow trout are most easily taken by trollers. Popular lures are the No. 2 Needlefish and Kastmasters. Shore fishing is also good when the surface water temperature is low. Baits like salmon egg/marshmallow combinations and inflated nightcrawlers score.

### Information/Bait/Tackle

Castaic Lake - Box 397, Castaic, CA 91310, (805)257-4050.
Castaic Boat Rental - (805)257-2049.

| Boating Facilities | Launching | Dockage | Fuel | Boat Rental |
|---|---|---|---|---|
| Castaic Lake Marina | multi-lane | Yes | Yes | Yes |

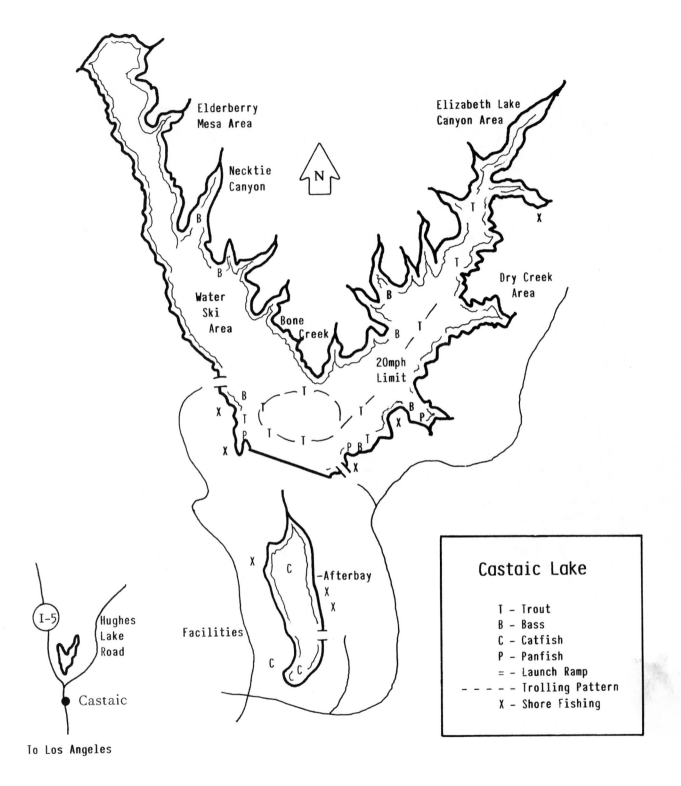

Elderberry
Mesa Area

Elizabeth Lake
Canyon Area

Necktie
Canyon

N

T

X

B

Dry Creek
Area

B

Water
Ski
Area

B

T

Bone
Creek

B

T

B

20mph
Limit

B

B       T       T

X       B

B   P

T       T

P   B   T

X

X   T   P

X

X

X

Afterbay

X

C

X   X

Facilities

C   C

I-5

Hughes
Lake
Road

Castaic

To Los Angeles

## Castaic Lake

T - Trout
B - Bass
C - Catfish
P - Panfish
= - Launch Ramp
- - - - Trolling Pattern
X - Shore Fishing

## Crowley Lake

Crowley Lake is probably the most popular mountain trout lake for Southern Californians. Crowley is planted each summer(after its trout season closes) with hundreds of thousands of small rainbow. By the next trout season opener in late April these plantings average almost a pound each. And in the early 1970's, Crowley held the state record for brown trout at 25 pounds, 11 ounces. There are special trout fishing regulations in effect at Crowley. These have changed, at times, from year to year, so be sure to read up on the current regulations when planning a trip. For instance, currently, only single, barbless, artificial lures are allowed after August 1st, with a limit of two, 18" minimum fish. Crowley also offers an abundant population of Sacramento perch. Crowley Lake is about 4 miles long, and there are complete boating facilities. It is located about 300 miles from Los Angeles, via Rte 395.

### Fishing Seasons   (+=good, -=fair)

| Species | J | F | M | A | M | J | J | A | S | O | N | D |
|---|---|---|---|---|---|---|---|---|---|---|---|---|
| Trout |  |  |  | + | + | + | + | - | - | - |  |  |
| Sacramento Perch |  |  |  | - | - | + | + | + | - | - |  |  |

### Fishing Tips

Historically, Crowley Lake has yielded many trout in the opening weeks of the season. But the larger trout are caught later in the season - June and July. This is also the time when Sacramento perch fishing is coming alive. Trout (mostly rainbow, some browns)are caught by the usual methods. Perch, which the Department of Fish and Game says threaten the trout fishery, are fun to catch and good to eat. And there is no limit. But don't catch more than you can clean and eat. Filleting is the most common cleaning technique. The record perch at Crowley is over 3½ pounds. The north end of the lake is best in the early part of the fishing season. Later the perch come near shore. Crappie jigs, weighted spinners, small Rapalas and Rebels, worms, nightcrawlers all work well. Look for the concentration of anglers and that's where the perch will be.

### Information/Bait/Tackle

Mammoth Sporting Goods - (619)934-8474.
Culver Sporting Goods - (609)872-8361.
Brock Sporting Goods - (619)872-3581.
Herron's Sporting Goods - (619)872-3741.

| Boating Facilities | Launching | Dockage | Fuel | Boat Rental |
|---|---|---|---|---|
| South Landing | Yes | Yes | Yes | Yes |

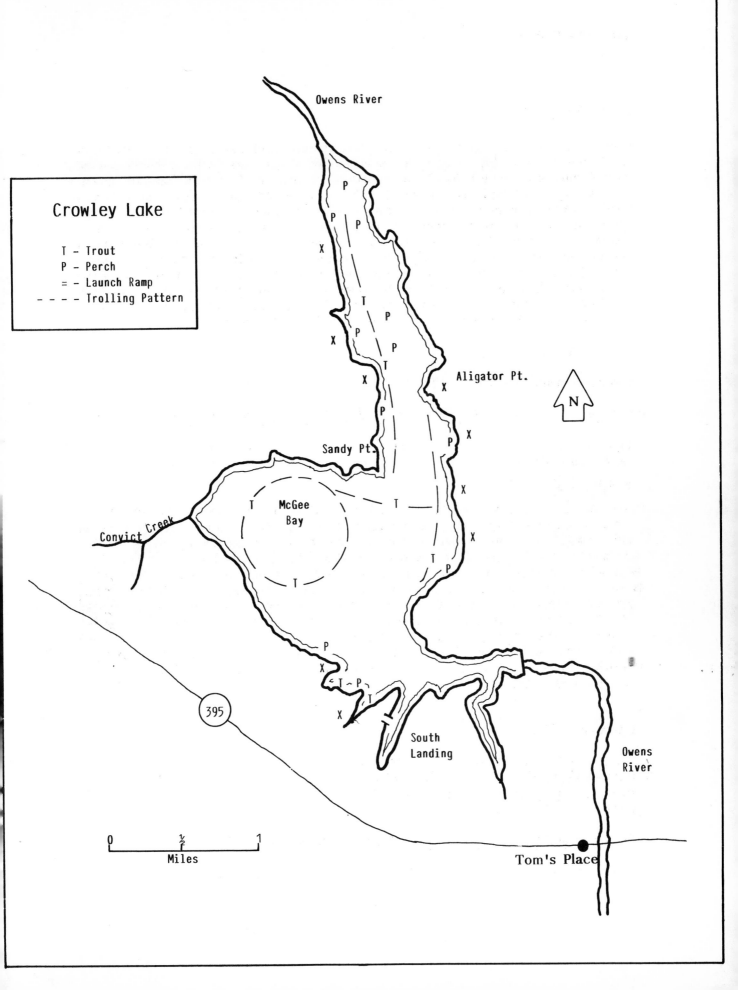

## El Capitan Lake

El Capitan Lake is a very fine dedicated fishing lake, located about 30 miles east and north of San Diego. It is primarily a day-use facility, but camping is available nearby. At maximum capacity El Capitan Lake is about 1100 acres, and has about 15 miles of shoreline. This canyon-style lake has a bushy shoreline at the north end that is one area that attracts the attention of bass anglers. Besides bass, El Capitan offers crappies and catfish. Crappie fishing is among the best in the San Diego area. El Capitan is open to anglers from about April thru the late fall, on Thursdays, Saturdays and Sundays. The boating speed limit is 10 mph and there is no swimming or body contact with the water. El Capitan Lake can be reached by taking Interstate 8 east to Lake Jennings Road Exit, then to El Monte Road.

### Fishing Seasons  (+=good, -=fair)

| Species | J | F | M | A | M | J | J | A | S | O | N | D |
|---------|---|---|---|---|---|---|---|---|---|---|---|---|
| Bass | | | | + | + | + | - | - | - | - | | |
| Catfish | | | | | - | - | + | + | + | - | | |
| Panfish | | | | + | + | + | - | - | - | - | | |

### Fishing Tips

Most bass caught at El Capitan are in the 1 to 3 pound range, but some much larger fish are caught. Work the ledges, drop offs and bushy areas. Live crawdads are a good bet here. Plastic worms and jigs also are local favorites. Catfishing(both channel and blue) is best in the warmer months. Try the north end shallows with cut mackerel. Spring is the best time for black crappies. The best area is from the Conejos on up to the north end. Many of these fish are in the 1-2 pound class.

### Information/Bait/Tackle

El Capitan Lake - (619)465-4500.
Current Fishing Information - (619)465-3474.

| Boating Facilities | Launching | Dockage | Fuel | Boat Rental |
|--------------------|-----------|---------|------|-------------|
| El Capitan Lake | Yes | Yes | Yes | Yes |

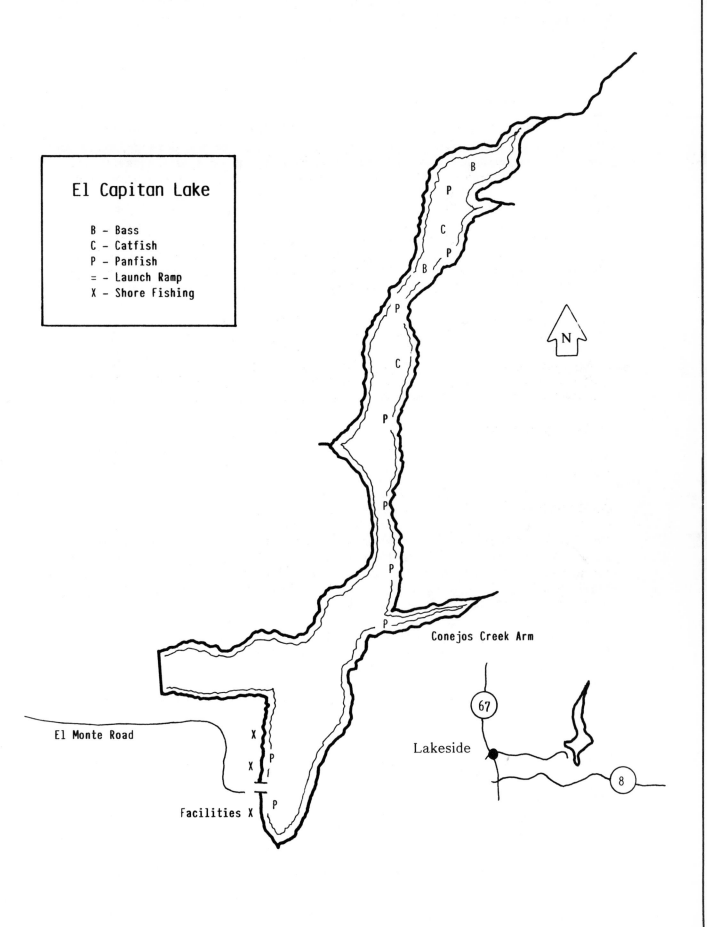

El Capitan Lake

B – Bass
C – Catfish
P – Panfish
= – Launch Ramp
X – Shore Fishing

N

Conejos Creek Arm

El Monte Road

Facilities X

Lakeside

67

8

## Gregory Lake

Lake Gregory is a fine mountain(elevation 4,500 feet) fishing lake that is sometimes overshadowed by two much larger and more famous fishing haunts(Big Bear and Silverwood) in the same vicinity. This exceptional trout lake is located in the San Bernadino Mountains approximately 72 miles east of Los Angeles and 14 miles north of San Bernadino. Lake Gregory has 4½ miles of shoreline (most of it providing fine shore fishing) and 120 surface acres of water. Private fishing boats are not allowed on the lake, but there is a boat house that rents electrically powered boats at a reasonable hourly rate. The boat rental season here starts the last Saturday in April and extends to the third Sunday in October, but shore anglers can go at it all year long. There is no charge for shore fishing. Bank anglers can fish from one hour before sunrise to one hour after sunset. There is no camping at the lake. Swimming and picnic facilities are provided June thru August.

**Fishing Seasons**   (+=Good, -=Fair)

| Species | J | F | M | A | M | J | J | A | S | O | N | D |
|---------|---|---|---|---|---|---|---|---|---|---|---|---|
| Trout   | + | + | + | + | + | - | - | - | - | + | + | + |
| Bass    |   | - | + | + | + | - | - | - | - | - | - |   |
| Catfish |   | - | - | - | - | - | + | + | + | + | - |   |
| Panfish |   | - | + | + | + | - | - | - | - | - | - |   |

### Fishing Tips

Rainbow trout are planted regularly in Lake Gregory. Catches are in the pan-size to 1½ pound range. Both boaters and shore anglers do well on trout depending on the whims of fish. All popular baits and lures work well. Two local favorites for still fishing are Velveta cheese and marshmallows. Largemouth bass were introduced into Lake Gregory several years ago by the Department of Fish and Game. Their purpose was to add a new fishery and at the same time to use the bass to control the massive population of small crappies. The plan seems to be working. Anglers are catching nice sized bass, and crappie stringers are holding bigger fish. Yellow and white mini-jigs are the most productive route to crappies. Largemouth bass anglers find most consistent success with a weedless rigged plastic worm. Water levels don't fluctuate much so the bass have good spawning opportunities.

### Information/Bait/Tackle

Lake Gregory Regional Park, Box 656, Crestline CA 92325. (714)338-2233.

### Boating Facilities

Lake Gregory has boat rental available from the last Saturday in April to the third Sunday in October. No private fishing boats.

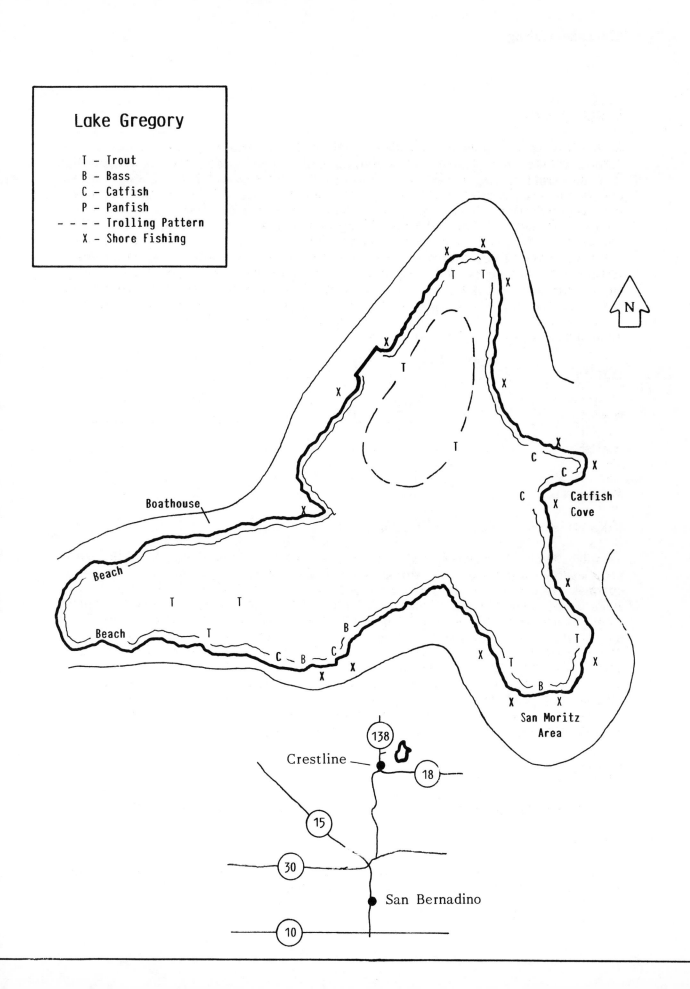

## Henshaw Lake

Besides being an almost world famous fishing lake, Henshaw has other attributes. Unlike many lakes in the greater San Diego area, it is open all year around, offers fishing every day of the week and has on-site camping facilities. This 1100 acre body of water is located on the southern slope of Polomar Mountain at 2700 feet above sea level. Henshaw offers rainbow trout, largemouth bass, catfish and panfish angling. Its shoreline is approximately 5 miles long. There is a 10mph speed limit on the water. A pool is available for swimming. Also, there are over 500 campsites, grocery store, snack bar, restaurant, bait and tackle shop, laundromat and hot showers. What more could any angler want? Lake Henshaw is located east of Highway 76, about 46 miles from Escondido.

**Fishing Seasons**  (+=good, -=fair)

| Species | J | F | M | A | M | J | J | A | S | O | N | D |
|---|---|---|---|---|---|---|---|---|---|---|---|---|
| Trout | + | + | + | + | - | - | - | - | - | - | + | + |
| Bass | | - | + | + | + | - | - | - | - | - | | |
| Catfish | | - | - | - | - | - | + | + | - | - | - | |
| Panfish | | - | + | + | - | - | - | - | - | - | - | |

**Fishing Tips**

Lake Henshaw is known for its lunker northern largemouths. The lake record is 13 pounds, 6 ounces. But, many fish are caught in the 3-4 pound class. Crawdads, plastic worms and nightcrawlers all work. Work both the man-made and natural underwater structures. Henshaw receives large plantings of both channel catfish and rainbow trout. These are all in the catchable size range, some trout going in the 3-5 pound class. Fish for catfish in the shallows. Crappie anglers score with red-and-white and pearl colored mini-jigs. Drift out in the lake early in the season; when they come in to spawn, fish for crappies in close.

**Information/Bait/Tackle**

Henshaw Resort, Santa Ysabel, CA 92070, (619)782- 3501.

| Boating Facilities | Launching | Dockage | Fuel | Boat Rental |
|---|---|---|---|---|
| Henshaw Resort | Yes | Yes | Yes | Yes |

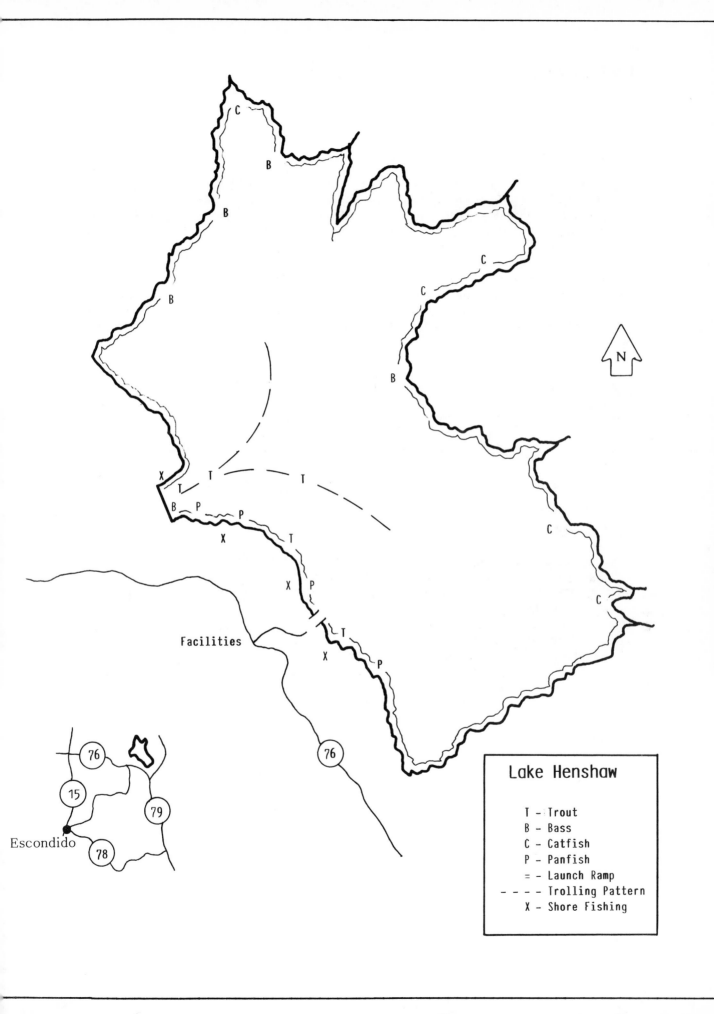

N

Facilities

Escondido

76

15

79

78

76

## Lake Henshaw

T – Trout
B – Bass
C – Catfish
P – Panfish
= – Launch Ramp
– – – – Trolling Pattern
X – Shore Fishing

## Hodges Lake

Lake Hodges is famous for its lunker Florida-strain largemouth bass. Because of this reputation, it is most fished of all the San Diego city lakes. And surprisingly, the lake is holding up well, producing fine catches of bass for most anglers. Hodges, about 1100 surface acres, is located just south of Escondido, on Interstate 15. It also offers excellent catfish, crappie and bluegill angling. Lake Hodges has outstanding cover and structures for bass. There are downed trees along grass banks, rocky points and drop-offs and plenty of shoreline cover like tules for spring flippin. Because this is a shallow lake(mean depth of 20 feet), it allows warmwater fish to utilize most of the lake. Hodges is open from about April thru November on Wednesdays and weekends. Hodges features boat rental, docks, launching ramps and a concession-tackle store.

### Fishing Seasons   (+=good, -=fair)

| Species | J | F | M | A | M | J | J | A | S | O | N | D |
|---------|---|---|---|---|---|---|---|---|---|---|---|---|
| Bass    |   | + | + | + | - | - | - | + | + | + |   |   |
| Catfish |   | - | - | - | - | - | + | + | - | - |   |   |
| Panfish |   | - | + | + | - | - | - | - | - | - |   |   |

### Fishing Tips

Hodges is such that one can do just about any type of bassing, from flippin, to spinnerbaits, to plastic worms, to surface plugs, to live bait. And they all work at times. Flippin in the tules is popular in the spring months. Data indicates that the basic plastic worm accounts for most of the action at Hodges. Four to six inch worms in brown, purple and blue are winners. Spinnerbaits (in white and chartreuse) are fished more in the summer through fallen trees. Shad and crawdad colored plugs and dark-colored jigs also catch their share of bass. Crappie fishing peaks in April and May, while catfishing is at its best in late summer. Good crappie locations include the Highway 15 bridge pilings and among the large trees near the shoreline leading to the bridge.

### Information/Bait/Tackle

Lake Hodges, Lake Drive, Escondido, CA 92025, (619)465-4500.
Current Fishing Information - (619)465-3374.

| Boating Facilities | Launching | Dockage | Fuel | Boat Rental |
|--------------------|-----------|---------|------|-------------|
| Lake Hodges        | 2 lanes   | Yes     | Yes  | Yes         |

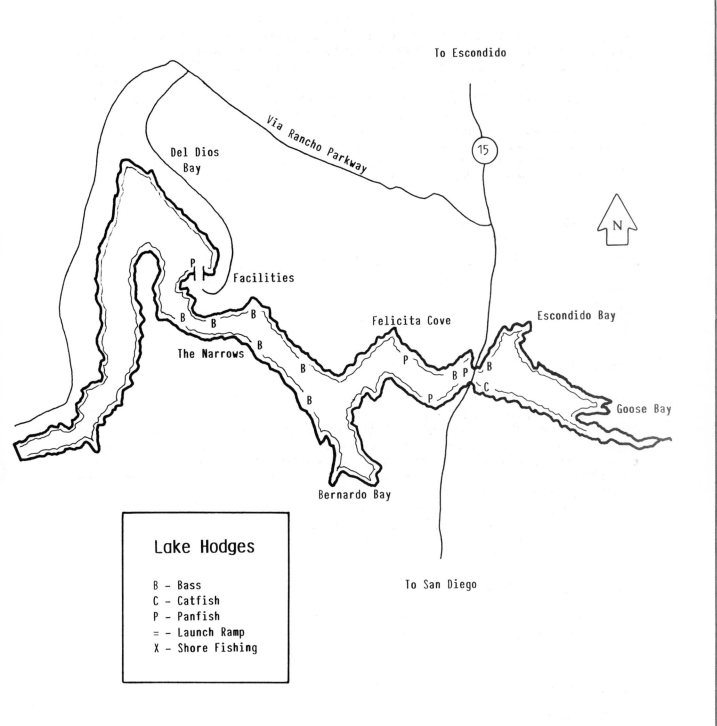

To Escondido

Via Rancho Parkway

15

N

Del Dios
Bay

P

Facilities

B
B
B

B

The Narrows

B

B

Felicita Cove

Escondido Bay

P

B P B

P C

Goose Bay

Bernardo Bay

To San Diego

Lake Hodges

B – Bass
C – Catfish
P – Panfish
= – Launch Ramp
X – Shore Fishing

## Irvine Lake

Irvine Lake is an urban, put-and-take(they put them in, you take them out) trout lake that rightfully boasts about the size of trout anglers catch. Irvine also offers largemouth bass, catfish, crappie and bluegill fishing. The lake records attest to the large fish to be caught. Rainbow - 13½ pounds. Largemouth - 14 pounds, 7 ounces. Catfish - 48½ pounds. Crappie - 4 pounds. Bluegill - 1 pound, 14 ounces. Irvine is a good-sized body of water at over 700 acres. Fish are stocked weekly - trout in the winter months and catfish in the summertime. Irvine offers rental boats, but also provides for launching of private craft. There is a 5mph speed limit on the entire lake. Despite the fishing access by boat, most of the fish at Irvine are caught by shore anglers. The lake is open to anglers, year around, starting at 6am, and there is a moderate per person fishing fee at this private lake.

### Fishing Seasons  (+=good, -=fair)

| Species | J | F | M | A | M | J | J | A | S | O | N | D |
|---|---|---|---|---|---|---|---|---|---|---|---|---|
| Trout | + | + | + | + | + | - |   |   |   | - | + | + |
| Bass |   | - | + | + | + | - | - | - | - | - | - |   |
| Catfish |   |   | - |   | - | + | + | + | + | + | - |   |
| Panfish |   | - | + | + | + | - | - | - | - | - | - |   |

### Fishing Tips

The favorite bait at Irvine is probably the inflated nightcrawler. Other approaches that float bait up off the bottom like floating commercial bait and marshmallow combinations are also good. A sliding sinker rig using about a #16 treble hook is fished on the bottom, or below a bobber. Lures, like spinners(Rooster Tails and Panther Martens) and spoons(Kastmasters and Phoebes) in smaller sizes are most productive in the early hours. These can either be trolled or cast from a boat or shore. Nightcrawlers are also good for bass. Summertime catfishing is best late in the day(Irvine has a 5-11pm night fishing session) in shallow areas. Crappies and bluegills are also usually caught near shore.

### Information/Bait/Tackle

Irvine Lake, Star Route, Box 38, Orange, CA 92667, (714)649-2560.

| Boating Facilities | Launching | Dockage | Fuel | Boat Rental |
|---|---|---|---|---|
| Irvine Lake | Yes | Yes | Yes | Yes |

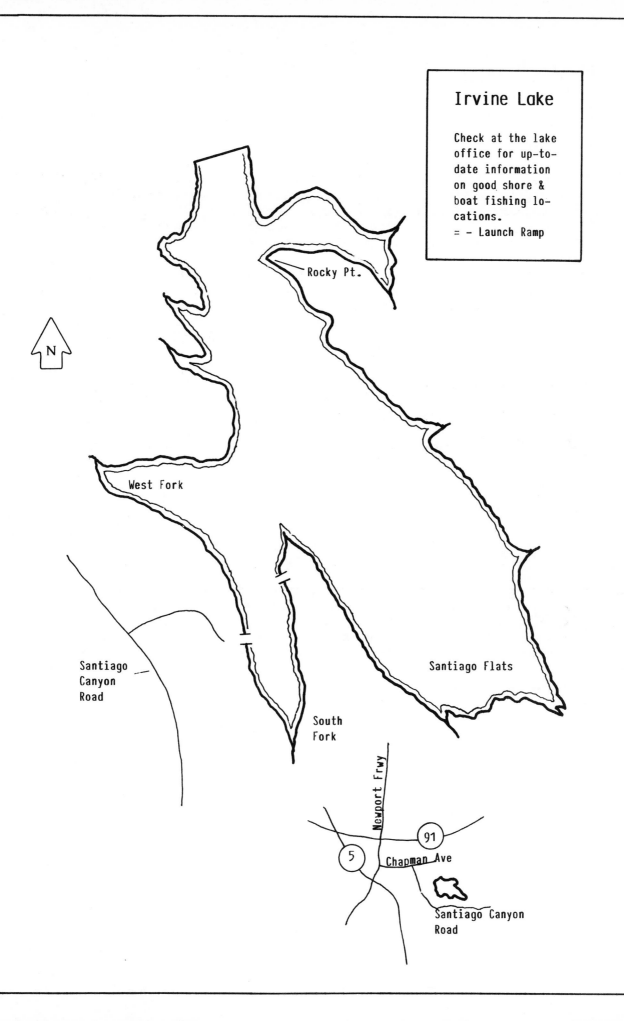

Irvine Lake

Check at the lake office for up-to-date information on good shore & boat fishing locations.
= - Launch Ramp

Rocky Pt.

N

West Fork

Santiago Canyon Road

South Fork

Santiago Flats

Newport Frwy

91

5

Chapman Ave

Santiago Canyon Road

## Isabella Lake

Isabella is one of the fine fishing lakes available to Southern and Central California anglers. This 11,400 acre lake is tucked up in the foothills about 45 miles northeast of Bakersfield. Most noteworthy at Isabella is the largemouth bass angling. 27,000 Florida-strain largemouth were planted in the early 1970's. Since then the lake record has steadily moved up to a current 18 pounds, 14 ounces! And fish in the 10 pound class are not uncommon. Rainbow trout hit year around but tend to go much deeper in the late spring and summer months. Catfish anglers do best from shore, catching 1-3 pounders, with an occasional lunker. Crappies and bluegills abound in the lake. Isabella has complete facilities with eight campgrounds around the lake. One note of caution. High winds can be a problem to boaters at Isabella, especially in the spring months. Find out about the high wind light warning system. Boaters need to get a safety permit at French Gulch Park Headquarters, during regular business hours, before launching.

**Fishing Seasons**   (+=good, -=fair)

| Species | J | F | M | A | M | J | J | A | S | O | N | D |
|---|---|---|---|---|---|---|---|---|---|---|---|---|
| Trout | - | - | + | + | + | + | + | - | - | - | - | - |
| Bass | + | + | + | + | + | - | - | - | + | - | | |
| Catfish | | | | | | | + | + | + | | | |
| Panfish | - | + | + | + | + | - | - | - | - | - | | |

### Fishing Tips

Bass is king at Lake Isabella. Good spots include the upper reaches of the north fork, where the old river channel is lined with dead trees. Another bass hot spot is the submerged Edison Canal. It is about 25 feet high and 25 feet wide and runs from up on the north fork to Engineers Point at the dam. This is a huge reef-like structure that provides excellent habitat for crawdads and big bass. A depth finder will help you trail it. Locals also watch the way gulls feed on the water. On an east wind anglers work the north end of the canal. On southwest winds they fish the northwest part of this structure. Live crawdads, plastic worms, pig-n-jigs and deep diving plugs are all good. Catfish anglers use clams and nightcrawlers at night. Trout trollers prefer Needlefish.

### Information/Bait/Tackle

Sierra Sporting Goods, Kernville - (619)376-2850.
Kern River Valley Visitors Council - (619)379-2805.
French Gulch Park Headquarters - (619)379-2806.

### Boating Facilities

There are a number of full service marinas on Lake Isabella. There are 6 launching facilities, primarily on the west and south sides of the lake.

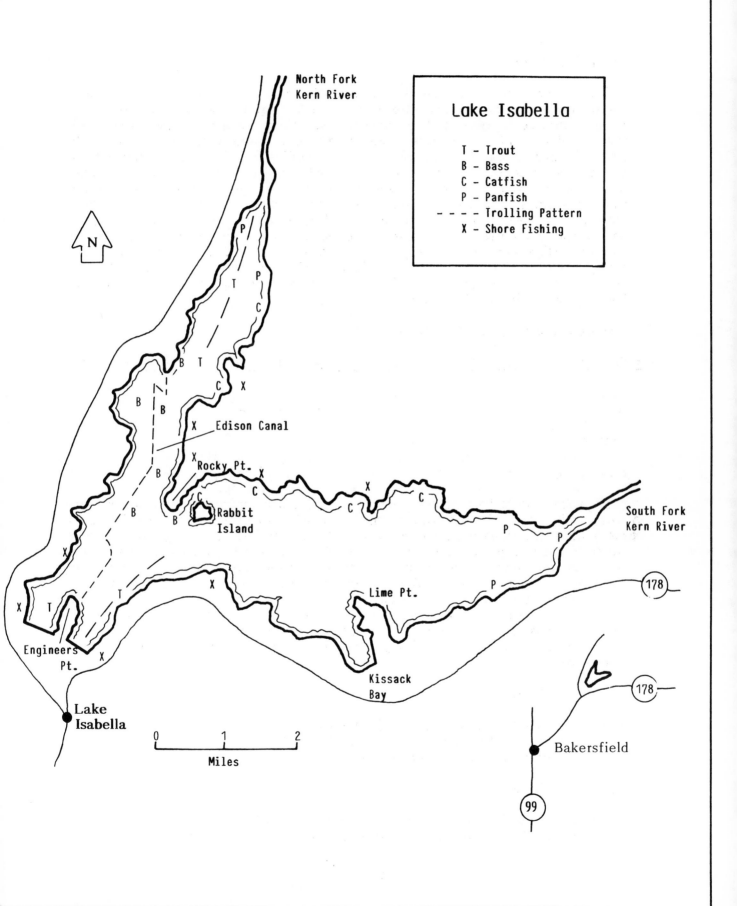

North Fork
Kern River

**Lake Isabella**

T – Trout
B – Bass
C – Catfish
P – Panfish
– – – – Trolling Pattern
X – Shore Fishing

N

Edison Canal

Rocky Pt.

Rabbit
Island

South Fork
Kern River

Lime Pt.

178

Engineers
Pt.

Kissack
Bay

178

**Lake
Isabella**

0        1        2
Miles

**Bakersfield**

99

## Lopez Lake

Lopez Lake, located between San Luis Obispo and Santa Maria off Hwy 101, provides excellent angling for trout, bass, catfish and panfish.  Known by some as an outstanding sailboarding spot, it's also a fine boating, camping and fishing locale.  Its 22 miles of drop-offs, rocky points and coves encompasses 950 surface acres of water.  The lake is in a beautiful hilly setting, surrounded by oak trees.  Almost 100,000 trout are planted by a combined effort of the Department of Fish and Game and San Luis Obispo County.  Lopez is open all year and has campsites, bait and tackle, grocery store, picnic areas and hiking trails.

**Fishing Seasons**   (+=good, -=fair)

| Species | J | F | M | A | M | J | J | A | S | O | N | D |
|---|---|---|---|---|---|---|---|---|---|---|---|---|
| Trout | + | + | + | + | + | - | - | - | - | - | + | + |
| Bass |  | - | + | + | + | - | - | - | - | + | - |  |
| Catfish |  | - | - | - | - | + | + | + | + | - | - |  |
| Panfish |  | - | + | + | + | - | - | - | - | - | - |  |

**Fishing Tips**

Trout fishing is at its prime in the winter and spring months, but dress warmly because the breeze off the Pacific can be chilling this time of year.  Rainbows range from pan-sized to about 3 pounds.  Trolling, near the surface in cool months and as deep as 40 to 60 feet in the summer is the most productive approach.  Lures like Super Dupers, Kastmasters and nightcrawlers are all good.  Bass anglers should concentrate at rocky points and drop-offs all over the lake, but especially in Lopez and Wittenburg arms.  Besides crappie jigs, they also take redworms and mealworms.  Catfish anglers using nightcrawlers sometimes hook up with large bass.

**Information/Bait/Tackle**

Lopez Lake, Rte. 2, Box 850, Arroyo Grande, CA 93420, (805)489-2095. Lopez Marina - (805)489-1006.

| Boating Facilities | Launching | Dockage | Fuel | Boat Rental |
|---|---|---|---|---|
| Lopez Marina | 4 Lanes | Yes | Yes | Yes |

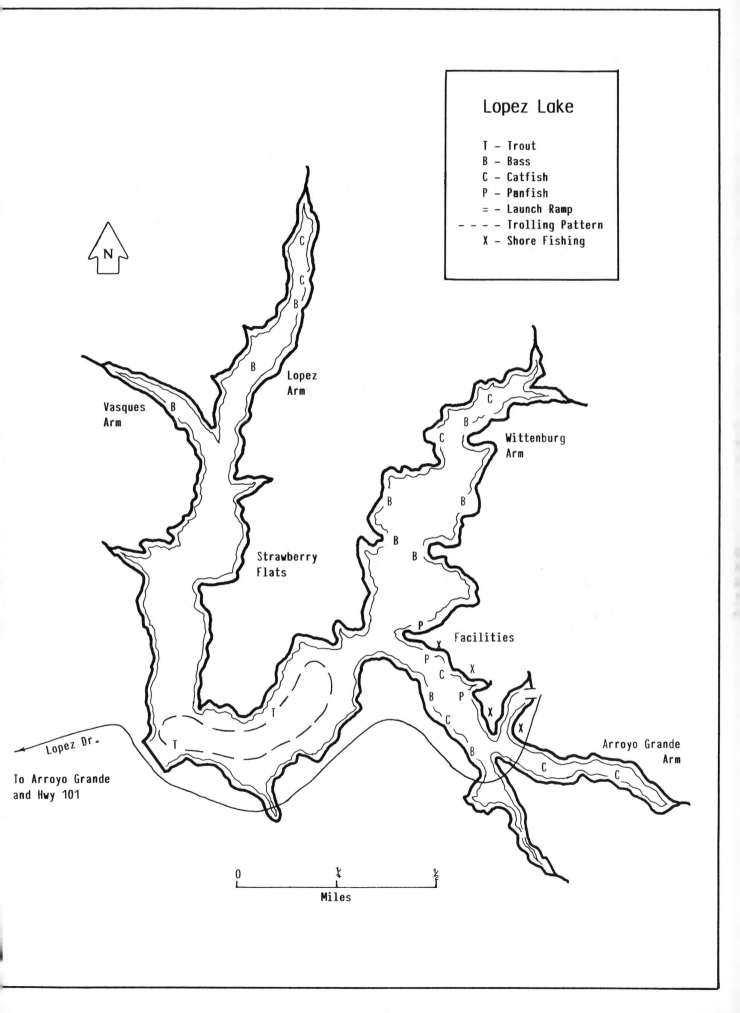

## Nacimiento Lake

Lake Nacimiento, which is just south of San Antonio Lake, provides one of the few white bass fisheries in California. White bass are prolific and can damage trout and striped bass fisheries. Therefore, the limit at Nacimiento for white bass has been removed but no **live** white bass may be in possession. No one wants white bass to take over other lakes. In addition to the excellent white bass fishing, there is also black bass, crappies, catfish and carp in Lake Nacimiento. This is a beautiful, big lake(18 miles long) that has an unusually large number of long narrow fingers and coves. Facilities at Nacimiento include store, campground and launch ramp. The lake has 165 miles of shoreline, surrounding 5,400 acres of water. It is located 17 miles northwest of the town of Paso Robles, and 241 miles from Los Angeles via Hwy 101 to Paso Robles.

**Fishing Seasons**  (+=good, -=fair)

| Species | J | F | M | A | M | J | J | A | S | O | N | D |
|---|---|---|---|---|---|---|---|---|---|---|---|---|
| White Bass | − | + | + | + | + | − | − | − | − | − | | |
| Bass | | − | + | + | − | − | − | − | − | | | |
| Catfish | | − | − | − | + | + | + | + | − | | | |
| Panfish | | − | − | − | − | − | − | − | − | | | |

**Fishing Tips**

White bass at Nacimiento spawn in the spring in the river that feeds the lake. This usually occurs in mid-April, when fishing is tremendous. Anglers boat up and then wade the river. Good lures are small feathered crappie jigs(white or yellow) or spinners. The key is to be careful not to spook the fish. Cast the lure in front of them and let it sink to the bottom. Retrieve in little jumps and you'll catch all the white bass you want. By sometime in May, all the white bass have moved out into the main lake. Anglers cast into feeding schools, at varying depths. Minnow-mimicking plugs like Rebels, Rapalas and Thin Fins with blue, black or gray backs and light colored bellies are popular. Good spinners include yellow and white Panther Martens and Roostertails. White bass average 2-3 pounds. Bluegills are available throughout the lake, especially at drop-offs and coves. Mealworms are suggested. Summers are good for catfish on anchovies and chicken livers. Spring is a good time for bowfishing for carp.

**Information/Bait/Tackle**

Nacimiento Resort, Bradley, CA 93426, (805)238-3256.

| Boating Facilities | Launching | Dockage | Fuel | Boat Rental |
|---|---|---|---|---|
| Nacimiento Resort | 3 Lanes | Yes | Yes | Yes |

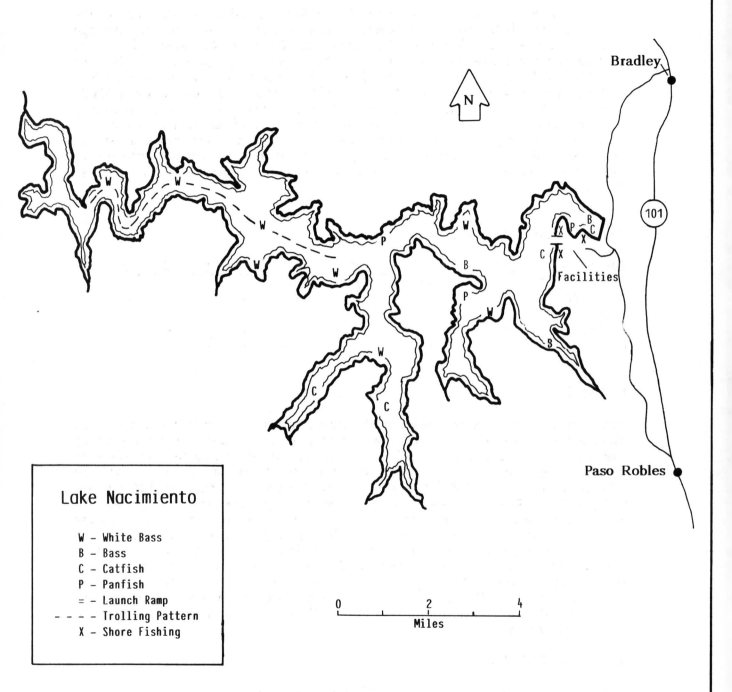

Bradley

101

Paso Robles

Facilities

Lake Nacimiento

W – White Bass
B – Bass
C – Catfish
P – Panfish
= – Launch Ramp
- - - – Trolling Pattern
X – Shore Fishing

0        2        4
        Miles

## Otay Lake(Lower)

Lower Otay Lake is one of the San Diego city lakes that is known for its great Florida-strain largemouth bass fishing. Anglers there catch large bass in good numbers. The average bass caught is just under 3 pounds and the lake record is 18 pounds, 12 ounces. Each fishing season, which runs from February to mid-October, anglers catch over 15,000 bass. Other fine features of Otay include its on-site camping and good bass shore fishing along the west shore. Lower Otay Lake, with 1100 surface acres of water and 13 miles of shoreline, is located in the vicinity of Chula Vista, about 20 miles from downtown San Diego and 2 miles from the Mexican border. Otay is open for fishing on Wednesday, Saturday and Sunday, from sunrise to sunset. Besides bass, Otay has good populations of healthy-sized catfish and bluegill.

**Fishing Seasons** (+=good, -=fair)

| Species | J | F | M | A | M | J | J | A | S | O | N | D |
|---------|---|---|---|---|---|---|---|---|---|---|---|---|
| Bass |  | - | + | + | + | - | - | - | - | + |  |  |
| Catfish |  | - | - | - | - | - | + | + | + |  |  |  |
| Panfish |  | - | + | + | - | - | - | - | - |  |  |  |

### Fishing Tips

As the fishing season opens many Otay anglers concentrate on live bait(crawdads and shiners) bass fishing in hopes of landing a trophy-sized, or lake record fish. Early season bassers also work plastic worms and pig-n-jigs in brown shades. As the fish move into shallow water and at dawn and dusk in the warm months, top water lures like Rapalas, Rebels and Zara Spooks work well. Flippin plastic worms and other offerings into the tules is also popular. Live shad, caught in the lake, are fished here for bass. Shore bass anglers have best results with live crawdads or shiners, and plastic worms. Nightcrawlers and mackerel pieces are good for catfish in the shallows of the Harvey Arm. Redworms and mealworms take bluegills.

### Information/Bait/Tackle

Lower Otay Lake, Chula Vista, CA 92010, (619)465-4500.
Current Fishing Information - (619)465-3474.

| Boating Facilities | Launching | Dockage | Fuel | Boat Rental |
|--------------------|-----------|---------|------|-------------|
| Otay Marina | Yes | Yes | Yes | Yes |

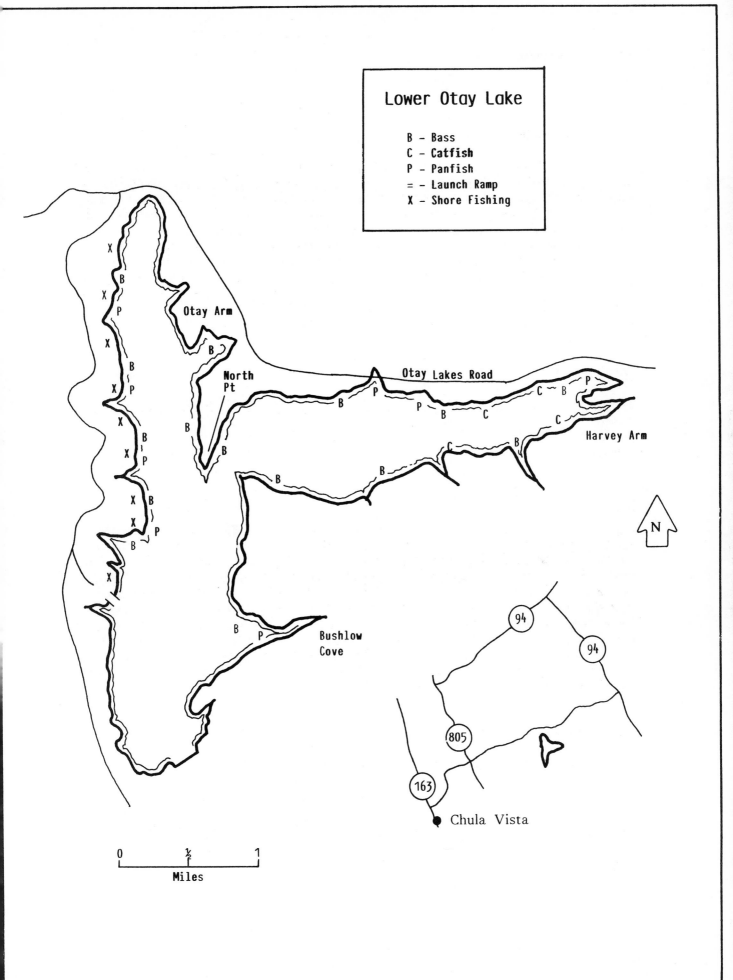

Lower Otay Lake

B – Bass
C – Catfish
P – Panfish
= – Launch Ramp
X – Shore Fishing

Otay Arm

North Pt

Otay Lakes Road

Harvey Arm

Bushlow Cove

N

94

94

805

163

Chula Vista

0    ½    1
Miles

## Perris Lake

Perris Lake is a fully developed recreational area run by the California Department of Parks and Recreation. It is a good-sized lake(2,400 surface acres) that is located 70 miles east of Los Angeles and 80 miles north of San Diego. This is a great place for a family or group outing. Anglers in the party can fish the lake early and late in the day. And swimmers, water skiers, jet skiers and sailboaters can enjoy the water during the warmth of the day. Perris offers anglers rainbow trout, Alabama spotted bass, catfish and bluegills. There are three 100-foot fishing piers and three launch ramps, as well as 450 campsites, picnicking, boat rental, stores, bait and tackle.

**Fishing Seasons** (+=good, −=fair)

| Species | J | F | M | A | M | J | J | A | S | O | N | D |
|---|---|---|---|---|---|---|---|---|---|---|---|---|
| Trout | + | + | + | + | − | − | + | + | − | − | + | + |
| Bass | | − | + | + | + | − | − | − | − | + | − | |
| Catfish | | − | − | − | − | + | + | + | + | − | − | |
| Panfish | | − | − | − | − | − | − | − | − | − | − | |

**Fishing Tips**

There are two rainbow trout peak fishing seasons at Lake Perris. The first is the normal winter trout season that is supported by regular planting. A second excellent trout bite occurs in the summer months when colder water is pumped into the lake, arousing the fish. Anglers take large(2-3 pound) holdover trout near the barrel line on live shad at these times. Alabama spotted bass are plentiful. The hot spot is the north side of Allesandro Island, and these fish are good size. The lake record is 9 pounds, 1 ounce. The easy way to catch them is with live crawdads or waterdogs. Plastic worms and pig-n-jigs are also good. Fish over the tire reef in this area. Catfishing is best after dark near the dam, and at the east end. Redworms, crickets and mealworms work good on the monster bluegills.

**Information/Bait/Tackle**

Lake Perris, 17801 Lake Perris Drive, Perris, CA 92370, (714)657-2179.

| Boating Facilities | Launching | Dockage | Fuel | Boat Rental |
|---|---|---|---|---|
| Lake Perris | 3 Ramps | Yes | Yes | Yes |

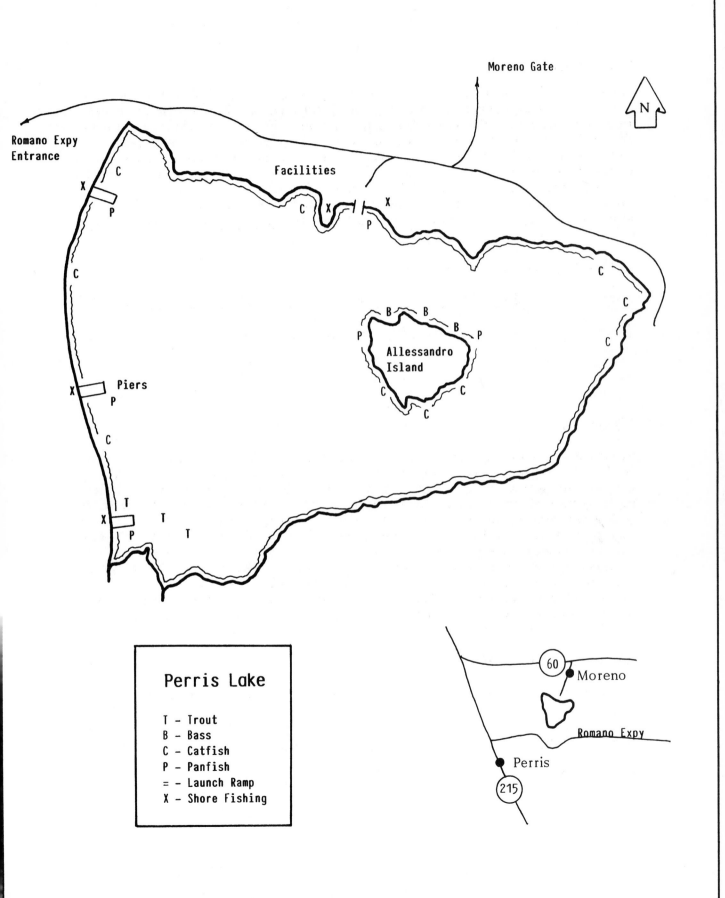

Moreno Gate

N

Romano Expy
Entrance

Facilities

X
C
P

C
X
P

C

X

C
C

C

Piers
X
P

B    B
B
P    Allessandro    P
Island
C    C
C

C

T
X    T    T
P

**Perris Lake**

T – Trout
B – Bass
C – Catfish
P – Panfish
= – Launch Ramp
X – Shore Fishing

60    ● Moreno

Romano Expy

● Perris

215

## Piru Lake

Lake Piru is a fine all-around outdoor reacreational facility that is about 50 miles north of Los Angeles. The fishing is good throughout the year, camping and other facilities are very nice, and all water sports(including waterskiing and swimming) are permitted. At capacity, Piru covers 1200 surface acres. There are about 250 campsites, a 5-lane concrete launch ramp, a tackle shop, snack bar and boat rental. Rainbow trout are planted in the winter months and this is the best angling time, especially for shore anglers along the west shore. But trollers who can get down will catch fish in the summer. Bass at Piru are the northern largemouth. These do not get as big as the Florida-strain, but most agree, they are easier to catch. Catfish, crappies and blue-gills are also plentiful.

### Fishing Seasons (+=good, -=fair)

| Species | J | F | M | A | M | J | J | A | S | O | N | D |
|---|---|---|---|---|---|---|---|---|---|---|---|---|
| Trout | + | + | + | + | - | - | - | - | - | - | + | + |
| Bass | | - | + | + | + | - | - | - | - | + | - | |
| Catfish | | | | - | + | + | + | + | + | - | - | |
| Panfish | | - | + | + | - | - | - | - | - | - | - | |

### Fishing Tips

In the winter months shore trout anglers work the west side of the lake. Floating baits like Zeke's and Velvetta cheese are productive. Casters also score with Kastmasters, Rooster Tails and Needlefish. Winter trolling is up near the surface, but summertime trolling means getting down 20-60 feet, usually with Needlefish, near the dam, or down the center of the lake. Early season bass anglers also work deep off the bottom in 15-60 feet of water. Plastic worms, live crawdads, pig-n-jigs and even inflated nightcrawlers score. When the bass come to shallow water to spawn(April) shore anglers toss plastic worms into Bobcat Cove and other west shore locations. Crappie season usually peaks in March and April. Fish brushy areas with white, green/yellow and pearl crappie jigs. Bluegills take over the panfishing action in the summer months. Use mealworms back in the coves.

### Information/Bait/Tackle

Lake Piru, Box 202, Piru, CA 93040, (805)521-1500.
Lake Piru Marina - (805)521-1231.

| Boating Facilities | Launching | Dockage | Fuel | Boat Rental |
|---|---|---|---|---|
| Lake Piru Marina | 5 Lanes | Yes | Yes | Yes |

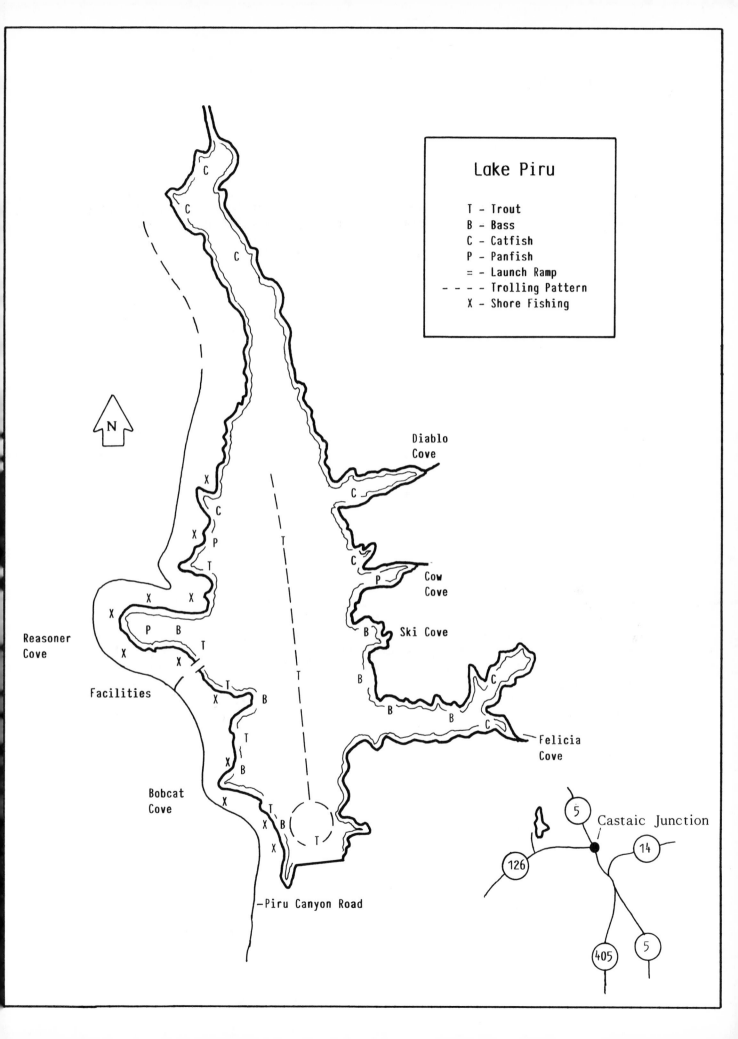

## Poway Lake

Lake Poway, run by the City of Poway, is a little lake(just 60 acres) with big fishing opportunities. It is located 3 miles east of Interstate 15 and northeast of the city of Poway. Shore fishing is very productive here. Private boats are not allowed, but boats(both row and electrically powered) are available for rent. Poway is stocked regularly with both pan-sized and larger rainbow trout and catfish. The lake record fish are impressive; trout-11 pound, 7 ounces; Florida-strain largemouth bass-17 pound, 8 ounces; catfish-18 pounds, 3 ounces. Speaking of catfish, Lake Poway allows night fishing, until midnight, during the peak summer catfishing season. And, unlike some other lakes, there is no extra charge over-and-above the modest daytime fee. At the lake there are bait and tackle, snack bar, horseback and hiking trails, picnic areas, a ballfield and playground area. Poway is open Wednesdays thru Sundays, all year long.

### Fishing Seasons  (+=good, -=fair)

| Species | J | F | M | A | M | J | J | A | S | O | N | D |
|---|---|---|---|---|---|---|---|---|---|---|---|---|
| Trout | + | + | + | + | + |  |  |  |  |  | + | + |
| Bass |  | + | + | + | + |  |  |  |  |  |  |  |
| Catfish |  | - | - | - | - | + | + | + | + | + | - |  |
| Panfish |  | - | - | - | - | - | - | - | - | - | - |  |

### Fishing Tips

Trout fishing begins in earnest in late October or November with a large planting, including a fair share of lunkers. About 1000 pounds are added each week until June. Nightcrawlers are probably the best bet, for both trolling and still fishing. Crawlers are inflated by shore anglers who also use corn and cheese. Trollers use light line(the water is very clear) and just a split shot in the cold water months. Spinners are also used by both shore anglers and trollers. Shinners and nightcrawlers are popular bait for bass at Poway. Lures that imitate shad are also good, as are plastic worms. Many of the bass caught are in the 3-4 pound range. A poway trout fishing instruction handout is available at the lake office.

### Information/Bait/Tackle
Lake Poway, Box 785, Poway, CA 92064, (619)748-2224.

### Boating Facilities

No private boats, but electrically powered boats and row boats are rented.

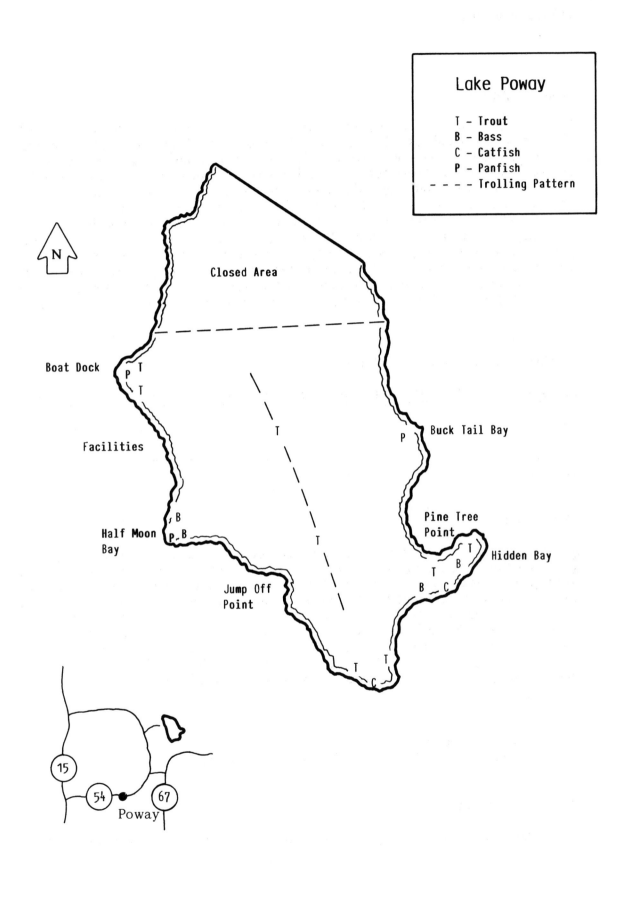

## Pyramid Lake

Pyramid Lake probably produces more striped bass per angler than any other lake in California. And trout are planted in Pyramid on a regular basis throughout most of the year. Pyramid Lake is part of the California Aquaduct System and is a day-use facility. It is located about 60 miles northwest of Los Angeles on Interstate 5. Pyramid Lake has about 1400 surface acres of water and 21 miles of shoreline. Most of the shoreline is accessible by boat only because of the rugged terrain. Facilities include a picnic area, marina, boat launching, hiking trails and store. Both swimming and water skiing are permitted. This is a very popular summer day-use facility. It's so popular, in fact, that many anglers prefer to come to the lake in the off season, when the fishing is at its peak and most of the people are somewhere else.

**Fishing Seasons**  (+=good, -=fair)

| Species | J | F | M | A | M | J | J | A | S | O | N | D |
|---|---|---|---|---|---|---|---|---|---|---|---|---|
| Striped Bass | - | + | + | + | + | - | - | - | - | - | + | + |
| Trout | + | + | + | + | - | - | - | - | - | - | + | + |
| Bass | | - | + | + | - | - | - | - | - | - | - | - |
| Catfish | | - | - | - | - | + | + | + | + | - | - | |
| Panfish | | - | + | + | + | - | - | - | - | - | - | |

**Fishing Tips**

Striped bass are nocturnal feeders, so many striper anglers concentrate their efforts at Lake Pyramid in the hours following dawn and before dusk. In fact, the avid striper hunters will get to the lake while it's still dark and wait for the gate to open at sunrise. The two most popular areas to fish for striped bass are near the park entrance and at the extreme other end of the lake, near the dam. Binoculars are useful to scan the water for striper feeding activity. Frequently stripers will surface near the dam. Casting surface plugs and spoons hooks these fish. Chart recorders(either paper or video) are also useful in finding striped bass. Jigging a spoon or leadhead jig is the best for stripers located down deep. Fishing for stripers soon after a trout plant, in the area of the plant, works well. Trolling is also productive, near the dam and along the rock wall, just below Interstate 5.

**Information/Bait/Tackle**

Pyramid Lake - Gate(805)257-2790; Marina(805)257-3330.
U.S. Forest Service, Saugus Ranger District, 27757 Bouquet Canyon Rd.,
    Saugus, CA 91350.

| Boating Facilities | Launching | Dockage | Fuel | Boat Rental |
|---|---|---|---|---|
| Pyramid Marina | 8 Lanes | Yes | Yes | Yes |

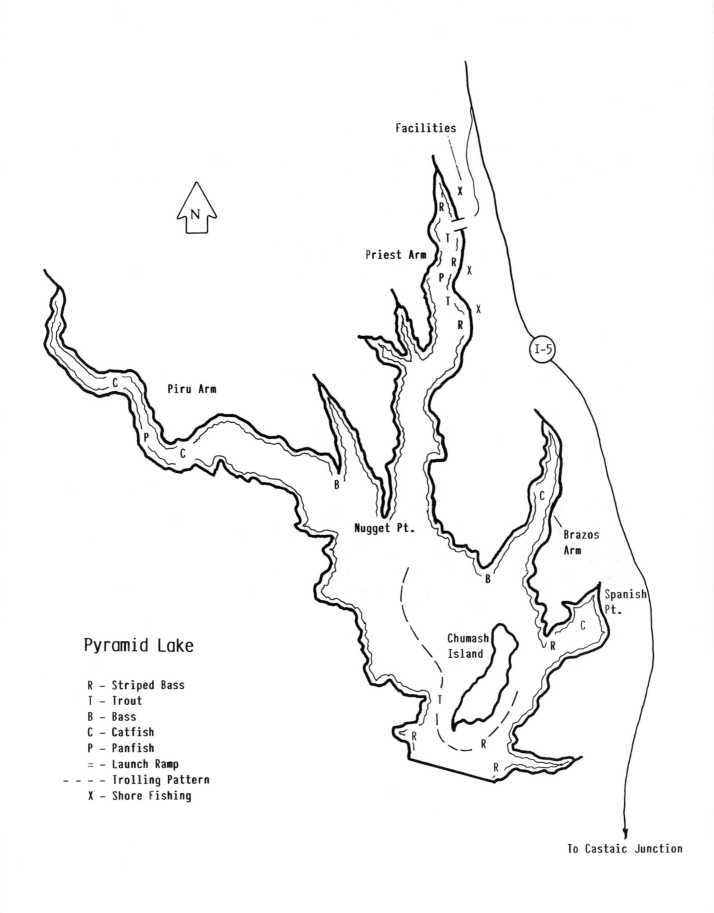

# Pyramid Lake

R – Striped Bass
T – Trout
B – Bass
C – Catfish
P – Panfish
= – Launch Ramp
- - - – Trolling Pattern
X – Shore Fishing

Facilities

Priest Arm

Piru Arm

Nugget Pt.

Brazos Arm

Spanish Pt.

Chumash Island

I-5

To Castaic Junction

N

## San Antonio Lake

San Antonio Lake is located in the extreme Southern end of Monterey County. Although this may not seem like a convenient Southern California fishing locale it is actually closer(250 miles) to Los Angeles than Crowley Lake(300 miles), for example, is to Los Angeles. San Antonio provides very good fishing for the usual species(trout, black bass, catfish and panfish), but in addition, it offers excellent striped bass fishing. The average striper caught is in the 15 pound range. Like Nacimiento, its sister reservoir, San Antonio is large(16 miles long, 5,500 surface acres). Its facilities are operated by the Monterey County Parks and Recreation Department. There are camping and launch ramps at three locations on the lake, as well as a restaurant, store and swimming.

### Fishing Seasons   (+=good, -=fair)

| Species | J | F | M | A | M | J | J | A | S | O | N | D |
|---|---|---|---|---|---|---|---|---|---|---|---|---|
| Trout | + | + | + | - | - | - | - | - | - | - | + | + |
| Bass |  | - | - | - | + | + | - | - | - | - | - |  |
| Striped Bass | - | + | + | + | + | + | - | - | + | + | + | - |
| Catfish |  | - | - | - | - | - | + | + | + | - | - |  |
| Panfish |  | - | - | - | - | - | - | - | - | - | - |  |

### Fishing Tips

One rule that seems to apply to all the fisheries in San Antonio is that the bite is best near shore early in the day and then moves into deeper water later in the day. So, if the action slows, move into deeper water rather than quit. Most trout are in the ½-1 pound range and hit on Kastmasters, Rooster Tails or salmon egg/marshmallow combinations. Striped bass are mostly caught trolling. Hopkins Spoons are a favorite trolling lure at San Antonio. Troll near the surface near shore in the mornings. Then move deeper and farther from shore later in the day. Harris Creek is one of the most productive spots on the lake for largemouth bass and crappies. Night fishing is allowed for all species and can be quite good for bass, crappies and catfish. Anchovy and mackerel bait, fished at night, is best for catfish. For largemouth bass, locals use purple and shad-colored leadhead jigs, crawdad-colored crankbaits, black and purple plastic worms and white spinnerbaits.

### Information/Bait/Tackle

Lake San Antonio, Bradley, CA 93426, (805)472-2311.

| Boating Facilities | Launching | Dockage | Fuel | Boat Rental |
|---|---|---|---|---|
| Lake San Antonio | 3 Ramps | Yes | Yes | Yes |

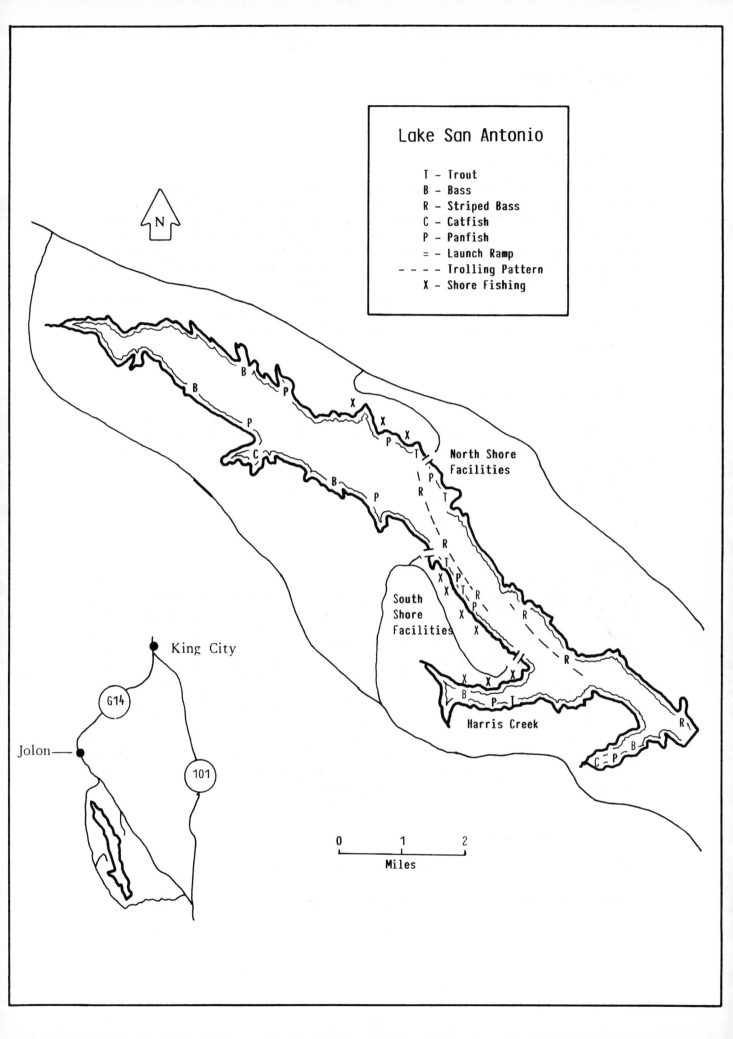

## San Vicente Lake

San Vicente Lake is one of the six lakes in the San Diego area that is owned by the city of San Diego and operated as a fishing lake as well as a reservoir. San Vicente(about 1100 surface acres) and the much smaller Lake Miramar (about 160 acres) are the two that function primarily as trout fisheries. But San Vicente Lake is more than a trout fishery. There are Florida-strain large-mouth bass(lake record is 18 pounds, 12 ounces), catfish(lake record is 38 pounds, 12 ounces), crappie and bluegill. San Vicente Lake is open for fishing from the end of September thru July 4th, each year, Thursdays thru Sundays. San Vicente is about 25 miles northeast of downtown San Diego. Facilities include boat launching, picnic area, boat rental and store.

### Fishing Seasons  (+=good, -=fair)

| Species | J | F | M | A | M | J | J | A | S | O | N | D |
|---|---|---|---|---|---|---|---|---|---|---|---|---|
| Trout | + | + | + | + | + | - | - | | - | - | + | + |
| Bass | | - | + | + | + | | | | | + | - | |
| Catfish | | | - | - | - | - | | | | - | - | |
| Panfish | | - | - | + | + | + | | | | - | - | |

### Fishing Tips

San Vicente Lake opens at the end of September, but usually at this time the lake temperature is still too warm for trout planting. Rainbow trout planting begins in early November, so trout anglers in October have only holdovers to pursue. Trolling is the approach of choice. The deepest part of San Vicente Lake is 150 feet below the spillway so, depending on fall water levels, the water and the holdover trout can be quite deep. In the cold months, best trout fishing is up in the arms at the marina and by the dam. Both bait anglers and lure casters do well up in the arms when water inflow is good. A sliding sinker rig is always good for trout and floating bait like marshmallow combinations and inflated nightcrawlers produce. The water is ultra clear, so use light, long leaders.

### Information/Bait/Tackle

San Vicente Lake, Lakeside, CA 92040, (619)465-4500.
Current Fishing Information - (619)465-3474.

| Boating Facilities | Launching | Dockage | Fuel | Boat Rental |
|---|---|---|---|---|
| San Vicente Lake | Paved | Yes | Yes | Yes |

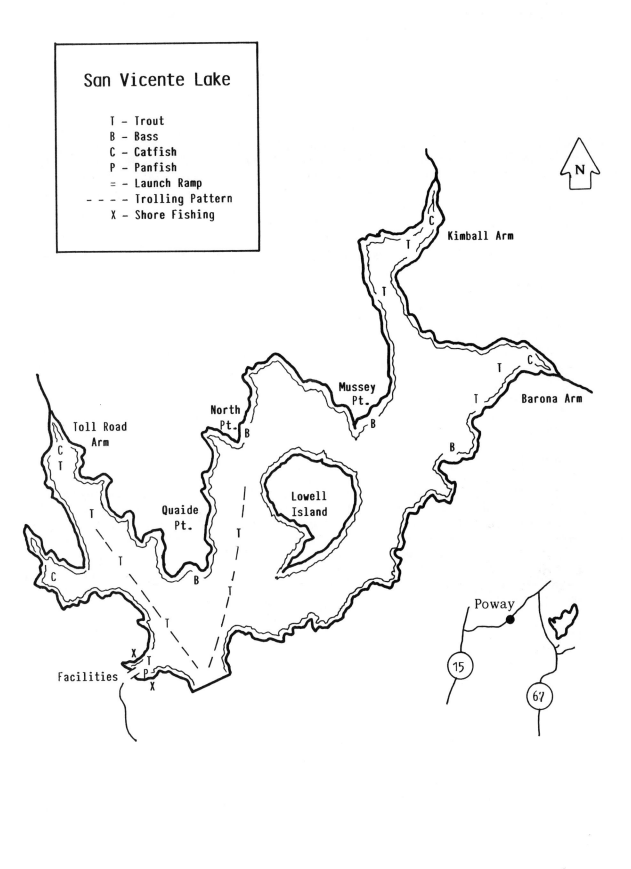

## Santa Ana River Lakes

For anglers who want to catch rainbow trout and catfish right near home, including some lunkers, this could be the place. Santa Ana River Lakes are located in the City of Anaheim, just north of Hwy 91(Riverside Freeway). Take Tustin Avenue north to La Palma. This facility is made up of three small lakes - Trout Lake(75 acres), Catfish Lake(12 acres), and Chris' Lake(10 acres). Fish are stocked weekly. Trout in the winter months and catfish in the summertime. Rental boats are available and private boats can be launched in Trout Lake. But shore angling is very popular at Santa Ana River Lakes. The lakes are open to anglers from 6am to 4pm and from 5pm to 11pm, seven days a week, all year long. There is a moderate, per person fishing fee at this private lake.

### Fishing Seasons  (+=good, -=fair)

| Species | J | F | M | A | M | J | J | A | S | O | N | D |
|---|---|---|---|---|---|---|---|---|---|---|---|---|
| Trout | + | + | + | + | + | - | | | | - | + | + |
| Catfish | | | | - | - | + | + | + | + | + | | |

### Fishing Tips

Some very large fish are planted at these lakes. Trout of 2-4 pounds, or more. Catfish of 1½ to up near 20 pounds are caught. All standard trout techniques take fish including trolling, still fishing and lure casting. Most popular trout baits are cheese and salmon eggs. Lures seem to work best early and late in the day. Mackerel, shrimp and nightcrawlers are used for catfish. Most anglers use 10-12 pound line. Good catfish locations in Catfish Lake are along the canal, Short-Pole-In-The-Water, and Power-Pole-In-The-Water. In Trout Lake the Bubbling Hole is good for catfish.

### Information/Bait/Tackle

Santa Ana River Lakes, 4060 E. LaPalma Ave., Anaheim, CA 92806, (714)632-7830.

| Boating Facilities | Launching | Dockage | Fuel | Boat Rental |
|---|---|---|---|---|
| Santa Ana River Lakes | Yes | Yes | Yes | Yes |

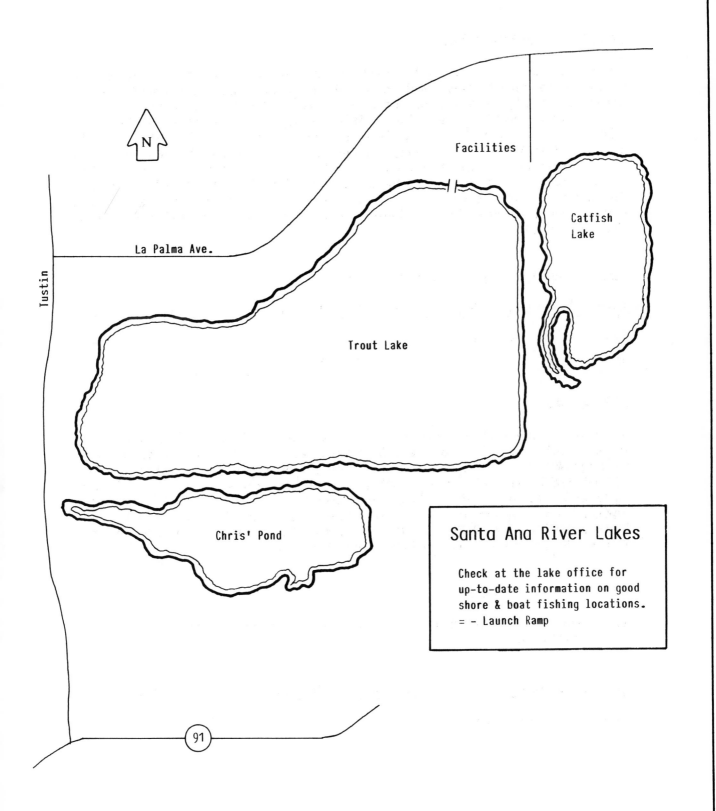

N

Facilities

Catfish
Lake

La Palma Ave.

Tustin

Trout Lake

Chris' Pond

**Santa Ana River Lakes**

Check at the lake office for
up-to-date information on good
shore & boat fishing locations.
= - Launch Ramp

91

## Santa Margarita Lake

Santa Margarita is an outstanding anglers lake. It is open throughout the year, has abundant supplies of striped bass, largemouth bass(northern strain), catfish (white, yellow and channel), crappie and bluegill. And summertime anglers will be happy to know that no waterskiing is permitted. In fact, swimming and wading are not allowed either(but there is an olympic-sized swimming pool for visitors). Other facilities include a picnic area, full service marina and store. There is no camping in the park itself, which is operated by San Luis Obispo County, but there are two private campgrounds just outside the gate (within several hundred yards of the lake). Santa Margarita Lake is a long (7 miles), narrow lake that covers 1100 surface acres. There are 22 miles of shoreline, surrounded by tree-studded foothills. Santa Margarita Lake is located about 220 miles north of Los Angeles, 8 miles off Hwy 101, north of San Luis Obispo.

**Fishing Seasons** (+=good, -=fair)

| Species | J | F | M | A | M | J | J | A | S | O | N | D |
|---|---|---|---|---|---|---|---|---|---|---|---|---|
| Striped Bass | - | + | + | - | - | - | - | - | - | + | + | - |
| Bass | | - | + | + | + | - | - | - | - | | | |
| Catfish | | - | - | - | - | + | + | + | + | - | | |
| Panfish | | - | + | + | + | - | - | - | - | - | - | |

**Fishing Tips**
The southern shore of Santa Margarita Lake, from Picnic Bay east to Salsipuedes Bay, provides a very long(7 miles) access area for shore anglers. However, there are numerous weedbeds that limit shore angling in many portions of this stretch. But persistent anglers are successful in locating fishable spots by exploring the shoreline. Summertime bass anglers take advantage of these weedbeds and rocky areas by working surface plugs near them in the early morning and late evening hours. Zara Spooks and Rapalas are two plugs that take largemouth bass. Santa Margarita striped bass anglers concentrate their efforts in searching for bass surface feeding activity. They boat within casting range of a boil and then toss Zara Spooks, Pencil Poppers and about 1 ounce Kastmasters with bucktail. Hair Raisers are also used in this technique. Trolling and vertical jigging are two other approaches for taking stripers, when they are down deep.

**Information/Bait/Tackle**

Santa Margarita Marina, Star Route, Box 36, Santa Margarita, CA 94353,
(805)483-5683.

| Boating Facilities | Launching | Dockage | Fuel | Boat Rental |
|---|---|---|---|---|
| Marina | Yes | Yes | Yes | Yes |

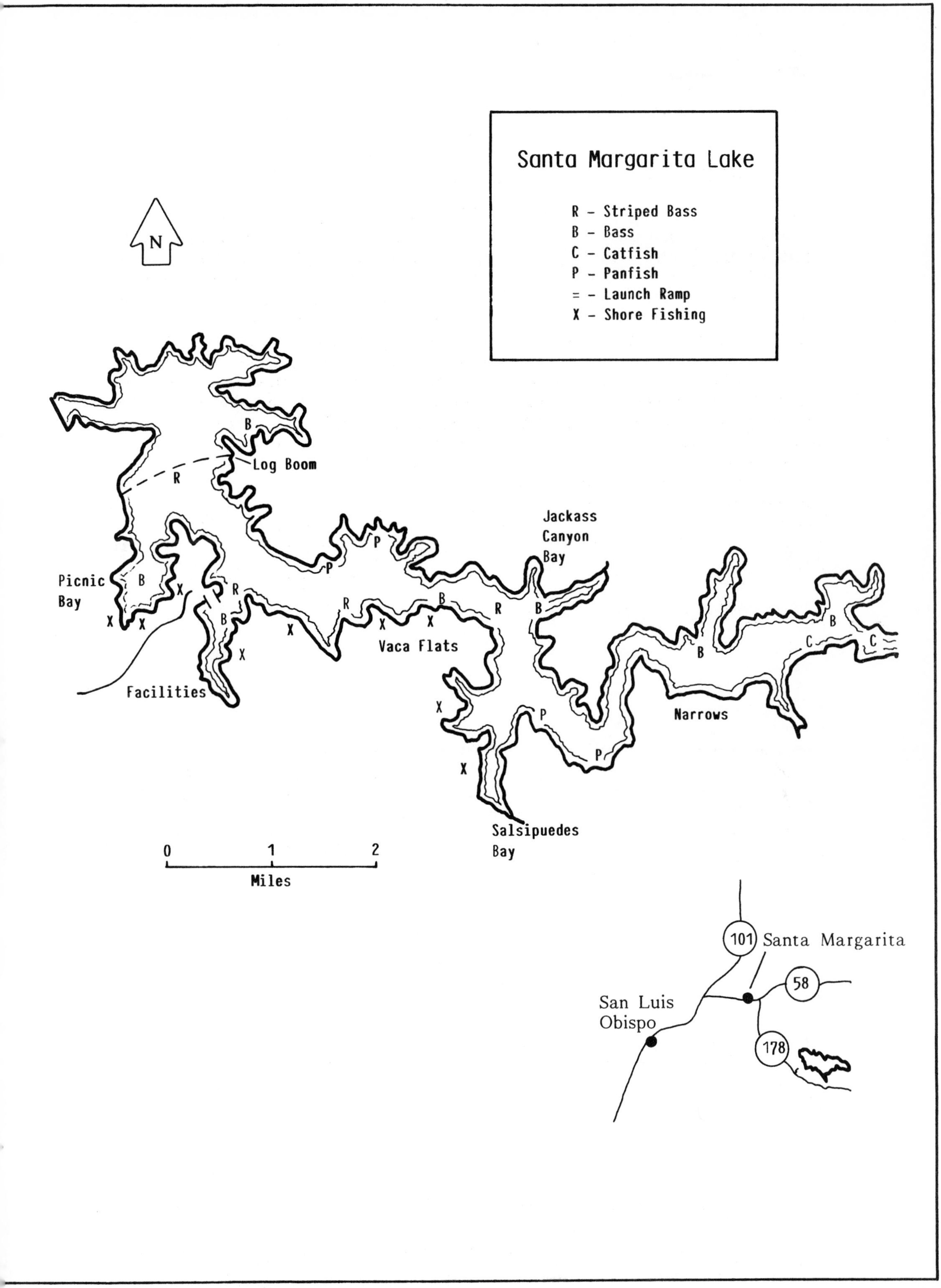

Santa Margarita Lake

R – Striped Bass
B – Bass
C – Catfish
P – Panfish
= – Launch Ramp
X – Shore Fishing

N

B
Log Boom
R

P
P

Jackass
Canyon
Bay

Picnic
Bay
B
X
R
X        B
X    X      X
B
X

R
X    X    R
Vaca Flats
B
R
B
B
C    B    C

Facilities

X
X
P

P
Narrows

X

Salsipuedes
Bay

0        1        2
Miles

101  Santa Margarita
58
San Luis
Obispo
178

## Silverwood Lake

Silverwood Lake is one of several reservoirs along the California Aquaduct that is known for its striped bass fishing. In fact, Silverwood is known for producing some of the largest land-locked stripers, a number in excess of 40 pounds. The lake record is 42 pounds, 12 ounces. But Silverwood is an all around fishery. Before stripers migrated in via the aquaduct, it was known for its trophy trout. And on top of all this, Silverwood is considered by many, as one of the top crappie producers in Southern California. Catfishing, especially at night, is also very good. Silverwood has a surface area of just under 1000 acres and a shoreline of 13 miles. It is located 85 miles east of Los Angeles and about 30 miles north of San Bernadino, on the edge of the high Mojave Desert. Silverwood Lake offers full recreational facilities. There are 135 developed campsites, launching ramps, boat rentals, hiking trails, etc. Waterskiing is permitted.

**Fishing Seasons**  (+=good, -=fair)

| Species | J | F | M | A | M | J | J | A | S | O | N | D |
|---|---|---|---|---|---|---|---|---|---|---|---|---|
| Striped Bass | - | + | + | + | + | + | - | - | - | + | + | - |
| Trout | + | + | + | + | + | - | - | - | - | - | + | + |
| Bass | | | + | + | + | - | - | - | - | + | - | |
| Catfish | | - | - | - | - | + | + | + | + | + | - | |
| Panfish | | - | + | + | + | - | - | - | - | - | - | - |

**Fishing Tips**

The best time for big stripers at Silverwood Lake is the spring and early summer months. Some of the best spots are the spillway, the dam and the rock quarry. Many of the most experienced anglers fish from shore in these areas, using surf casting equipment. Lures like a 3 ounce Kastmaster that imitate injured minnows seem to work best. Silver and white colors are preferred. Many bait anglers use a sliding sinker rig with a 3 foot leader, about a 1/0 bait holder hook and a whole anchovy. It's always a good idea to keep your eyes peeled for shad to boil up on the surface. Cautiously casting shad imitations into these striper feeding fringes can produce fish. Catfishing anglers use cut anchovies and mackerel. Largemouth bass go for nightcrawlers and dark-colored plastic worms.

**Information/Bait/Tackle**

Silverwood Lake, Star Route, Box 7A, Hesperia, CA 92345, (619)389-2281/2303 Marina - (619)389-2320.

| Boating Facilities | Launching | Dockage | Fuel | Boat Rental |
|---|---|---|---|---|
| Silverwood Marina | Paved | Yes | Yes | Yes |

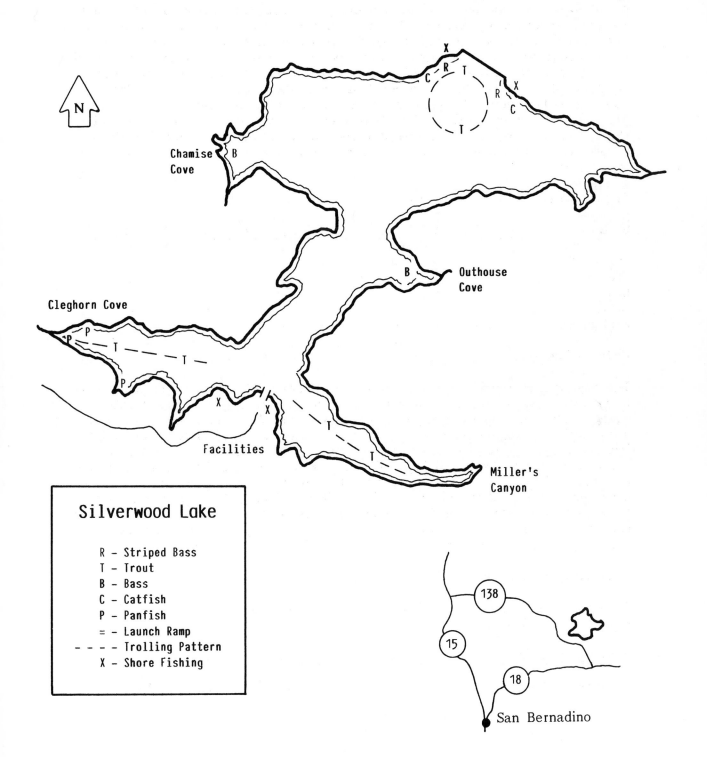

N

X
C R T
T R X
T C

Chamise
Cove
B

Outhouse
Cove
B

Cleghorn Cove
P
P T T
P

Facilities
X
X T
T

Miller's
Canyon

Silverwood Lake

R – Striped Bass
T – Trout
B – Bass
C – Catfish
P – Panfish
= – Launch Ramp
- - - – Trolling Pattern
X – Shore Fishing

138
15
18
San Bernadino

## Skinner Lake

Lake Skinner is a fine fishing lake and it is surrounded by the very nice 6,000 acre Lake Skinner Park. Lake Skinner is located about 90 miles southeast of Los Angeles and about 70 miles northeast of San Diego. It's 9 miles from Rancho California, east of Interstate 15 in Riverside County. The lake is owned by the Metropolitan Water District and leased to the Riverside Parks Department. This is a dedicated fishing lake with no bodily contact with the water and a 10mph speed limit on the water. Skinner is 1200 surface acres with about 14 miles of irregular shoreline. Fishing is a year-around activity with rainbow trout, largemouth bass(northern-strain), catfish and panfish. Facilities include 200 campsites, 2 launch ramps, a half-acre swimming lake with beaches, picnic areas, boat rentals and store. This is a picturesque setting at 1500 feet elevation.

**Fishing Seasons**   (+=good, -=fair)

| Species | J | F | M | A | M | J | J | A | S | O | N | D |
|---------|---|---|---|---|---|---|---|---|---|---|---|---|
| Trout | + | + | + | + | + | - | - | - | - | + | + | + |
| Bass |  | - | + | + | + | - | - | - | - | - |  |  |
| Catfish |  | - | - | - | - | + | + | + | + | - | - |  |
| Panfish |  | - | + | + | + | - | - | - | - | - |  |  |

### Fishing Tips

Trout are probably the best known fishery at Lake Skinner. Rainbows are planted almost weekly, alternately by the Department of Fish and Game, or by the Riverside Parks Department. This planting extends from October to May. In colder months shore anglers do well with bait and lures in the south arm. Trollers also do well, both in cool months and when the water temperature increases. The peak bass season runs from March through May. Skinner does not have many large bass, but they are plentiful. Average fish run from 1-2 pounds. Plugs work good in spring. Anglers in summer work the north shore in the early morning and the south shore at dusk. Fall bass anglers seem to score best with plastic worms. Although Lake Skinner is a newer lake(opened in 1976), catfish in the 10-15 pound range are common.

### Information/Bait/Tackle

Lake Skinner, 37701 Warren Rd., Winchester, CA 92396, (714)926-3360. Riverside County Parks Department - (714)787-2551.

| Boating Facilities | Launching | Dockage | Fuel | Boat Rental |
|--------------------|-----------|---------|------|-------------|
| Lake Skinner Marina | 2 Ramps | Yes | Yes | Yes |

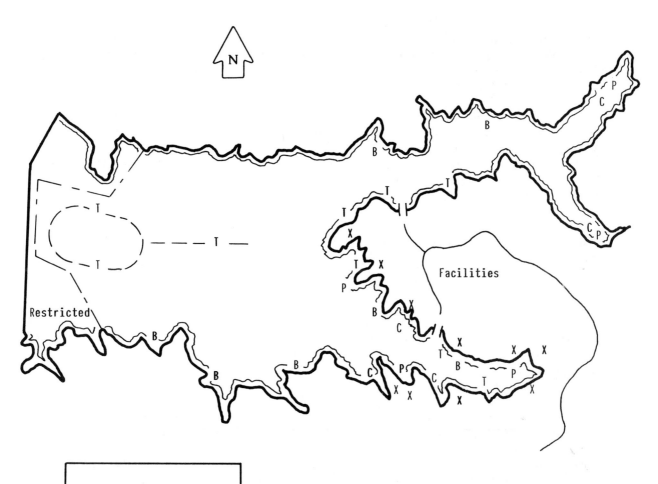

N

Restricted

Facilities

Lake Skinner

T – Trout
B – Bass
C – Catfish
P – Panfish
= – Launch Ramp
- - - – Trolling Pattern
X – Shore Fishing

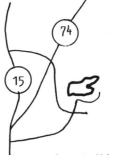

74

15

Rancho California

## Success Lake

Success Lake is a very fine fishery. It is located about midway between Fresno and Bakersfield, near Porterville, on the Tule River. This reservoir which is under the jurisdiction of the U.S. Army Corps of Engineers, holds 2400 surface acres of water, with 30 miles of shoreline. Success has trout, largemouth bass(northern strain), catfish and panfish, as well as an up and coming striped bass fishery. This combination provides year around activity for the angler. There are about 100 developed campsites at the Tule area and an almost equal number of primitive campsites at the Rocky Hill area. All types of water activities are permitted including swimming and waterskiing. Other facilities include a full service marina, 3 launch ramps, store, hot showers and wildlife management area. Hunting, in season, is permitted in the Kincaid Coves section of the lake.

### Fishing Seasons  (+=good, -=fair)

| Species | J | F | M | A | M | J | J | A | S | O | N | D |
|---|---|---|---|---|---|---|---|---|---|---|---|---|
| Trout | + | + | + | + | - | - | - | - | - | + | + | + |
| Bass | | - | + | + | + | - | - | - | - | + | - | |
| Striped Bass | | - | + | + | + | + | - | - | + | + | + | - |
| Catfish | | - | - | - | - | + | + | + | + | - | - | |
| Panfish | - | + | + | + | - | - | - | - | - | - | | |

### Fishing Tips

Largemouth bass anglers concentrate on the coves at the north end of the lake when the fish move into shallow water to spawn. Live baits, including shad from the lake and waterdogs are productive this time of year. Another good bet is plastic worms, especially browns and purples with glitter. Later season bassers work dropoffs and other structures all over the lake. Trout seekers tend to work near the dam, the launch areas and up near the north fork of the Tule River. Often, planted trout from the river are caught in this part of the lake. In the spring, striped bass are caught by trollers using deep-running type lures that immitate either small trout or shad. The Kincaid Coves are also great areas for crappies when they spawn in the spring. And the upper end of these coves are good for bluegills throughout summer. The marina is also a good fishing area.

### Information/Bait/Tackle

Success Lake, Box 1072, Porterville, CA 93258, (209)784-0215.

| Boating Facilities | Launching | Dockage | Fuel | Boat Rental |
|---|---|---|---|---|
| Success Marina | 3 Ramps | Yes | Yes | Yes |

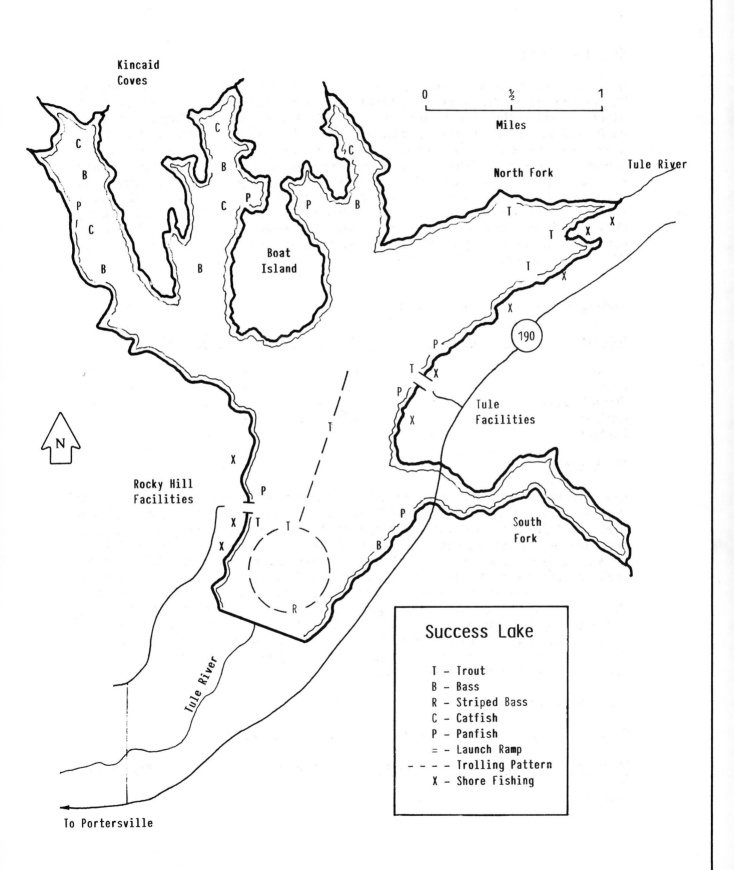

Kincaid
Coves

North Fork

Tule River

190

Tule
Facilities

Boat
Island

South
Fork

N

Rocky Hill
Facilities

Tule River

To Portersville

## Success Lake

T – Trout
B – Bass
R – Striped Bass
C – Catfish
P – Panfish
= – Launch Ramp
– – – Trolling Pattern
X – Shore Fishing

0    ½    1

Miles

## Sutherland Lake

Lake Sutherland is another in the "chain" of San Diego City fishing lakes. Sutherland is a warm water fishery that offers largemouth bass(Florida-strain), catfish and bluegill angling, from March to late fall, on Fridays, Saturdays and Sundays. This is a day-use facility that is nestled in the rolling hills 7 miles northeast of Ramona, 138 miles southeast of Los Angeles and 45 miles northeast of San Diego. Sutherland Lake covers about 550 acres when filled to capacity. There is a 10mph speed limit on the lake. The nearest camping facility is about 5 miles west of Ramona on Hwy 67. Facilities at the lake include a store, boat launching, picnic area and boat rental. As is true at all San Diego City lakes, there is a modest, per person daily fishing fee.

### Fishing Seasons  (+=good, -=fair)

| Species | J | F | M | A | M | J | J | A | S | O | N | D |
|---------|---|---|---|---|---|---|---|---|---|---|---|---|
| Bass    |   |   | + | + | + | - | - | - | - | - |   |   |
| Catfish |   |   | - | - | - | - | + | + | + | + |   |   |
| Panfish |   |   | - | - | - | + | + | + | - | - |   |   |

### Fishing Tips

Sutherland is not as famous a Florida-strain largemouth bass fishery as several of the other San Diego City lakes. But because of this, it's probably less crowded and less hectic. Anglers here consistently catch stringers of bass in the 2-4 pound range. And Sutherland does produce its share of fish in the over 5 pound category. The current lake record is 15 pounds, 8 ounces. The north shore is a favorite spot for bassers. It actually extends from west of the dam(there is a restricted area in front of the dam) up into the Mesa Grande Arm. Plastic worms and pig-n-jigs work good along the rocky out-croppings. Usually an annual surface bite begins at Sutherland along the west shore in March or April. Rapalas, poppers and prop plugs take them. Cat-fishing is most productive in the Santo Ysabel Arm using cut mackerel.

### Information/Bait/Tackle

Lake Sutherland, Box 429, Ramona, CA 92065, (619)465-4500.
Current Fishing Information - (619)465-3474.

| Boating Facilities | Launching | Dockage | Fuel | Boat Rental |
|--------------------|-----------|---------|------|-------------|
| Sutherland Marina  | Yes       | Yes     | Yes  | Yes         |

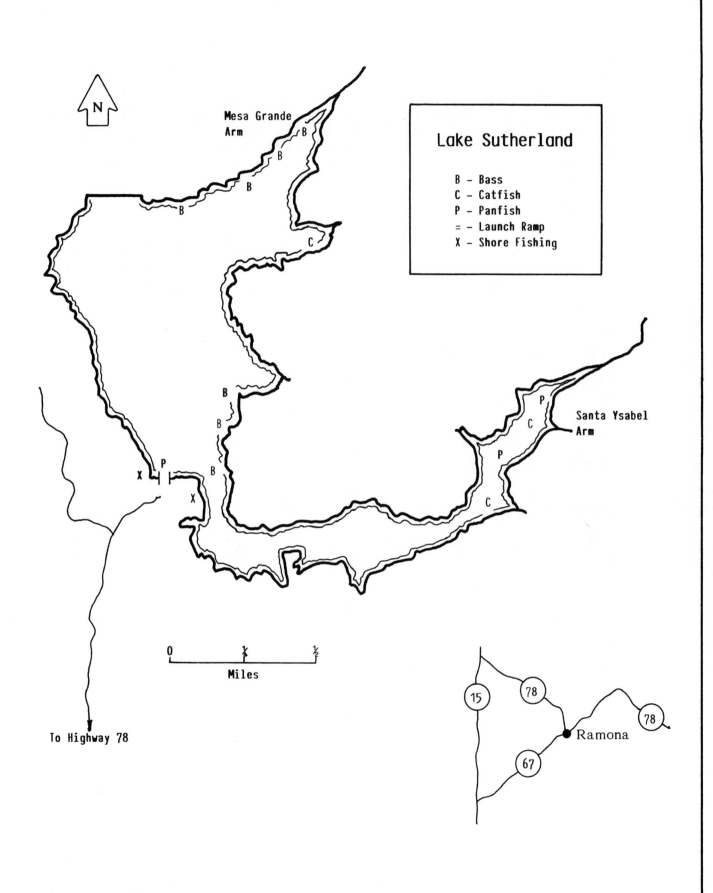

N

Mesa Grande
Arm

B
B
B
B
C

Lake Sutherland

B – Bass
C – Catfish
P – Panfish
= – Launch Ramp
X – Shore Fishing

B
B
B

P
C

Santa Ysabel
Arm

X P
X

P

C

0    ¼    ½
Miles

To Highway 78

15    78
78
67    Ramona

## Wohlford Lake

Lake Wohlford is a fine, small fishing lake located a short distance(about 6 miles) northwest of Escondido. It's about 120 miles from Los Angeles and about 40 miles from San Diego, off Interstate 15. The City of Escondido owns the reservoir and it is maintained in conjunction with the Escondido Mutual Water Company. This is a lake that is convenient to the urban area, yet still offers a get-away-from-it-all atmosphere. Lake Wohlford opens each year around January(call for exact date) and remains open for fishing until September, or so. There is an unpaved launch ramp and a boat speed limit of 5mph. But many anglers fish from shore here. There is good access all around the lake and the shoreline is pretty much unobstructed. Rainbow trout are the quarry early in the season(they are planted weekly). But Wohlford also offers very good-sized largemouth bass(lake record is 19 pounds, 12 ounces), catfish and panfish. There are two(Lake Wohlford Resort and Oakvale Park) private campgrounds right near the lake.

### Fishing Seasons  (+=good, -=fair)

| Species | J | F | M | A | M | J | J | A | S | O | N | D |
|---|---|---|---|---|---|---|---|---|---|---|---|---|
| Trout | + | + | + | + | + | - | - | - | - | | | |
| Bass | | - | + | + | + | - | - | - | - | | | |
| Catfish | | - | - | - | - | + | + | + | + | | | |
| Panfish | | - | + | + | + | - | - | - | - | | | |

### Fishing Tips

Rainbow trout plants extend from January through early summer. A good spot for shore anglers is in the vicinity of the launch ramp and dock. Two other prime areas are the small bay opposite the launch ramp and near the dam along the barrel line. All of the popular methods of taking trout work well at Lake Wohlford. Bait anglers are encouraged to use a sliding sinker rig and to keep hands or eyes on the rod or line to detect pick-ups. It's also always advisable to float the offering up off the bottom. Inflate nightcrawlers, or add a small marshmallow to cheese or salmon egg baits. Floating cheese and marshmallow baits are available commercially. Fishing hours at Wohlford are from 6am to 5pm.

### Information/Bait/Tackle

Lake Wohlford Resort, Box 204, Escondido, CA 92027, (619)749-2755.
Oakvale Park, Box 268, Escondido, CA 92025, (619)749-2895.

| Boating Facilities | Launching | Dockage | Fuel | Boat Rental |
|---|---|---|---|---|
| Lake Wohlford | Unpaved | Yes | Yes | Yes |

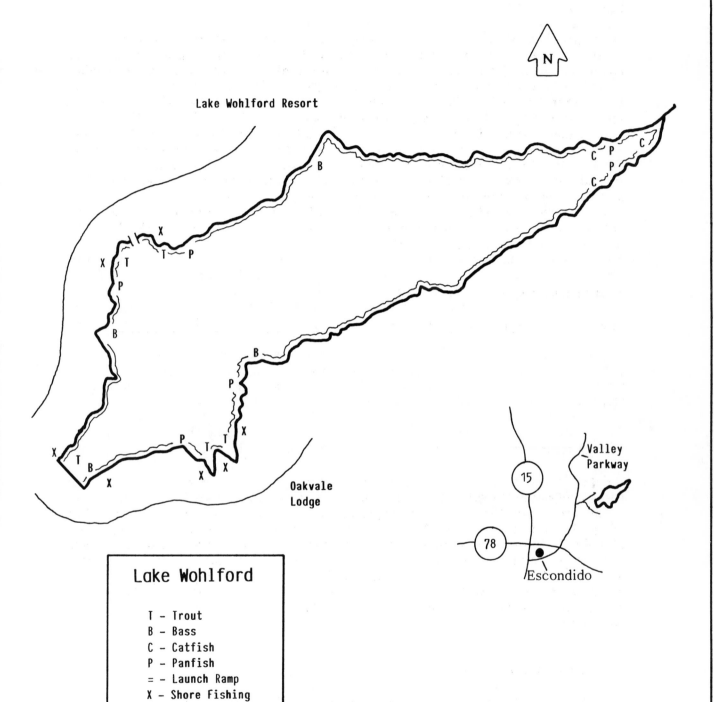

Lake Wohlford Resort

Oakvale Lodge

Valley Parkway

15

78

Escondido

N

**Lake Wohlford**

T – Trout
B – Bass
C – Catfish
P – Panfish
= – Launch Ramp
X – Shore Fishing

# Salton Sea Fishing

The Salton Sea, to say the least, is a unique place to fish. This is a very large (45 miles by 17 miles) inland saltwater sea. Its water level is about 230 feet below sea level, and is a little more salty than the Pacific Ocean. Four species of saltwater fish provide great fishing action in this shallow(average depth is less than 20 feet) oval. Species include the orangemouth corvina that average 5-15 pounds, as well as several smaller fish that make the Salton Sea a great place for kids to experience the joy of catching lots of fish. As a matter of fact, the catch rate per angler here is greater than at any other inland fishing locale in California. This is the result of diligent Department of Fish and Game efforts that began in the 1950's.

The Salton Sea is located about 140 miles southeast of Los Angeles and is surrounded by desert. The climate is very enjoyable in the cooler months. Summer temperatures often rise over 100°, moving anglers to fish early and late in the day. Surface water temperatures reach over 90° in the summer and fall to as low as 55° in the winter.

There are good facilities here, including the Salton Sea State Park. Marinas, launch ramps, boat rental, motels and campgrounds are mostly near the state park or near Salton City. There is also a marina at Red Hill. All together there are about 8 launching facilities.

The fishing is good almost all year at the Salton Sea. But the bite of the various species varies a great deal, depending on the season.

**Fishing Seasons** (+=good, -=fair)

| Species | J | F | M | A | M | J | J | A | S | O | N | D |
|---|---|---|---|---|---|---|---|---|---|---|---|---|
| Corvina | - | - | - | + | + | + | - | - | + | + | | |
| Sargo | + | + | + | + | - | - | - | - | - | - | + | + |
| Tilapia | - | - | - | - | - | + | + | + | - | - | - | - |
| Gulf Croaker | - | - | - | + | + | + | + | + | + | + | - | - |

## Catching Corvina

Orangemouth corvina is by far the largest and most sought after fish in the Salton Sea. The lake record fish(and world record) is 36 pounds, 8 ounces! Many are caught in the 5-15 pound range. And this long, sleek fish is fantastic eating. Many compare it favorably with such great ocean-caught eating fish as halibut and rockfish.

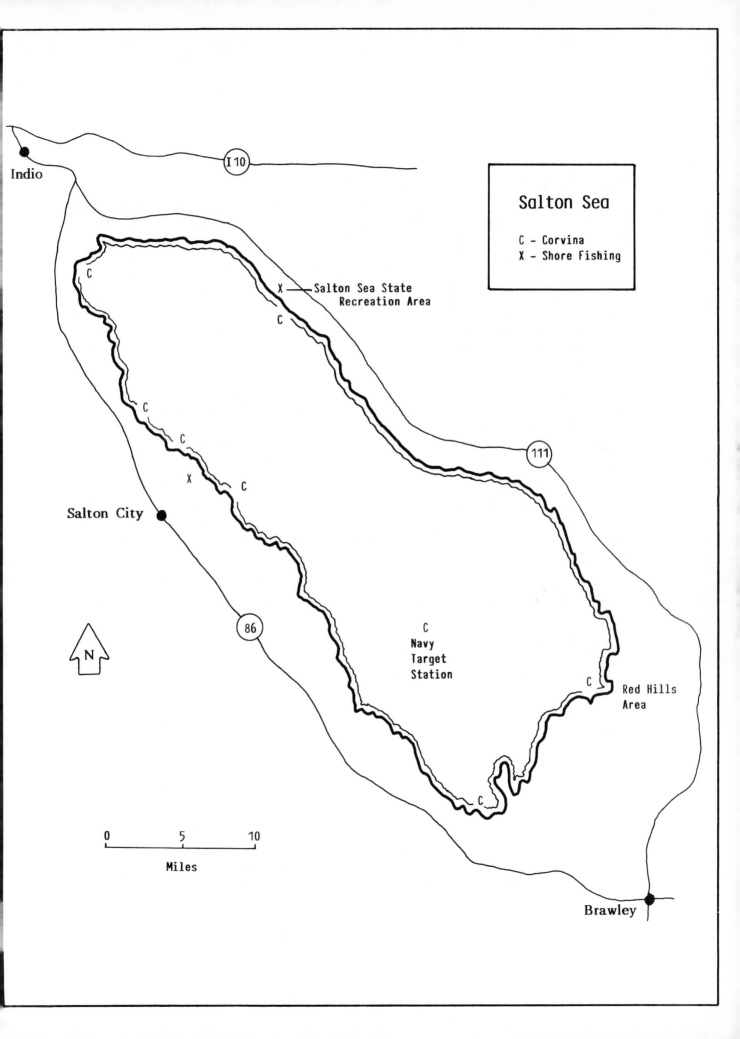

Indio

I 10

**Salton Sea**

C – Corvina
X – Shore Fishing

C

X —— Salton Sea State
Recreation Area

C

C

111

C

C

X

C

Salton City

C

86

N

C
Navy
Target
Station

C
Red Hills
Area

C

0      5      10

Miles

Brawley

There are several ways to take these fish, depending on the season. Corvina seek water temperatures in the 70-85° range. This means they are in shallower water in the late spring and early summer, then retreat to deeper water in the heat of late summer. In winter, when climatic conditions are right to produce warmer shallow water in the Red Hill area, they move in to feed in water as shallow as 4 feet. Their other winter hangout is down deep.

Trolling, casting and live bait fishing are all productive at the Salton Sea, depending on the season and on what seems to be working. Among the trolling lures that produce, the most popular is the Thin Fin Shad(about 3½ inch). Use the sinking type in red, green or yellow. The locally produced Lunker Lure is also popular, as are Hopkins Spoons, Kastmaster and Krocodile Spoons(all in 1/2-3/4 ounce). Minnow-shaped plugs like Rebels also produce. Troll slowly, and make sure the lure taps the bottom once-in-a-while.

When the corvina are in the deeper parts of the lake, vertical jigging with a wobbly spoon(like a Hopkins) is productive. Jig up and down from the bottom to 2 feet above the bottom. Some anglers leave their motor running and chum with canned corn. The noise and corn seem to stimulate a bite.

Live bait fishing is a tried-and-true method of taking corvina, especially from late spring to mid-July. The most popular bait is mudsuckers. Tilapia, sargo and croaker are also used. From shore, live bait fishing is done on the bottom using a sliding sinker rig. Match hook size to bait size.

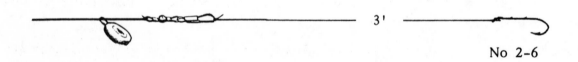

No 2-6

Bait is either nose hooked or the hook is put through the back at the dorsal fin. From a boat, most anglers use a rubber core sinker, also about 3 feet up from the hook.

In winter, the corvina are sometimes found in a feeding boil in shallow water in the Red Hill area. A most productive approach is casting a Thin Fin type lure, and retrieving it medium to slow, yet with an erratic action.

Many a crovina are caught by shore anglers at the sea. One technique(called "arm pit fishing") is popular. After wading out from a beach, anglers either cast out live bait or cast and retrieve lures(the same as used in trolling). Several jetties around the lake also produce corvina for shore anglers.

## Catching Tilapia

Tilapia, originally a native of the Middle East and Africa, are prolific breeders and there are literally millions in the Salton Sea. These good eating fish are generally caught in the ½-3 pound range.

The most popular method for catching tilapia, especially from shore, is to use bait on what is basically a surf fishing rig, or crappie rig.

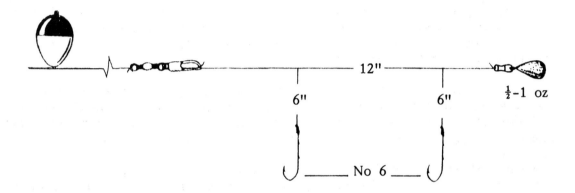

Popular baits include a piece of nightcrawler or a whole redworm. It sometimes helps to keep the bait moving, and, at times, anglers put a kernal of corn on the hook before the worm. Corn improves the visibility. This rig can be fished under a bobber, or from a boat.

Jigging Kastmasters and Hopkins Spoons(about ½ ounce) up and down right off the bottom in 10-20 feet of water is often a good way to take larger tilapia. This is done from a drifting boat. A good spot is from Avenue 81 south to Desert Shores.

## Catching Sargo

Sargo are native to Southern California ocean waters where they are called China croaker. These ½-2 pound fish like to hang out around old submerged buildings, trees or rock jetties. Boat anglers like to fish the sunken buildings just south of the town of North Shore. The Salton Sea State Recreation Area has a good jetty for sargo fishing.

Sargo should be fished right on the bottom. Popular baits are nightcrawlers, shrimp, or canned whole-kernal corn. Corn is the most productive. Anglers put 3 or 4 kernals on one hook. Chumming, or throwing corn into the water is often done to stimulate the bite. This is legal in the sea.

The same rig as used for tilapia can be used for sargo.  Or a one hook or two hook sliding sinker rig can be used:

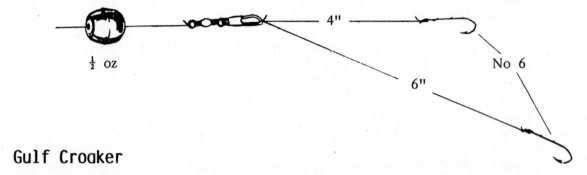

½ oz    4"    No 6    6"

## Gulf Croaker

Gulf croaker, averaging in the 8-12 inch range, are easier to catch in the warmer months.  They travel in large schools, and are not fussy eaters.  Popular offerings include minnows, nightcrawlers, redworms, and pieces of anchovy.  They can be caught all over the lake in the summertime using a tilapia rig.  Casting small trout spoons and spinners also works.  Whole croaker are a popular bait for corvina fishing.

## Tackle and Equipment

One of the beauties of Salton Sea fishing is that only one rod and reel combination is needed to participate in all the fishing fun.  The most popular rig is

- .  Spinning Reel

- .  6½-7½ foot medium action spinning rod

- .  10-15 pound monofilament line

Baitcasting equipment is also popular, as is spin surf casting equipment for long-cast shore fishing.  Boat anglers need a landing net.

## Cleaning and Cooking

Corvina are most often filleted.  The white, sweet meat is delicious prepared almost any way.  Tilapia are also filleted.  Try to avoid cutting into the stomach cavity.  It has an unpleasant odor.  Skinless fillets can be baked, broiled, fried, poached or smoked.  Sargo are also filleted.  Remember to remove the dark meat along the lateral line.  Sargo are excellent smoked, or fillets are excellent when breaded and deep fried.  Gulf croaker are filleted, but even with the skin on, they have a mild flavor.  Deep frying is a popular preparation method.

# Colorado River Lakes Fishing

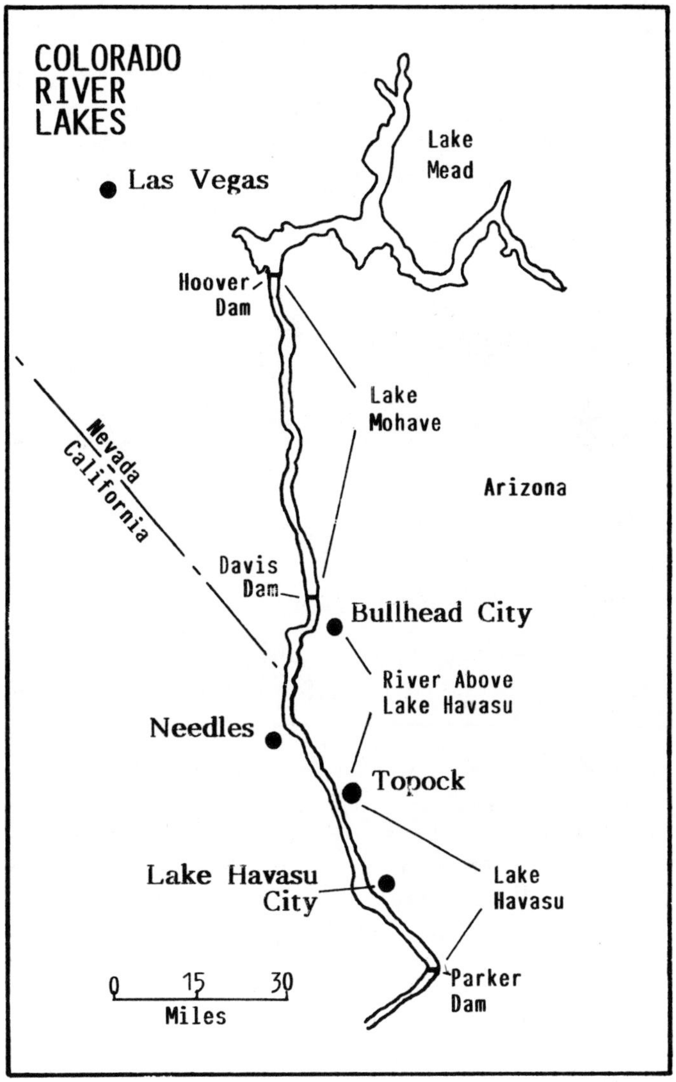

In 1935, Hoover Dam was completed to form Lake Mead. Three years later Lake Havasu was formed by the completion of Parker Dam. And then in 1953, Davis Dam was completed to form Lake Mohave. These dams, besides satisfying hydroelectric, water storage and flood control needs, have created three marvelous, huge, year around fishing and recreation lakes.

Although all water sports, including houseboating and waterskiing, are a part of the scene at the Colorado River Lakes, the common denominator of much activity on the water, is fishing. Rainbow trout, largemouth bass, catfish, panfish, and in recent decades, monster-sized striped bass, are the attractions. Prime trout waters are the Bullhead City area of the river above Lake Havasu and all of Lake Mohave. Largemouths are caught in all three Colorado River Lakes, as are catfish and panfish. Prime striper waters are Lake Havasu and Lake Mead. In these big waters, striper anglers have found that the graph-type depth sounders are extremely helpful in locating fish off underwater points and other structures. Striper are taken by casting to surface feeding fish and shoreline structures, and by trolling and bait fishing.

COLORADO RIVER LAKES

Las Vegas

Lake Mead

Hoover Dam

Nevada
California

Lake Mohave

Arizona

Davis Dam

Bullhead City

River Above Lake Havasu

Needles

Topock

Lake Havasu City

Lake Havasu

0    15    30
Miles

Parker Dam

## Lake Havasu

Lake Havasu, the home of The London Bridge, is an immense and varied fishing and recreation locale.  It is located in the desert between California and Arizona and extends from Davis Dam down to Parker Dam. In essence, Havasu is actually two distinct waters.  First, there is the river portion from Davis Dam down to about Topock.  Just below Davis Dam the water runs cold, even in summer, over a rock and rubble stream bed that is an excellent rainbow trout habitat.  Down river at about the state line the stream bed changes to sand, as the water flows through Topock Swamp.  These are good bass, catfish and crappie fishing areas.  Lake Havasu itself, has a varied shoreline, with marshlands and secluded coves.  It varies in width from 3 miles to less than ½ mile.  There are abundant camping facilities, launch ramps and over 15 resorts.

### Fishing Seasons   (+=good, -=fair)

| Species | J | F | M | A | M | J | J | A | S | O | N | D |
|---|---|---|---|---|---|---|---|---|---|---|---|---|
| Striped Bass | | | + | + | + | - | - | - | - | + | + | |
| Trout | + | + | | - | - | - | - | - | - | - | + | + |
| Bass | | | - | + | + | - | - | - | - | + | + | |
| Catfish | | - | - | - | - | + | + | + | + | - | - | |
| Panfish | + | - | - | - | - | | | | | | + | + |

### Fishing Tips

In the winter striped bass are usually concentrated in the deeper waters of the main lake.  A traditional winter hot spot is the Havasu Spring area, near Parker Dam.  In early spring, striper start their move to shallower water.  March and April they are in the upper lake and lower river.  By May fishing is good all the way up to Davis Dam.  In the warm summer months, following the migration, stripers are spread out and fish are caught just about everywhere.  Just below Davis Dam, surf casting equipment is used to reach the white water with larger jigs.  Most of the river section is too shallow to troll, so bait angling and casting and retrieving are productive.  Casters drift about 30 feet offshore and cast to shore like largemouth bass anglers.  November, December and January are prime months for crappie in the Topock Bay area.  In Lake Havasu proper, trolling, casting and spoon jigging are productive methods of taking striper.  Good striper spots include Grass Island, Skier's Island, Sod Farm, Pilot Rock, Red Rock and outside of Steamboat Bay.

### Information

Lake Havasu Area Chamber of Commerce, 65 N. Lake Havasu Ave., Lake Havasu, AZ 86403, (602)855-4115.

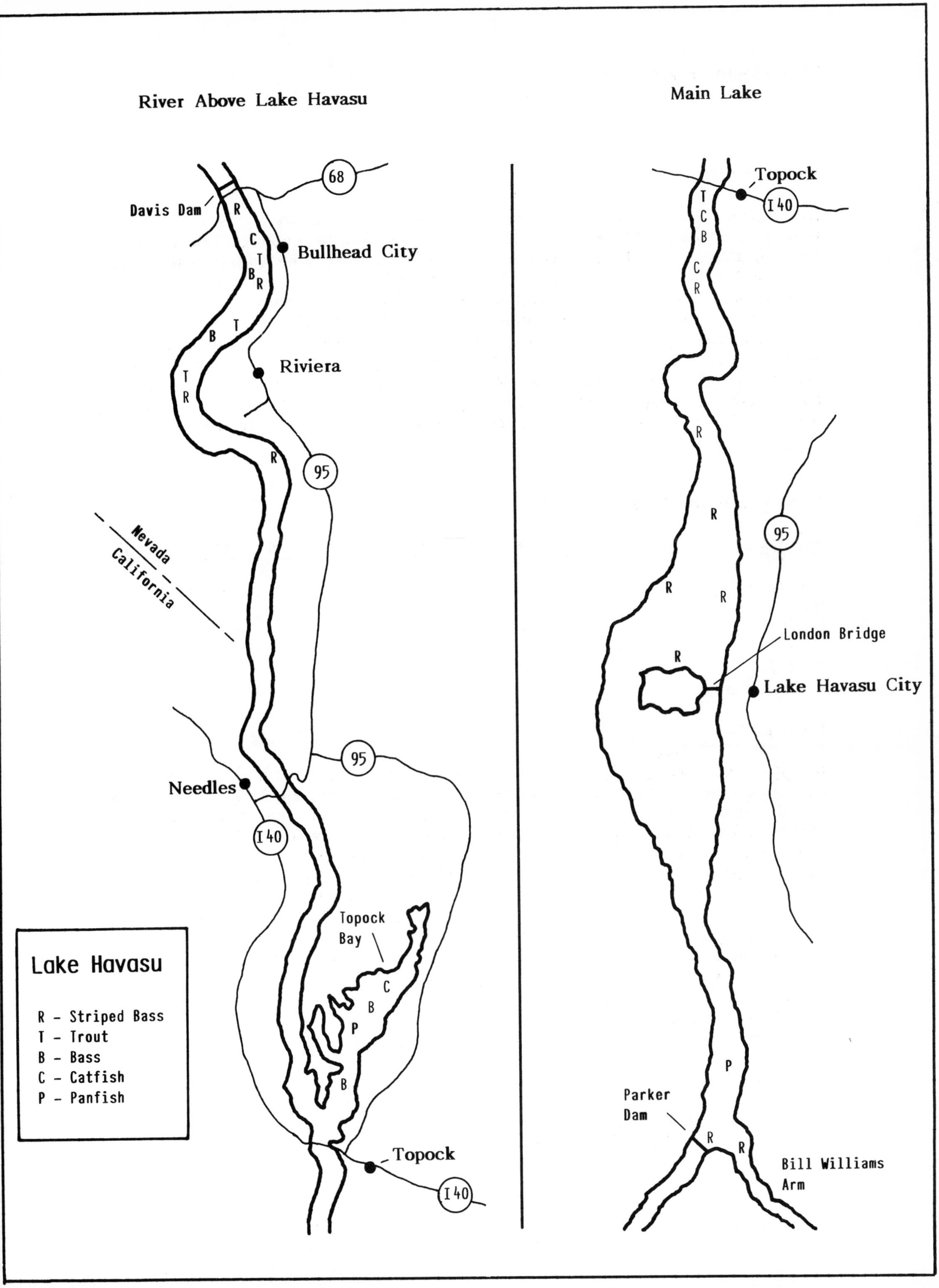

## River Above Lake Havasu

Davis Dam

68

R
C
T
B
R

● Bullhead City

B T

T R

● Riviera

R

95

Nevada
California

95

Needles ●

I 40

Topock
Bay

C
B
P

B

● Topock

I 40

### Lake Havasu

R – Striped Bass
T – Trout
B – Bass
C – Catfish
P – Panfish

## Main Lake

● Topock

I 40

T
C
B
C
R

R

R

R

R

R

95

London Bridge

● Lake Havasu City

Parker
Dam

P

R
R

Bill Williams
Arm

## Lake Mohave

Lake Mohave, located along the southernmost tip of Nevada, is a marvelous fishing grounds. This stretch of the Colorado River, between Hoover Dam and Davis Dam is 71 miles long. Now that's a long lake! The widest point, south of Cottonwood, is about 4 miles. The upper part of the lake is characterized by narrow canyon waters, whereas the southern reaches offer a mosaic of secluded coves, rocky cliffs and sandy beaches. Most facilities are concentrated in the Willow Beach, Cottonwood Cove and Lake Mohave Marina(near Davis Dam) areas of the lake. These include camping, boat rental, launch ramps, full service marinas, etc. If one didn't know that Mohave was a Colorado River Lake on the border between Nevada and Arizona, its prime fishing attractions would suggest it was located in the Sierra somewhere. That's because rainbow trout, largemouth bass and catfish are the main bill-of-fare.

### Fishing Seasons  (+=good, -=fair)

| Species | J | F | M | A | M | J | J | A | S | O | N | D |
|---|---|---|---|---|---|---|---|---|---|---|---|---|
| Trout | + | + | - | - | - | - | - | - | - | - | + | + |
| Bass | | - | + | + | + | - | - | - | - | - | - | |
| Catfish | | - | - | - | - | + | + | + | + | - | - | |

### Fishing Tips

The winter months of November, December, January and February are prime trout times at Mohave, although they are taken all year long. The lake record rainbow is 16 pounds, 4 ounces. Trolling, using leadcore line, is the most popular approach. Downriggers also work. Regular trout anglers score most consistently with Needlefish(both rainbow and frog patterns). Proper trolling depth depends on season and water temperatures. Bass anglers new to Mohave must make adjustments because of its exceptionally clear water. Approach casting targets quietly and slowly, and try your best to get that first cast exactly where you want it. Plastic worms(purple or brown) are popular, as is live bait fishing with water dogs. Most anglers hook them up through the lips, like a small bait fish. Catfishing peaks in the hot summer months. Frozen baits and commercial formulas score.

### Information/Bait/Tackle

Lake Mead National Recreation Area, 601 Nevada Highway, Boulder City, Nevada 89005, (702)293-4041.
Willow Beach Resort, Boulder City, Nevada 89005, (702)767-3311.
Cottonwood Cove Marina, Cottonwood Cove, Nevada 89046, (702)297-1464.
Lake Mohave Marina, Bullhead City, Arizona 86430, (602)754-3245.

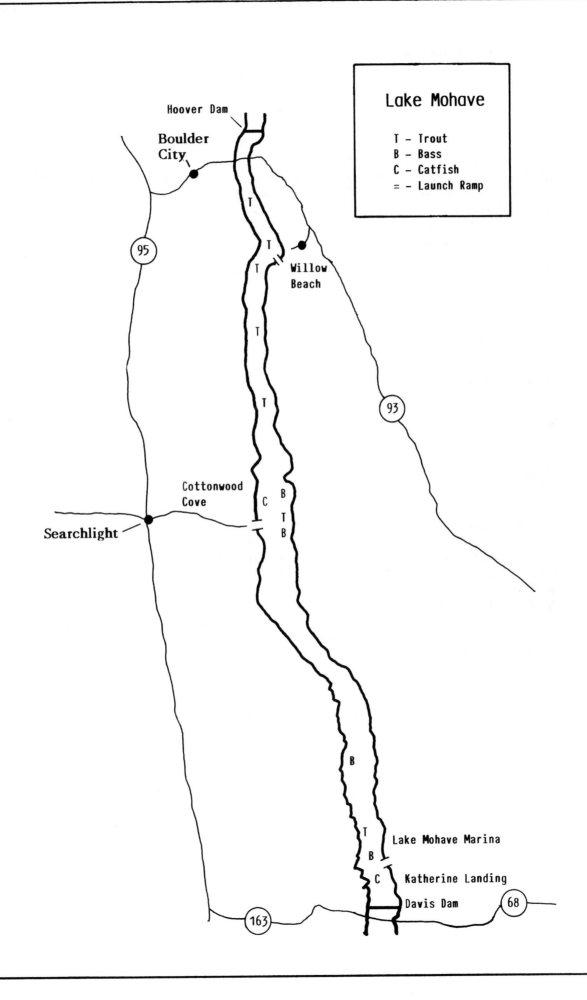

Lake Mohave

T – Trout
B – Bass
C – Catfish
= – Launch Ramp

Hoover Dam

Boulder City

95

Willow Beach

93

Cottonwood Cove

Searchlight

Lake Mohave Marina

Katherine Landing

Davis Dam

163

68

## Lake Mead

Lake Mead is an immense reservoir that was formed in the mid 1930's by the completion of Hoover Dam. It has 550 miles of shoreline surrounding 225 square miles of water. This ever changing shoreline is highlighted by steep canyon walls, wide gravel beaches and hundreds of little coves. From one end to the other, Mead measures 115 miles. Located just east of Las Vegas, all types of water-related activities are available including fishing, houseboating, waterskiing and boat camping. Lake Mead is known for excellent largemouth bass and striped bass fishing. Other fisheries include catfish and panfish.

It has been the sight of countless largemouth bass tournaments. Surveys indicate that 60% of angling time, on a year around basis, is aimed at stripers. In the summer, this rises to 90%!

**Fishing Seasons** (+=good, -=fair)

| Species | J | F | M | A | M | J | J | A | S | O | N | D |
|---|---|---|---|---|---|---|---|---|---|---|---|---|
| Striped Bass | - | + | + | + | + | - | - | - | + | + | - | |
| Bass | - | + | + | + | - | - | - | - | + | - | | |
| Catfish | - | - | - | - | + | + | + | + | - | - | | |

**Fishing Tips**

Since this is such a big lake, and since striper move from day-to-day and by season, the key to catching them is finding them. Some anglers first make telephone calls to bait shops, marinas, etc., to help narrow down the search area. Graph recorders are also extremely helpful as are tip-offs like feeding birds. When the stripers aren't in shallow water or surface feeding, look for them out off points, in 20-70 feet of water. Stripers at Lake Mead follow their favorite food, the threadfin shad. In winter the stripers are down deep, eating those shad. As water temperatures increase, the shad and stripers move up closer to the surface. By fall the shad are often being eaten by stripers in shallow water. But no matter the season, stripers are feeding nearer to shore in early morning and late evening. At midday, the sun on the water drives the striper down. Favorite among bait anglers at Mead are frozen anchovies. A popular spoon for spoon jigging is the Hopkin's Shorty 45. Trollers use Sassy Shad, Cordell Redfin, large Rebels, Rapalas, etc. Water dogs are popular largemouth bass baits.

**Information**

Lake Mead National Recreation Area, 601 Nevada Highway, Boulder City, Nevada 89005, (702)293-4041.

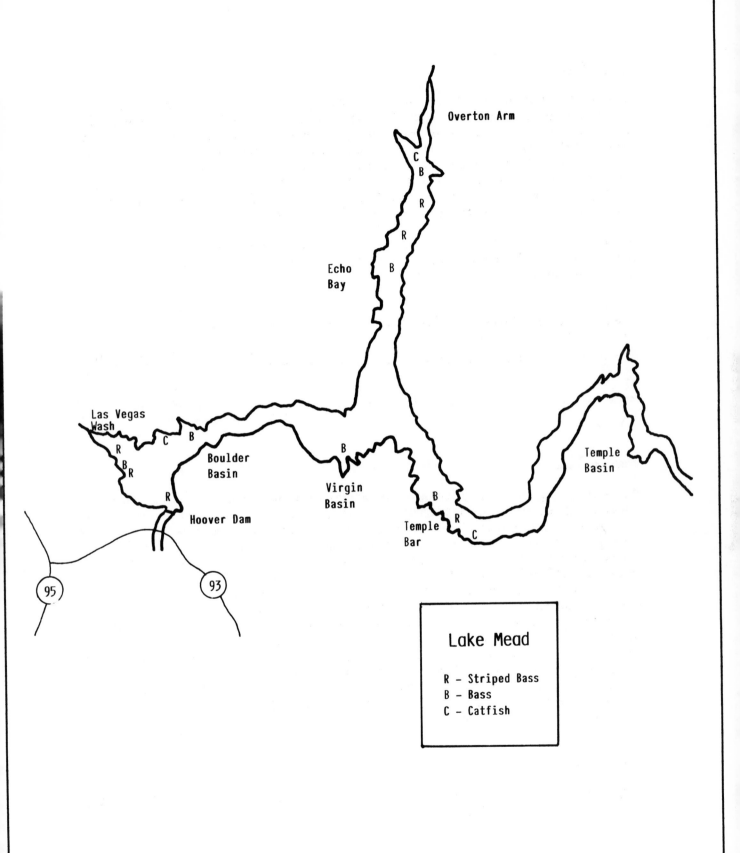

Overton Arm

Echo
Bay

Las Vegas
Wash

Boulder
Basin

Virgin
Basin

Temple
Basin

Temple
Bar

Hoover Dam

95

93

Lake Mead

R – Striped Bass
B – Bass
C – Catfish

# Mountain Trout Fishing

There are numerous, easily accessible mountain trout fishing opportunities available to Southern California anglers. In this section some of the best are profiled in detail. These include the many lakes and streams in the stretch of the eastern Sierra along Rte 395 from Bishop to Bridgeport. Next comes the fine fishing in the western Sierra out of Bakersfield and Fresno. And finally, several opportunities right at the backdoor of Los Angeles area anglers are described.

Trout fishing takes the angler to some of the most beautiful spots in this most beautiful state. This point was eloquently made back in 1894 when David Starr Jordan, writing at the conclusion of a State Fish Commission report, said, "In writing on the trout of California, one does not willingly lay down the pen at the end. The most beautiful of fishes, the most charming of lands, where the two are connected, one wishes to say something better of them than has been said. It is with regret that he lets fall the pen in confession of inability to say it."

Much has changed in California in the last 90 or so years. But the beauty of many of our mountain lakes and streams, and of our trout has not. In this section a wide variety of enriching and productive trout fishing locations are profiled.

### Fishing Tips

The success of a stream fishing experience depends on many factors including the amount of snowfall, the runoff, timing of insect hatches, weather patterns, etc. Generally, trout fishing is better in the spring and fall, than it is in the summer. But summer fishing is often productive. When summer comes on, veteran stream anglers follow 60-65° water temperature up to higher elevations as backroads become passable. In July and August, a good spot is the cool tailwaters below dams. Summer lake anglers use trolling methods that will take their offering to deeper and cooler waters.

One approach that always seems to produce more and larger trout is to contradict human nature. Most anglers park at a stream access point, walk to the water and begin to fish. So the pros have found that it's always better to hike for say 15 minutes along a stream before fishing. This will get you beyond the overworked and underpopulated spots into some really good fishing action.

Once fishing in a stream, the most productive anglers aren't afraid to get into the water. Don't just wade around the edges and fish from convenient spots. Get in the water with chest waders, if necessary, and move to the spots that provide access to the most likely holes.

## EASTERN SIERRA TROUT

With some variation, the trout season in the eastern Sierra runs from the last Saturday in April through October 31st(check regulations).

Take a look at the map on the right of this page. On it are shown some of the best and most famous lake and stream trout fishing areas in all of California. Let's work our way up Rte 395 starting at Bishop and you'll see what we're talking about.

## Bishop Area Trout

The town of Bishop is one of the centers for eastern Sierra trouting. Elevation varies in the Bishop area from 7,000 ft. to 9,000 ft. Lower elevation fishing is usually more popular in the cooler months. Streams and lakes at higher elevations are more popular in the warmer months since air and water temperatures are cooler and most of the higher elevation waters are closed to fishing in the winter months. The main streams and lakes in the Bishop area are shown on the next page.

The Lower Owens River, from Pleasant Valley Reservoir downstream to Five Bridges Rd. is a wild trout water. Only artificial lures may be used and there is a 2 fish limit. But this stream is open all year around. The catch here is native brown trout.

Four other streams in the area(South Fork of Bishop Creek, North Fork of Bishop Creek, Upper Rock Creek and Big Pine Creek) have much in common. They are all stocked weekly with catchable sized rainbows. Typical fish are 8-12 inches. This maintains a high catch-per-angler ratio throughout the summer months. Also these streams are all about the same size - about 10 to 20 ft. wide. Average water depth is several feet

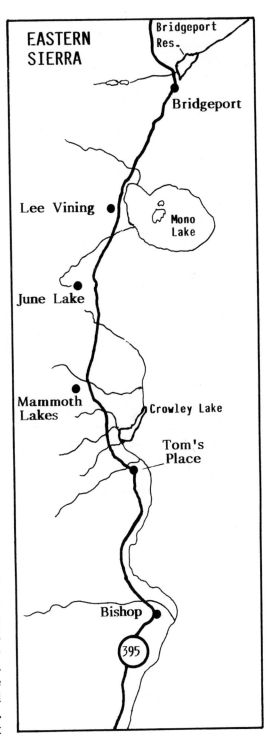

but there are holes five to six feet deep.

Big Pine Creek also offers a marvelous hike-in fishing opportunity. The adventure begins at Big Pine, on Rte 395, south of Bishop. Take Big Pine Creek Road for 11 miles to the campground. There are seven beautifully maintained lakes on the trail that leads out from here. They range in size from 4-5 acres to over 25 acres, at altitudes of about 10,000 to over 11,000 feet. These lakes are inhabited by both rainbow and eastern brook trout. Of course the lakes (and streams) that are more remote receive less fishing pressure. Because of the altitude, this is a trip best taken after the ice melts. Suggested months are June through August.

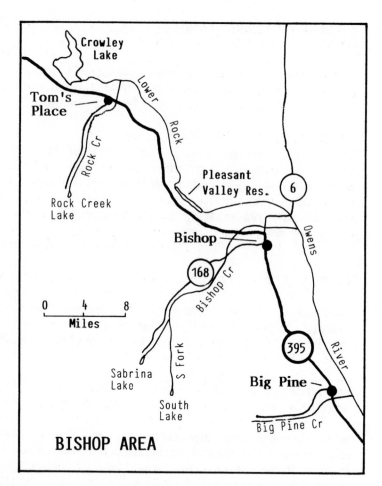

**BISHOP AREA**

Lower Rock Creek, which runs from Tom's Place parallel to Rte 395 to Pleasant Valley Reservoir is a very special trout stream. This stream holds both wild and planted fish including some very large browns and rainbows. The upper reaches of the stream, accessible by a good trail, is a small clear water area that harbors many wild brown trout.

The last mile of Lower Rock Creek, before it empties into Pleasant Valley Reservoir, has an entirely different character. At the Los Angeles DWP power plant, Lower Rock Creek is joined by waters from Pine Creek and the Owens River Aqueduct system, to produce a large river. Here trophy sized browns and rainbows are caught. Nightcrawlers, Rapalas, Rebels, and Mepps and Rooster Tail spinners are the top producers.

And don't overlook the fine little lakes in the Bishop area. There is South, Sabrina and North Lake on the Bishop Creek Road, all accessible by car. Boats can be rented at South and Sabrina Lakes. And at the head of Rock Creek is Rock Creek Lake, which also has boat rentals.

Maps of the region are available by writing Inyo National Forest, 798 Main St. Bishop, CA 93514. Their phone number is 619-873-4207. The John Muir Wilderness Map is $1.00. It has topographical information. The Bishop Chamber of Commerce can be reached at 619-873-8405. Fishing information is available at Culver's Sporting Goods, 619-872-8361 and Brock's Sporting Goods, 619-872-3581.

## Crowley Lake and Vicinity

There are two full pages on Crowley Lake in this book, in the Lake Fishing Section. But it deserves mention here because it is probably the most popular mountain trout lake for Southern California anglers. It was formed by a dam at the end of a long valley and is a key link in the City of Los Angeles' water system. Crowley is planted with hundreds of thousands of small rainbow trout each summer. By the next opening day, these fish average almost one pound each.

Thousands of anglers fish Crowley on its opening weekend each year. And most catch fish using a sliding sinker rig and bait, like salmon eggs, cheese and worms. Larger fish are usually caught later in the season by trollers pulling Rebels, Rapalas(both in the 5 to 7 inch size range) and Needlefish. In the early 1970's Crowley held the record for brown trout with a 25 pound, 11 ounce fish. Crowley Lake is located about 30 miles north of Bishop.

Convict Lake is just up Rte 395 a short ways past Crowley Lake. Many consider it one of the most beautiful spots in the eastern Sierra, with rugged peaks surrounding clear, cold waters. Launch ramp, cabins, boat rental, grocery, restaurant, etc., support anglers in pursuit of rainbow and brown trout. Fishing is best in late spring and early fall, but also holds up well in the summer months. From this base camp, it's possible to hike to about 6 small mountain lakes and numerous streams to enjoy fine fishing and spectacular scenary. Convict Lake itself is about 1 mile long by a ½ mile wide. It is at an elevation of 7600 feet so summer daytime temperatures are in the mid 70's.

Hot Creek gets its name from the hot springs naturally-heated waters. Although the upper part of this stream is private, there is a wild trout fishery in the one mile long Hot Creek Gorge stretch. The hot springs are also located in the gorge. Fishing here is catch-and-release, barbless, artificial lures and the quarry is native brown trout. A well maintained gravel road leads to Hot Creek. It's about 30 miles north of Bishop. Turn right near the east end of Long Valley Airport. Hot Creek was once considered one of the best fly fishing streams in the west and it can still provide much enjoyment.

The Upper Owens River feeds Crowley Lake. It is a meadow stream with open banks. It's a good fly fishing stream. Concentrate on the undercut banks in late evening. Several-pound browns hold in these areas. Access to the Upper Owens River is at Benton Crossing. Go north from Rte 395 at Witmore Hot Springs for about 6 miles. You can fish upstream or downstream from Benton

Crossing. Going downstream early in the season might catch you some rainbows that come up from Crowley Lake to spawn. Locals use streamers and nymphs.

## Mammoth Lakes Area Trout

The Mammoth Lakes Area is only a short way(about 12 miles) up Rte 395 from Crowley Lake. The town of Mammoth Lakes serves as a launching point for a wide variety of trout fishing experiences, including lake fishing, stream fishing, day-hike fishing and pack-in fishing. There is an immense assortment of twisting creeks, and secluded mountain lakes. Lodging, camping facilities and other amenities are plentiful in the Mammoth Lakes area.

One of the most popular destinations here is Twin Lakes. They are just out of town on Highway 230. They offer complete facilities and good fishing. Twin Lakes is actually three lakes joined by a small stream. They are weedy and range in depth to about 40 or 50 feet. Brook trout, browns and rainbow are all available. Most trout are pan-sized, but some range up to 5 to 6 pounds.

Also accessible by car are four more lakes located right near Twin Lakes. Lake Mary, Lake Mamie, Horseshoe Lake and Lake George all offer housekeeping cottages and/or camping facilities and good trouting. Lake Mary is the largest of the four, with depths of up to 60 feet, and is a favorite for trolling. The other three are productive, using a variety of techniques. After the ice clears, they are planted regularly during the summer.

Some of the favorite day-hike fishing lakes in the Mammoth Lakes area are Arrowhead, Skelton, Wood and Barney Lakes. These lakes are generally not reachable early in the trout season because of snow on the trails. But they are all along the same trail. It begins near the Lake Mary campground.

If you're interested in other day-hike and pack-in fishing excursions in the Mammoth Lakes area, the Mammoth Ranger District of the Inyo National Forest offers(for about $1.00) a Mammoth Trails Booklet. It provides complete information on about 15 different hikes, of varying length and degree of difficulty. The Mammoth Ranger Station is at Box 148, Mammoth Lakes, CA 93546.

Fly anglers new to the area should check with Mammoth tackle outlets to determine which offering works best in these waters. A good source is Mammoth Sporting Goods, 619-934-8474. Mammoth Visitors Center can be reached at 619-934-2505. And the Mammoth Lakes Chamber of Commerce is at 619-934-2712.

## June Lake Loop Trout

The next fine fishing spot, known as June Lake Loop, is about 18 miles north of Mammoth Lakes up Rte 395. It consists of 4 Lakes off of Rte 395. They are all reached by taking Highway 158 out of June Lake Junction. The first lake you'll hit, just about 2 miles out of town is June Lake(160 acres). Next, in order, comes Gull Lake(64 acres), Silver Lake(80 acres) and finally Grant Lake (1,100 acres). These lakes are at an elevation of about 7,000 feet and offer spectacular eastern Sierra mountain scenery. All these lakes have developed facilities including campgrounds, boat rentals, etc. Lodging is available at some lakes as well as in the town of June Lake.

In June Lake itself, trolling and casting are probably the most popular and productive approaches. Good offerings include Rooster Tails, Mepps, Super Dupers, Rapalas and Rebels. Spinners are best in yellow or black while silvers and golds are good in Rapalas and Rebels.

Gull Lake, the littlest, is regarded as a good baitfishing opportunity. There are both rainbow and brook trout in Gull Lake that go for nightcrawlers, cheese, salmon eggs and worms. The bottom of Gull Lake is a little marshy, so it's best to try and float your offering up off the bottom. Use a worm inflator, floating bait or marshmallow combination to accomplish this.

In Silver Lake and the inlet area of Rush Creek, both bait and lures are productive. In Rush Creek proper, above Silver Lake, worms and salmon eggs take both stocked fish and native trout.

Grant Lake is another spot for the trollers. They use flasher/nightcrawler combinations, Rapalas and Phoebes. Bright colors, like gold, work well in this lake. Grant Lake also offers good shore fishing opportunities. Toss spinners or bait like cheese, eggs or worms.

Information on the June Lake Loop Area is readily available. For general and accommodation information call the Chamber of Commerce at 619-648-7584. Camping information is available from the United States Forest Service in the town of Lee Vining at 619-647-6525. A good source of fishing information is Ernie's Tackle in June Lake at 619-648-7756.

## Bridgeport Area Trout

Our last local, up Rte 395, in the eastern Sierra is Bridgeport. It offers excellent and widely diverse trouting experience. Here in a beautiful setting are lakes, rivers and streams that provide many trout, some very large. All these waters are located within 20 miles of Bridgeport, a full facility resort town.

The most prominent trout water in the Bridgeport area is Bridgeport Reservoir. It is featured in the Lake Fishing Section of this book, but deserves mention here, also. This lake is large(about 3,000 acres), but not deep. In the early part of the season, trollers do well(down about three to four colors of leadcore line) with black/white and black/gold Rapalas and Rebels and with Needlefish and Flatfish. In the summer months, weed growth restricts trolling. At this time, bait anglers do well with nightcrawlers, red salmon eggs and cheese. Bridgeport Reservoir has complete recreational and boating facilities.

Flowing out of Bridgeport Reservoir toward Nevada is the East Walker River. This is a trophy brown trout fishery. Browns average 2-5 pounds here, but range up to 9 pounds. Minimum size in the East Walker is 14 inches with a two-fish limit and only single, barbless hooks on artificial lures may be used. Anglers wade this river in chest waders. Submerged roots and overhanging branches add to the character of the East Walker. Anglers use spinning gear or fly casting equipment. Fly anglers use a 4-pound test tippet for dry flies and 8-pound for streamers. Good fly patterns include Mayflys, Caddis, Grasshoppers, Yellow Stoneflies and Woolly Worms. Best streamers are No. 2 black-white and No. 2 black-yellow Marabous. Dawn and dusk are the best times to fish the undercut banks of this sizeable stream.

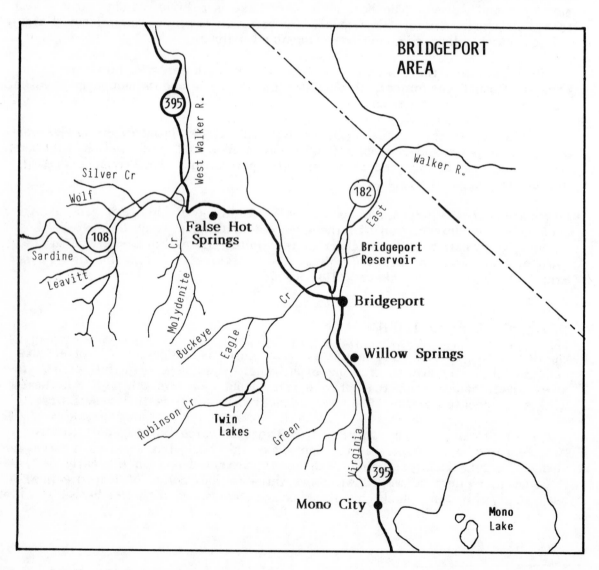

Another gem(or should we say gems) is Twin Lakes. Big browns are also the order of the day here. Fish in the ten pound range are not uncommon. And Lower Twin currently holds the California brown trout record at 26 pounds and 5 ounces, set in May 1983. Fishing techniques are similar to those in the Bridgeport Reservoir, but weed growth is not a problem in the Twins. These big browns feast on planted rainbows, small kokanee salmon as well as crawdads. Troll Rapalas and Rebels that imitate these. Best fishing for very large brown trout in the Twin Lakes is late April to early May and then again near the end of the season in late October. Twin Lakes are located about 12 miles southwest of Bridgeport at an elevation of about 7,000 feet. There is camping and a full service marina at the lake.

By the way, planted brood stock rainbow, pan-sized planted rainbow and small kokanee are abundant in Twin Lakes. Trolling works well on all these fish throughout the summer months. Go deeper as the water warms up.

Upper Robinson Creek, which flows into the Twin Lakes is a good rainbow fishery. Spinning anglers use spoons such as Hot Shots and Phoebes. Fly anglers score with floating line and Zug Bug Nymphs.

In addition to Robinson Creek there are literally scores of other small, productive trout streams. Some of the best known are Buckeye, Eagle, Swauger, Leavitt, Sardine, Wolf, Silver, West Walker and Molydenite. Many smaller streams are lightly fished. But it's important to remember to fish these waters slowly and carefully. Walk quietly. Crawl up to pools in meadows. Keep your shadow off the water. Move upstream so you stay behind the fish. Trout fishing in small streams is akin to stalking in a hunt.

Trail and camping information in the Bridgeport area is available from the United States Forest Service, Bridgeport Ranger District, Box 595, Bridgeport, CA 93517. Telephone is 619-932-7070. Fishing information is available at Ken's Alpine Shop and Sporting Goods in Bridgeport at 619-932-7707.

## WESTERN SIERRA TROUT

The western slopes of the southern Sierra Mountains provides enormous opportunities for anglers in pursuit of trout. And there is a special treat in store for trouters here. It's the golden trout. This is a highly colored fish that originally was limited to a few streams in the Upper Kern River drainage, at elevations of from about 6,300 feet to 10,500 feet. The extremely beautiful appearance of the golden trout, and the fact that it is a native son(or daughter?) has resulted in it being designated as the State Fish of California.

As early as the 1870's man has extended the range of the golden trout, by transplanting wild fish or stocking hatchery-reared fish. Golden trout are now available in many streams and lakes in the upper drainages of the southwestern Sierra.

These fish don't grow big(ranging in size from 8-14 inches) because of the high altitude and cold waters they inhabit isn't abundant in food. But goldens are feisty, great eating and very beautiful. Their name in Latin translates as "pretty in the water," and that they are. By the way, rainbow, brown and brook trout are also abundant in these waters.

## Fresno Area Trout

Highway 168 out of Fresno is a gateway to some marvelous trout fishing. Within one to two hours drive up this route are a half dozen fine lakes and many productive trout streams. Let's start with the lakes and then move on to a beautifully scenic day-hike or pack-in stream trout excursion.

Shaver Lake is about 55 miles from Fresno at an altitude of about 5,600 feet. It is a popular all-around watersports area. There are good boating, camping and resort facilities on the 2,000 surface acre lake. Shaver Lake, beside brown, rainbow and brown trout, also has largemouth bass, catfish and panfish. Nightcrawlers are a popular bait for trout at Shaver, for both trollers and bait anglers. Two possible vehicles side-trips from Shaver Lake are Wishon Reservoir and Courtright Reservoir. The trip starts by taking Dinkey Creek Road, off Rte 168, just south of Shaver Lake Heights. There are some good, little trout streams in this backcountry.

The next lake up Rte 168 is Huntington. Just north of Shaver Lake take the cutoff to the town of Big Creek. The beginning of the lake is about 10 miles along this road(a few miles past Big Creek). Huntington Lake is about 4 miles long and ½ mile wide, with 14 miles of shoreline. It's at an elevation of 7,000 feet in the Sierra National Forest. There are forest service campsites as well as a number of private resorts. Huntington Lake has rainbow, brown and brook trout, as well as kokanee salmon.

Proceeding up Rte 168, a total of about 100 miles from Fresno is Mono Hot Springs. Here at an elevation of about 7,500 feet are two delightful small mountain lakes(Edison and Florence) and access to great stream trout fishing in the Bear Creek drainage and the John Muir Wilderness. Edison Lake, about 6 miles north of Mono Hot Springs, and Florence Lake, about 8 miles in the other direction, both offer excellent fishing for rainbow, brown and brook trout.

The Bear Creek drainage consists of over fifty lakes(from 1 acre to 125 acres) and about 25 miles of streams. It's possible to catch golden, brown, rainbow and brook trout all in the same day in Bear Creek!

Bear Creek flows southeasterly for about 20 miles and empties into the South Fork of the San Joaquin River, near Mono Hot Springs. Bear Creek, including the East, West and South forks, and its Hilgard and Orchard Creek tributaries all contribute to the flow of clear, cold water from a 11,000 foot elevation.

Unlike some of the more southerly golden trout streams, Bear Creek runs through forests of pines and cottonwoods. Trail heads are located at either Bear Dam or Edison Lake. Backpacking anglers often spend the first day hiking into the junction of the north and south forks of Bear Creek. A base camp here(9,500 feet) allows for day hikes to lakes like Orchid, Sandpiper, Medley, Apollo, etc.

Many anglers carry light or ultra-light spinning gear which allows them to fish dry or wet flies in streams(using a plastic casting bobber) and also fish spinners and spoons in the lake waters. Dry flies that work include the Adams, Mosquito and Renegade. Good wet flies imitate dark ants or mosquitos. Producers include Zug Bugs, Woolly Worms, Black Gnats and Royal Coachman in sizes of 10-14. Since the fish are all pan-sized, 2 or 4 pound test line is sufficient. Popular spinners like Rooster Tails, Mepps, and Panther Martins, and Kastmaster-like spoons are effective.

Maps are essential when backpacking. You'll want the U.S. Geological Survey Topographic Map of the Mt. Abbot Quadrangle. The Sierra National Forest, 1130 "O" St., Fresno, CA 93721,(209-487-5155) has a forest map that is useful in locating campsites. Finally, the best time to make this trip is mid to late June through September.

## Bakersfield Area Trout

Bakersfield area trout focuses on the Kern River Basin. First there is Lake Isabella, which was formed by a dam built on the main fork of the Kern River. It is fed by both the main fork of the Kern River and the South Fork of the Kern River. Of course the Upper Kern River drainage was the original home of California's golden trout. This is a gorgeous and delicious trout, that is now plentiful in many high elevation streams in the southern Sierra.

Lake Isabella is an 11,000 acre waterway with about 38 miles of shoreline. It is about 8 miles long and has an elevation of 2,600 feet. This lake is about 45 miles from Fresno and about 160 miles north of Los Angeles. Trout fishing at Isabella is best in late spring and early fall. Rainbows range in size from pan size to over 3 pounds. Bank bait fishing is best near the dam using salmon eggs, marshmallows, cheese and nightcrawlers. Trollers and bait anglers fish deeper in the warm months. Kastmasters, Needlefish and Rapalas are local favorites for trolling near the dam and in deep open water. Boaters should get familiar with Isabella's system of wind warning lights. Two pages of this book, in the Lake Fishing Section, are devoted to Lake Isabella fishing.

Starting at Kernville, the main fork of the Kern River runs almost straight north from Lake Isabella. This river is planted with trout for about 16 miles up to the Johnsondale Bridge. But there is also a significant native population of browns and rainbows. Most of the fish caught here are small, but it's not uncommon to tie into trout in the 4 pounds class. The most popular angling approach is using salmon eggs(singly or in pairs)on about a number 12 hook.

Fly anglers score well with Mosquitos, Stone Nymphs and at times Black Gnats and Black Ants. Use about a number 14. A local nymph, called a Flip's Bug is a big winner. It's often fished with a casting bubble and possibly some split shot to help bump it on the bottom. The most popular spinners are Panther Martin(gold or silver)in small sizes(1/32 and 1/16 ounce) and Rooster Tails(yellow, white) in 1/16 ounce size.

The possibility also exists that stream anglers might hook into a king salmon. They were planted into Isabella recently and have been known to move up into the cooler waters of the Kern River. Fishing information on the Kern River is available at Sierra Sporting Goods in Kernville(619-376-2850).

For those who enjoy scenic backpacking combined with golden trout angling the upper Kern River drainage is a delight. It is here, in the dry southern mountains, that the goldens outlook was enhanced by the designation of 306,000 acres of the Sequoia National Forest as the Golden Trout Wilderness Area. Golden trout are believed to be a second cousin to the rainbow that evolved because of geographical isolation as glaciers moved into the area. These fish only thrive in high altitude waters.

Some of the best golden trout waters are the Rocky Basin Lakes and the head-water of the South Fork of the Kern River. These and other good waters(like) Golden Trout Creek) are arduous hikes over the eastern crest of the Sierra. Or there is the Eastern Sierra Flying Service in Lone Pine that takes anglers to Tunnel Meadows, on the South Fork.

The South Fork of the Kern River, which is only a small stream in its head-waters, flows for about 20 miles through a gorge. One way to get there is to pack-in from the BLM Long Valley Campground. You can reach this locale by taking 178 from Fresno, past Lake Isabella, and then up Cranbrake Road. Or from Rte 395, take Ninemile Canyon Road west. Follow the signs. It's about 25 miles from the main highway. From this campground it's about a 3 mile hike to the South Fork of the Kern River. The New Army Pass trailhead, an alternate trip, can be reached by taking Lubken Canyon and Horseshoe Meadow Roads for about 16 miles off of Rte 395, about 4 miles south of Lone Pine. These pack-ins should only be taken by experienced, well-equipped anglers. The weather and fishing are best in late August and September. Information is available at the Chief Ranger's Office, Sequoia and Kings Canyon National Forest Parks, Three Rivers, CA 93271(209-563-3306).

## Los Angeles Mountain Trout

There are several excellent mountain trout fishing locations near the Los Angeles area, including two designated wild trout streams. All of these can be found in the mountains rimming the Los Angeles basin.

Let's take a look at the wild trout streams first. In these waters there is no planting and only artificial flies or lures with single barbless hooks may be used. Some wild trout streams are catch-and-release(limit of zero) and others have reduced limits. These can change depending on angling pressure and fish populations, so it's wise to be aware of current limits.

As of this writing, our first wild trout stream, Deep Creek in the San Bernadino Mountains has a limit of 2, with a minimum size of 6 inches. These regulations apply from the headwaters at Little Green Valley to Deep Creek confluence with Willow Creek. Deep Creek is near Hespina. Take the Bear Valley Road exit off northbound Interstate 15(Barstow Freeway). A detailed map of Deep Creek is available from the U.S. Forest Service, Arrowhead Ranger Station, Rim Forest, CA 92378.

Deep Creek is known for pool after pool of crystal clear water. Experts say that Renegades and Woolly Worms are best for browns, while Royal Coachman are food for rainbows. Larger flies take larger fish. Number 10-14 are worth a try. If you can't interest bigger ones, slip down to number 18 or even number 22 for smaller fish. There are no overnight facilities in the Deep Creek area so save enough energy to climb back to your car.

Our second wild trout stream near Los Angeles(about 30 miles north of the downtown area) is the West Fork of the San Gabriel River. This stretch of river forms the southern border of the San Gabriel Wilderness and is reached by going north on Hwy 39, off Interstate 210(Foothills Freeway) near Azuza(between Arcadia and Glendora). A map of the area is available from most U.S. Forest Service offices in the Mt. Baldy Ranger District, 110 N. Wabash Avenue, Glendora, CA 91740. Currently this wild trout stream is catch-and-release.

Although a service road runs along the designated wild trout section of this stream (it leads to Cogswell Reservoir), no vehicles are allowed to use it. Some anglers take advantage of this right-of-way by pedaling bicycles from place to place along the stream. The wild river designation applies from the gate near Hwy 39 up to the reservoir, a distance of about 5½ miles.

The West Fork is a very good fishing spot in the spring and fall. Summer anglers are advised to fish early and late in the day. Good flies to try include a dark Parachute(about size 18), Caddis(size 18 and 20), Royal Coachman(size 14), Mosquitos, Red Ants and Royal Wulffs. Fish are not big here - probably about 8 to 10 inches. Spinners like the Colorado are also good bets.

The San Gabriel Mountains have more to offer anglers, beside the West Fork. There is also the North Fork and the East Fork of the San Gabriel River, Bear Creek, San Dimas Reservoir, San Gabriel Reservoir and Crystal Lake.

The North and West Forks are right in the vicinity of the wild trout waters, as is Bear Creek.  The North Fork is accessible from Rte 39 along its entire length, whereas the East Fork requires use of a hiking trail that parallels it.  These waters are heavily planted and heavily fished.  Most anglers use salmon eggs and nightcrawlers, but flies are also popular.

Bear Creek runs north off of the West Fork right into the San Gabriel Wilderness.  Fishing can be quite good, but the terrain is difficult.  A backpacking permit is required.

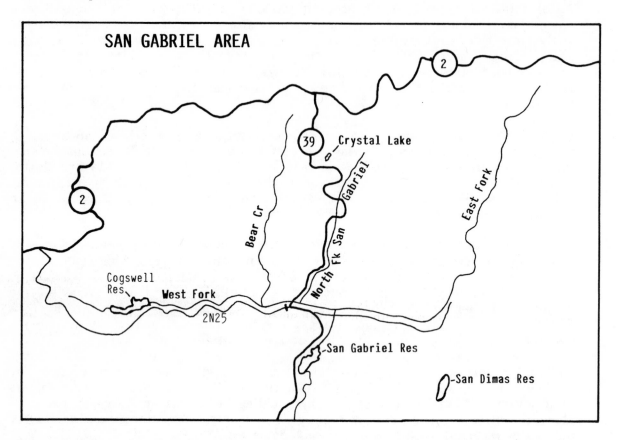

Crystal Lake is a tiny(7 acre) trout water, off Rte 39, along the North Fork.  Since you can drive right up to it, it is heavily fished.  It offers planted rainbow, as well as some bass and catfish.

San Gabriel Reservoir is also conveniently located right near Rte 39.  But you can't drive to it.  And, in fact, its banks are so steep that hiking along it is no easy task.  But the rewards to determined anglers are many.  Many of the trout that are planted upstream in the San Gabriel River end up in San Gabriel Reservoir.  And because of the difficult terrain this lake is lightly fished.  So the trout are larger(14 inches or more) and less leary. Bait, spinners and spoons are suggested here.

San Dimas Reservoir is another reservoir in the vicinity. It's a lower elevation, 35 acre lake that is regularly stocked with channel catfish. So after you've got your limit of trout or tire of releasing fish in the West Fork, hop in your car and get some catfish at San Dimas. It's reached from San Dimas Canyon Road out of Glendora. The best catfishing is at the north and south end of the lake, along the eastern shoreline. By the way, when conditions permit, trout are also planted at San Dimas.

There are a number of campgrounds in the San Gabriel River Area. For information call the main office of the Angeles National Forest in Pasadena at 213-557-0050. A reliable source for fishing information is Charter Oaks Tackle in Glendora(818-335-1617).

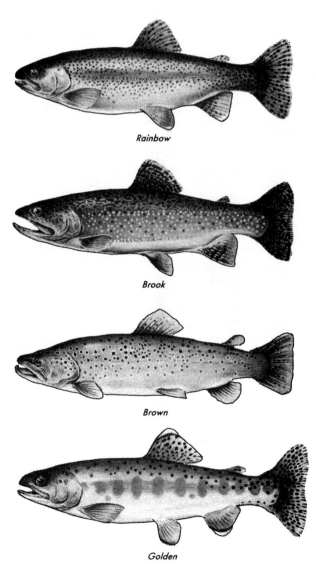

*Rainbow Trout*—Native of California, found in nearly all lakes and streams where water temperatures do not exceed 70 F for any length of time. Dark, bluish-green back, black spots on back and tail, red stripe on sides, silvery belly. Spawns on gravel bars in fast, clear water. Most suitable of all trout for artificial propagation and highly regarded as a game fish for its fighting qualities.

Rainbow

*Brook*—Native of Atlantic coastal area, found in many mountain lakes and spring-fed streams throughout the state. Dark olive, worm-like lines on back and sides, red spots along sides, belly reddish-orange to lemon, lower fins red tipped with white. Well suited to hatchery production. Unlike other species, it may spawn in shallow areas of lakes having spring seepage.

Brook

*Brown*—A native of Europe, generally the hardest of California inland trouts to catch. Plentiful in many Sierra streams and scattered elsewhere throughout the State. The record fish in California weighed 25 pounds. Dark brown on back with black spots, shading to light brown with red spots on sides. The only trout with both black and red spots on its body.

Brown

*Golden*—State fish of California, the golden trout is native to the high country of the Kern River watershed, and now is found in many lakes and streams in the Sierra from Mt. Whitney north to Alpine County. Medium olive back, shading down the sides to brilliant golden belly and reddish-orange stripes from head to tail, crossed with olive vertical bars. Lower fins golden-orange.

Golden

# Pacific Ocean Fishing

The coastal waters of the Pacific Ocean offer an immense variety of fishing opportunities.  There are numerous sport fishing party boats and launching facilities for those who want to fish the bays, islands and open ocean.  Shore fishing facilities include miles of beaches and rocky coastlines, as well as numerous piers, jetties, breakwaters and fishing barges.

Fishing can and does go on all year long.  There's live bait fishing for bonito, barracuda, bass and yellowtail.  There's drift fishing for halibut and bottom fishing for lingcod and rockfish.  Trollers pursue albacore, bonito and striped marlin.  Surf casters work the breakers for perch, croaker and halibut while more agile souls work rocky shores for the likes of opaleye, halfmoon, kelp bass and cabizon.  And finally, there are the pier, barge, jetty and breakwater anglers who catch a little bit of everything.

But ocean fishing can be dangerous.  Anglers are lost every year.  Breakers wash fishermen off rocks.  People fall overboard.  Wind warnings are foolishly ignored.  Equipment fails.  But don't let this scare you away from fishing.  Do enjoy the marvelous experience of ocean fishing, but be prepared, be careful and error on the side of caution.

**Fishing Seasons**   (+=good, -=fair)

| Species | J | F | M | A | M | J | J | A | S | O | N | D |
|---|---|---|---|---|---|---|---|---|---|---|---|---|
| Albacore |   |   |   |   |   | - | + | + | - | - |   |   |
| Barracuda |   | - | - | - | + | + | + | - | - | - | - |   |
| Bonito | - | - | - | - | - | - | - |   | + | + | + | + |
| Calico Bass | - | - | - | - | + | + | + | + | - | - | - | - |
| Grunion |   |   | + |   |   | + | + | + |   |   |   |   |
| Halibut | - | - | + | + | + | + | + | + | + | - | - | - |
| Lingcod | + | + | - | - | - | - | - | - | - | - | + | + |
| Marlin(Striped) |   |   |   |   |   |   | - | + | + | - |   |   |
| Rockfish | - | - | - | - | - | + | + | + | - | - | - | - |
| White Sea Bass | - | + | + | + | + | - | - | - | - | - | - | - |
| Yellowtail |   | - | + | + | + | - | - |   | + | - |   |   |

## Fishing Tips

The bite of most saltwater species is less predictable than that of their freshwater cousins.  So success on an ocean fishing outing depends, to a great extent

---

This section is based on Angler's Guide To The United States Pacific Coast(U.S. Dept. of Commerce).

on going at the proper time. There are many sources of fishing information that can be helpful to the saltwater angler. Ocean oriented bait and tackle shops and party boat operators are always worth a phone call. There are several outdoor newspapers that are also very helpful, as are local daily papers. A drive to the shore to meet the party boats as they come in and to ask the pier anglers how they're doing is also worth considering.

Ocean bottom structure is also an important consideration, as shown below;

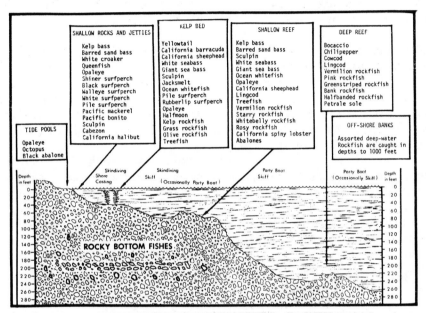

*Species taken most commonly in rocky bottom habitats according to depth.*

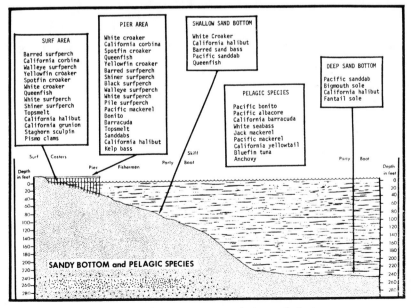

*Species taken most commonly in sandy bottom and pelagic habitats according to depth.*

## San Diego Area

In the San Diego area the major offshore sport fishing grounds are about Mexico's Coronado Islands and near the Point Loma and La Jolla kelp beds. Some of the finest marine angling facilities for fishing in local and distant waters are to be found in San Diego Harbor and Mission Bay. San Diego is the principal port for long-range fishing trips to off the coast of Baja California. It is also one of the major ports for albacore sport fishing from July through October, with most fishing within 40 to 100 miles west and southwest of San Diego. Sometimes in early summer, albacore also will appear near the Coronado Islands. Occassionally, trips by modern well-equipped sport fishing boats are made to San Clemente Island for yellowtail and kelp bass and to offshore banks for rockfishes.

Variations in the offshore bottom topography have a pronounced influence on where different species are caught. The coastal shelf off San Diego is widest from Point Loma south to the Coronado Islands, averaging about 20 fathoms in depth. Here the bottom is sand, sand shell, and mud and sand, over which sand bass, white seabass, California halibut, and sizable quantities of forage fish such as the northern anchovy are frequently taken. Although the bottom is generally sandy from the Coronado Islands north, nearshore rocky reefs are to be found off Imperial Beach, Point Loma and La Jolla.

Off Point Loma the shelf is about 3 miles wide and becomes narrower off La Jolla and to the north; offshore the bottom depth descends to about 600 fathoms. The edge of the shelf is generally the inner limit of late summer fishing for striped marlin. Excellent fishing areas for rockfishes also can be found along the shelf edge.

Several submarine canyons cut into the nearshore shelf; the two most prominent are the Coronado Canyon and the La Jolla Canyon. These canyons provide good habitats along their upper edges for rockfishes, sheephead, kelp bass and bottom-tail grouper.

The Coronado Islands are the property of Mexico, and a Mexican fishing license must be obtained before fishing about any of the three islands. When fishing from a commercial sport fishing boat, the foreign fishing license fee is usually included in the cost of the trip. These islands constitute the most productive area in Southern California for fishing yellowtail, which are taken there during late spring through summer. The north end of the North Coronado Island is excellent for yellowtail fishing, and anglers usually experience a good morning bite. The "Middle Ground," between North Coronado and Middle Coronado, is also good for yellowtail and for white seabass in spring. Other game fishes taken by anglers around the Coronado Islands are: Pacific barracuda, Pacific bonito, rockfishes(olive, kelp and grass), lingcod, ocean whitefish, sculpins, and kelp bass. Pacific barracuda are taken April through October(summer best), and Pacific bonito are caught in summer - the remaining species are taken year round. Between the Coronado Islands and the mainland coast, fishing is good

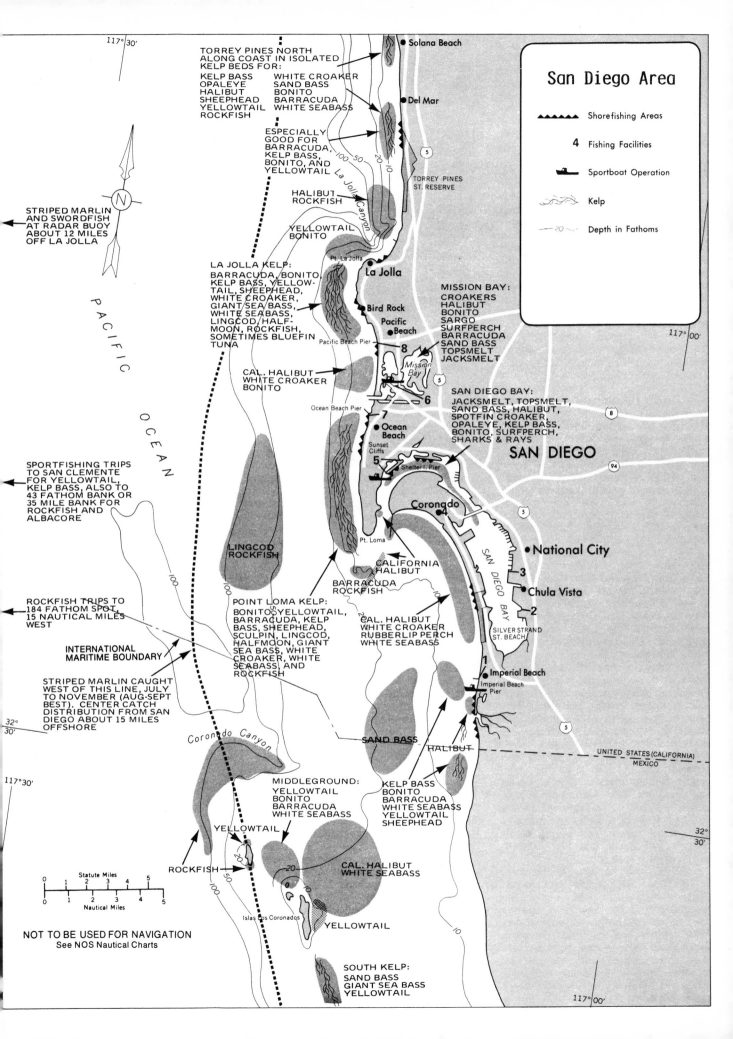

**San Diego Area**

⊾⊾⊾⊾ Shorefishing Areas

**4** Fishing Facilities

🛥 Sportboat Operation

〰〰 Kelp

—20— Depth in Fathoms

117° 30'

117° 00'

117° 30'

117°30'

TORREY PINES NORTH
ALONG COAST IN ISOLATED
KELP BEDS FOR:
KELP BASS        WHITE CROAKER
OPALEYE          SAND BASS
HALIBUT          BONITO
SHEEPHEAD        BARRACUDA
YELLOWTAIL       WHITE SEABASS
ROCKFISH

ESPECIALLY
GOOD FOR
BARRACUDA,
KELP BASS,
BONITO, AND
YELLOWTAIL

HALIBUT
ROCKFISH

YELLOWTAIL
BONITO

STRIPED MARLIN
AND SWORDFISH
AT RADAR BUOY
ABOUT 12 MILES
OFF LA JOLLA

LA JOLLA KELP:
BARRACUDA, BONITO,
KELP BASS, YELLOW-
TAIL, SHEEPHEAD,
WHITE CROAKER,
GIANT SEA BASS,
WHITE SEABASS,
LINGCOD, HALF-
MOON, ROCKFISH,
SOMETIMES BLUEFIN
TUNA

CAL. HALIBUT
WHITE CROAKER
BONITO

SPORTFISHING TRIPS
TO SAN CLEMENTE
FOR YELLOWTAIL,
KELP BASS, ALSO TO
43 FATHOM BANK OR
35 MILE BANK FOR
ROCKFISH AND
ALBACORE

ROCKFISH TRIPS TO
184 FATHOM SPOT,
15 NAUTICAL MILES
WEST

INTERNATIONAL
MARITIME BOUNDARY

STRIPED MARLIN CAUGHT
WEST OF THIS LINE, JULY
TO NOVEMBER (AUG-SEPT
BEST). CENTER CATCH
DISTRIBUTION FROM SAN
DIEGO ABOUT 15 MILES
OFFSHORE

POINT LOMA KELP:
BONITO, YELLOWTAIL,
BARRACUDA, KELP
BASS, SHEEPHEAD,
SCULPIN, LINGCOD,
HALFMOON, GIANT
SEA BASS, WHITE
CROAKER, WHITE
SEABASS, AND
ROCKFISH

LINGCOD
ROCKFISH

CALIFORNIA
HALIBUT

BARRACUDA
ROCKFISH

CAL. HALIBUT
WHITE CROAKER
RUBBERLIP PERCH
WHITE SEABASS

MISSION BAY:
CROAKERS
HALIBUT
BONITO
SARGO
SURFPERCH
BARRACUDA
SAND BASS
TOPSMELT
JACKSMELT

SAN DIEGO BAY:
JACKSMELT, TOPSMELT,
SAND BASS, HALIBUT,
SPOTFIN CROAKER,
OPALEYE, KELP BASS,
BONITO, SURFPERCH,
SHARKS & RAYS

**SAN DIEGO**

PACIFIC OCEAN

Solana Beach

Del Mar

TORREY PINES
ST. RESERVE

Pt. La Jolla

La Jolla

Bird Rock

Pacific
Beach

Pacific Beach Pier

Mission
Bay

Ocean Beach Pier

Ocean
Beach

Sunset
Cliffs

Shelter I. Pier

Coronado

Pt. Loma

National City

Chula Vista

SILVER STRAND
ST. BEACH

Imperial Beach

Imperial Beach
Pier

SAND DIEGO BAY

La Jolla Canyon

Coronado Canyon

SAND BASS

HALIBUT

KELP BASS
BONITO
BARRACUDA
WHITE SEABASS
YELLOWTAIL
SHEEPHEAD

MIDDLEGROUND:
YELLOWTAIL
BONITO
BARRACUDA
WHITE SEABASS

YELLOWTAIL

ROCKFISH

Islas Los Coronados

YELLOWTAIL

CAL. HALIBUT
WHITE SEABASS

SOUTH KELP:
SAND BASS
GIANT SEA BASS
YELLOWTAIL

UNITED STATES (CALIFORNIA)
MEXICO

100

50

20

10

100

100

50

20

10

50

20

10

20

0

10

Statute Miles
0  1  2  3  4  5

Nautical Miles
0  1  2  3  4  5

NOT TO BE USED FOR NAVIGATION
See NOS Nautical Charts

for white seabass in spring and early summer, when squid are spawning in this area. This is also a good fishing location for California halibut during the spring. North of the Coronado Islands along the edge of the Coronado Submarine Canyon in deep water, bottom anglers catch rockfishes(chilipepper, bocaccio, vermillion, yellowtail, gopher and canary).

The Point Loma kelp beds and deep water immediately northwest of the Point are good fishing spots. Near shore, rockfishes(olive, grass, vermillion and kelp) are commonly taken near the kelp beds; offshore in deeper water, bocaccio, chilipepper, gopher, canary and greenstriped rockfishes are caught.

Fishing the La Jolla kelp bed has become increasingly popular in recent years. Statistics indicate there are more anglers, catching greater numbers of fish, from this area than from any other location along the California coast. Off Point La Jolla, California halibut sometimes are taken on the flats to the north and south of the La Jolla Submarine Canyon.

North of La Jolla begins a near continuous kelp bed that extends northward along the coast. There is limited amount of fishing off the kelp beds at Del Mar and in adjacent areas to the north and south for kelp bass and rockfishes (kelp, olive, grass and vermillion). Yellowtail and Pacific bonito sometimes are taken in and about these kelp beds.

| Location | Sport Fishing Boats | Pier Fishing | Boat Rental | Launch Ramp | Jetty Fishing |
|---|---|---|---|---|---|
| 1-Imperial Bch | + | + | | | |
| 2-Chula Vista | | | | + | |
| 3-National City | | | | + | |
| 4-Coronado | | | | + | |
| 5-Shelter I. | + | + | | + | |
| 6-Mission Bay | + | | + | + | + |
| 7-Ocean B. Pier | | + | | | |
| 8-Pacific B. Pier | | + | | + | |

Several public piers, located in bays or along the open coast, allow the marine anglers to catch resident shore fishes and sometimes migratory species such as

Pacific bonito and Pacific barracuda. The outer coast has two public fishing piers. The Ocean Beach public fishing pier is a good place for surfperches(barred, pile, walleye, and kelp). Pacific bonito, Pacific mackerel, white seabass, sharks (sand, brown smoothhound and leopard), queenfish, jacksmelt, California halibut, and sculpin. To the south, the Imperial Beach fishing pier just north of the Mexican border has, at times, good fishing for pile and rubberlip surfperches in winter and spring, and walleye and shiner surfperches all year. Sharks, rays, white croaker, Pacific sanddab, Pacific bonito, jacksmelt, Pacific barracuda, white seabass(small), cabezon, sculpin, and "rock" crabs are also taken from this pier.

San Diego Bay has some fishing about the municipal piers for sculpins, jacksmelt, pile surfperch, topsmelt, sharks and rays. The major public sport fishing pier in San Diego Bay is on Shelter Island, near the entrance to the bay. Off the pier and along the rocky shore nearby, anglers catch surfperches(shiner, black, rubberlip and pile), jacksmelt, topsmelt, sandbass, sculpin, sharks, rays, Pacific bonito and California halibut. Anglers fish for the same array of shore species from the south side of Shelter Island and 1 mile east off Harbor Island.

Mission Bay offers excellent pier, shore or small-boat fishing. Bay fishermen frequently catch yellowfin and spotfin croakers, small Pacific bonito and Pacific barracuda, California halibut, shiner and rubberlip surfperches, topsmelt, jacksmelt, spotted sand bass, sharks and rays.

The open coast offers shore fishing along both rocky and sandy shores; the species of fish caught depends upon which of these two shoreline types is being fished. Some of the better shore fishing areas are near Del Mar and Torrey Pines, and from Coronado to Imperial Beach.

The major sandy-shore fishes are the surfperches, croakers, corbina and grunion. The barred surfperch is common and comprises about 70% of the shore angler's surfperch catch. It is taken throughout the year; December through March is considered best. Others such as shiner, white, rainbow, rubberlip and silver surfperches are available all year. The walleye surfperch also is taken most of the year over sandy bottom, as well as around pier pilings and jetties. Catches of California corbina are taken off the sandy shore all year, but are greatest during July through September. Spotfin croaker are taken all year, but summer fishing is best, especially along beaches extending north from Imperial Beach. Yellowfin croaker are caught on some sandy shores during the summer run, but these locations will vary according to movements of the fish. The white croaker or kingfish is taken off most sandy beaches.

Grunion is one of the favorite fishes on the open-coast sandy beach. This small silvery fish enters the surf zone to spawn during periods of high tides in late spring and summer from March to September. They may be captured by hand in such popular fishing areas as La Jolla, Pacific Beach, Mission Beach, Ocean Beach, along the Coronado Strand(Silver Strand) and Imperial Beach. The best time to search for grunion is the second, third, and fourth nights after a full moon and for a 3-hour period after a high tide.

Along rocky portions of the coast at La Jolla, Bird Rock, and Sunset Cliffs and about Point Loma, the species commonly taken are opaleye(best in spring), halfmoon, surfperches(black, shiner, walleye and pile), rockfishes(kelp, grass and brown), kelp bass and occasionally sargo and cabezon. Opaleye, halfmoon and rockfishes are available to the rocky shore angler all year.

## Solana Beach to Dana Point

This fishing area, geographically between the population centers of San Diego and Los Angeles, is a growing one for marine sport fishing operations. New facilities such as the extensive small-boat harbor at Dana Point(Dana Harbor), and the excellent small-boat basin at Oceanside now make many coastal fishing areas accessible to the small-boat angler. About 15 miles of coastline from Oceanside north to near San Mateo Point is the property of the U.S. Marine Corps and is part of the Camp Pendelton complex. Access to this area was very limited; however, in the north a portion of the coast(San Onofre Bluffs State Beach) and greater access to the shore is being given the public.

The coastal shelf is very narrow off this section of coast, extending only 2 to 3 miles offshore before reaching a depth of 50 fathoms or more. Sand and gray sand predominate the bottom nearshore, with some rocky areas such as those found north of Oceanside and along the coast from south of San Mateo Point northward. This hard bottom stratum allows for development of kelp, which in turn provides an attractive environment for kelp bass and the brown types of rockfishes. Offshore in deeper water the bottom type is gray and green mud and the coastal shelf descends to a depth of 300 to 400 fathoms within 8 to 10 miles offshore. Along the edge of the shelf, in deep water, are several places where rockfishes may be taken.

| Location | Sport Fishing Boats | Pier Fishing | Boat Rental | Launch Ramp | Jetty Fishing |
|---|---|---|---|---|---|
| 1-Encina Bay | | | | | + |
| 2-Oceanside Pier | | + | | | |
| 3-Oceanside Hbr | + | | | + | + |
| 4-San Clemente | | + | | | |
| 5-Dana Harbor | + | + | + | + | + |

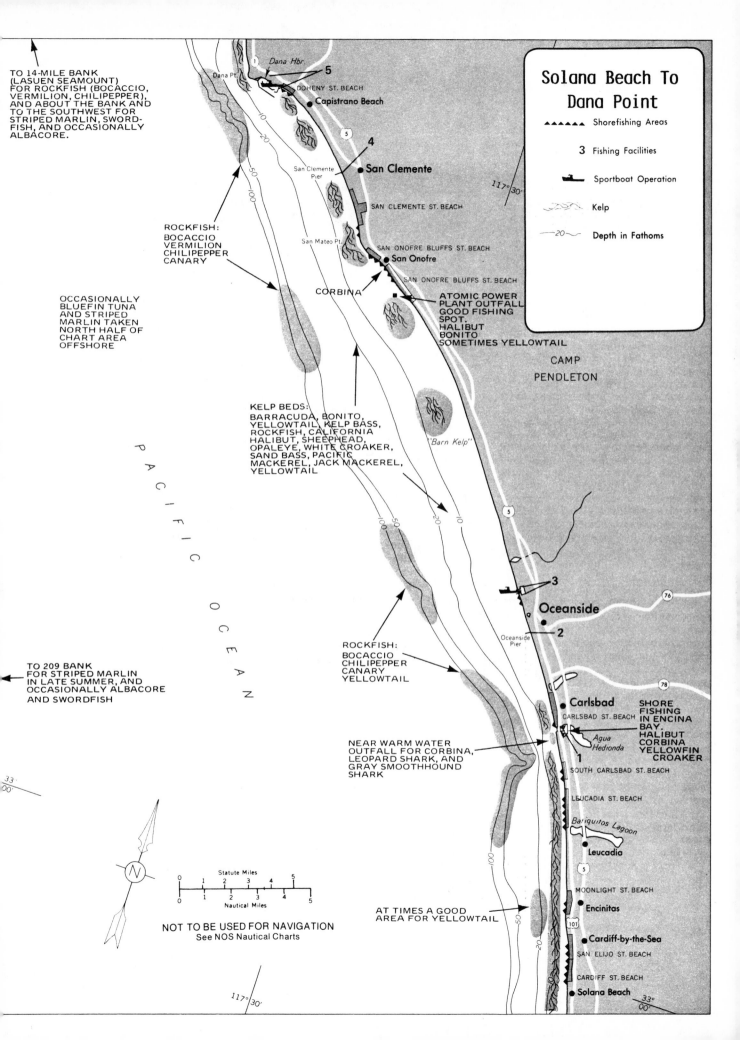

TO 14-MILE BANK
(LASUEN SEAMOUNT)
FOR ROCKFISH (BOCACCIO,
VERMILION, CHILIPEPPER),
AND ABOUT THE BANK AND
TO THE SOUTHWEST FOR
STRIPED MARLIN, SWORD-
FISH, AND OCCASIONALLY
ALBACORE.

ROCKFISH:
BOCACCIO
VERMILION
CHILIPEPPER
CANARY

OCCASIONALLY
BLUEFIN TUNA
AND STRIPED
MARLIN TAKEN
NORTH HALF OF
CHART AREA
OFFSHORE

KELP BEDS:
BARRACUDA, BONITO,
YELLOWTAIL, KELP BASS,
ROCKFISH, CALIFORNIA
HALIBUT, SHEEPHEAD,
OPALEYE, WHITE CROAKER,
SAND BASS, PACIFIC
MACKEREL, JACK MACKEREL,
YELLOWTAIL

ROCKFISH:
BOCACCIO
CHILIPEPPER
CANARY
YELLOWTAIL

TO 209 BANK
FOR STRIPED MARLIN
IN LATE SUMMER, AND
OCCASIONALLY ALBACORE
AND SWORDFISH

NEAR WARM WATER
OUTFALL FOR CORBINA,
LEOPARD SHARK, AND
GRAY SMOOTHHOUND
SHARK

AT TIMES A GOOD
AREA FOR YELLOWTAIL

PACIFIC OCEAN

Dana Hbr.
Dana Pt.
5
DOHENY ST. BEACH
● Capistrano Beach

4
San Clemente Pier
● San Clemente
SAN CLEMENTE ST. BEACH

San Mateo Pt.
SAN ONOFRE BLUFFS ST. BEACH
■ San Onofre
SAN ONOFRE BLUFFS ST. BEACH

CORBINA

ATOMIC POWER
PLANT OUTFALL
GOOD FISHING
SPOT.
HALIBUT
BONITO
SOMETIMES YELLOWTAIL

CAMP
PENDLETON

"Barn Kelp"

3
Oceanside
2
Oceanside Pier

76

78

Carlsbad
CARLSBAD ST. BEACH
Agua Hedionda
1
SOUTH CARLSBAD ST. BEACH

SHORE
FISHING
IN ENCINA
BAY.
HALIBUT
CORBINA
YELLOWFIN
CROAKER

LEUCADIA ST. BEACH
Batiquitos Lagoon
● Leucadia
5
MOONLIGHT ST. BEACH
● Encinitas
101
● Cardiff-by-the-Sea
SAN ELIJO ST. BEACH
CARDIFF ST. BEACH
● Solana Beach

117° 30'

33° 00'

**Solana Beach To
Dana Point**

▲▲▲▲▲  Shorefishing Areas

3  Fishing Facilities

⛵  Sportboat Operation

〰〰  Kelp

—20—  Depth in Fathoms

N

Statute Miles
0  1  2  3  4  5

Nautical Miles
0  1  2  3  4  5

NOT TO BE USED FOR NAVIGATION
See NOS Nautical Charts

Sport fishing boats are available at the port of Dana Harbor and at Oceanside. These boats fish the coastal kelp beds and offshore in deep water for rockfishes and other species. During albacore season they run offshore to 60 Mile Bank (60 miles southwest of Point Loma), to the 43 Fathom Bank(35 miles west of Point Loma), and sometimes beyond San Clemente Island. The 209 Bank, about 35 miles west of the mainland, is one of the better fishing areas for striped marlin and swordfish, and albacore occasionally are taken here during July or August.

Immediately offshore from Solana Beach north to off Carlsbad and from San Mateo Point to San Clemente are substantial kelp beds. Although the kelp beds in this area are not as extensive as those off Point Loma to the south, or off the Santa Barbara coast farther north, they do provide a suitable habitat for kelp bass, sand bass and rockfishes(kelp, grass, olive, and vermillion) and also attract coastal migrants such as Pacific barracuda and Pacific bonito. Yellowtail and white seabass are sometimes taken near the kelp as are jack and Pacific mackerels(July to September), opaleye, white croaker and kelp rockfish. Nearshore rocky reefs provide a habitat suitable for many species such as opaleye, grass and kelp rockfishes, halfmoon, cabezon and black surfperch.

Rockfishing is often productive along the edge of the narrow coastal shelf, in water 30 to 100 fathoms deep over rocky, sharp-sloping areas. Anglers fish off Carlsbad to Oceanside and north to Dana Point for boraccio, chilipepper, canary, and yellowtail species of rockfishes.

Bluefin tuna and striped marlin are taken occasionally off the San Clemente Coast in late summer, even less frequently, however, in recent years.

Two public fishing piers are available along this stretch of coast. One is at San Clemente where surfperches(barred, walleye and rubberlip), California halibut, sculpins and the usual array of sharks and rays are caught. The second is the Oceanside fishing pier, good at times for runs of California halibut(spring and summer best), sculpin, sargo, jacksmelt, white croaker(kingfish), queenfish, occasionally small white seabass, Pacific bonito, and Pacific barracuda(in summer), kelp and sand bass and barred and walleye surfperches. In addition, there is shore fishing from the jetty systems at Dana Harbor and Oceanside.

The extensive sandy-shore beaches from Solana Beach to San Clemente are productive areas for the surf angler. Some of the better, or at least more popular surf fishing areas are found near San Mateo Point where corbina are taken from July through September. Farther south, there is excellent spotfin croaker and barred surfperch fishing along San Onofre Bluffs State Beach near the northern boundary of Camp Pendleton. Fishing is good 3 miles south of Carlsbad, particularly about the entrance to the cooling-water inlet of the steam-electric generating plant where, because of a constant inflow of water from the ocean, the small bay has a high concentration of California halibut, corbina and yellowfin croaker. Other good shore fishing spots are north of Leucadia and near San Elijo Lagoon, just north of Solana Beach. Surfperches frequently taken along the sandy shores are the barred(winter, spring best), walleye shiner, calico (December to March best), and silver species. Other fishes taken by the surf angler are the white and yellowfin croaker and California halibut. Grunion runs are known to occur on these beaches in late spring and early summer.

The shore from San Mateo Point to San Clemente has only a few isolated areas where rocky-shore species can be taken.

## Los Angeles Area

A great diversity of fishing areas and facilities are available from Laguna Beach to Point Vicente. Many types of angling opportunities are available along rocky and sandy shores, from jetties and piers, in bays and over offshore kelp beds and deepwater fishing grounds. The coastline is oriented generally in a north-west-southwest direction with about one-half composed of sandy beaches; the rest is a rocky shore interlaced with small sandy beaches.

Major sport fishing boat facilities are available at three locations in the Los Angeles-Long Beach Harbor area; one at Long Beach and two at San Pedro. Smaller sport boat operations are available at the Belmont Shore, Huntington Beach and Seal Beach piers. Newport Beach and Balboa have extensive sport boat and pier facilities.

South of Newport Beach to off Laguna Beach the coastal shelf is very narrow, about 2 miles - sometimes less - in width. The bottom nearshore is mostly sand and mud interspersed with rocky areas. Because of the narrow shelf, open ocean species such as bluefin tuna and striped marlin sometimes migrate to within a short distance of the shore.

From about Newport Beach west toward Long Beach and Point Fermin, the coastal shelf widens to its greatest width in Southern California. The nearshore bottom is primarily sand, gray sand and mud and provides a good habitat for California halibut. In the wider part of the coastal shelf, the bottom types are sand, shells, green sand and green mud. Along the outer edge of the coastal shelf, the bottom descends to a depth of 250 to 300 fathoms, providing good rockfishing locations. The bottom reaches depths greater than 400 fathoms near the middle of the San Pedro Channel.

South of Newport are scattered small kelp beds where a number of coastal species such as barracuda, kelp bass, sand bass, white croaker, bonito, California halibut, sheephead and rockfishes(kelp, olive, grass, and vermillion) are caught. Occasionally, yellowtail and white seabass are landed. Off Laguna Beach, over deepwater rocky areas, anglers fish for bocaccio, chilipepper and canary rock-fishes. Southeast of Newport Beach, and northwest of Laguna Beach over the coastal shelf, is a kelp area where several of the brown species of rockfishes are commonly taken. Bluefin tuna and striped marlin have been caught just offshore a short distance from Laguna Beach, although not commonly in recent years.

| Location | Sport Fishing Boats | Pier Fishing | Boat Rental | Launch Ramp | Jetty Fishing |
|---|---|---|---|---|---|
| 1–Aliso Pier | | + | | | |
| 2–Newport Bay | + | | + | + | + |
| 3–Balboa Pier | | + | | | |
| 4–Newport Pier | | + | | | |
| 5–Huntington Pier | | + | | + | |
| 6–Huntington Hbr | | | | + | |
| 7–Seal Bch Pier | + | + | | | |
| 8–Alamitos Bay | | | | + | + |
| 9–Belmont Pier | + | + | + | | |
| 10–Golden Shores | | | | + | |
| 11–Long Beach | + | | | | |
| 12–San Pedro | + | | + | + | |
| 13–22nd St Lndg | + | | | | |
| 14–Cabillo Bch | | + | | | + |

Farther offshore to the west is Lasuen Seamount, widely known as "14 Mile Bank" or "58 Fathom Spot." This is an excellent bottomfishing area for rock-fishes(bocaccio, vermillion and chilipepper), and in summer, striped marlin and swordfish are taken near the surface about the Seamount and to the southwest. Albacore also are caught here during the summer, but like bluefin tuna, only occasionally in recent years.

Off Newport, in the Newport Submarine Canyon, sablefish(blackcod), a species usually associated with more northern latitudes, can be taken in deep water. On rare occasions during the spring, coho(silver) salmon have been caught off Newport. Since deep water is close to shore off Newport, striped marlin are taken on occasions only a short distance south of the Newport Harbor entrance.

From Huntington Beach west over nearshore sandy bottom, there is good fishing for many of the bottom species; California halibut is one of the more important fishes caught in this area.

The "horseshoe kelp" bed, south of Los Angeles Harbor, has been reduced in size over the years and the kelp growth is now under the surface. However, this spot sometimes is good for Pacific barracuda, Pacific bonito, kelp bass, yellowtail, jack and Pacific mackerels and rockfishes(olive, kelp and vermillion).

The greater Los Angeles Harbor-San Pedro Bay area, being readily accessible

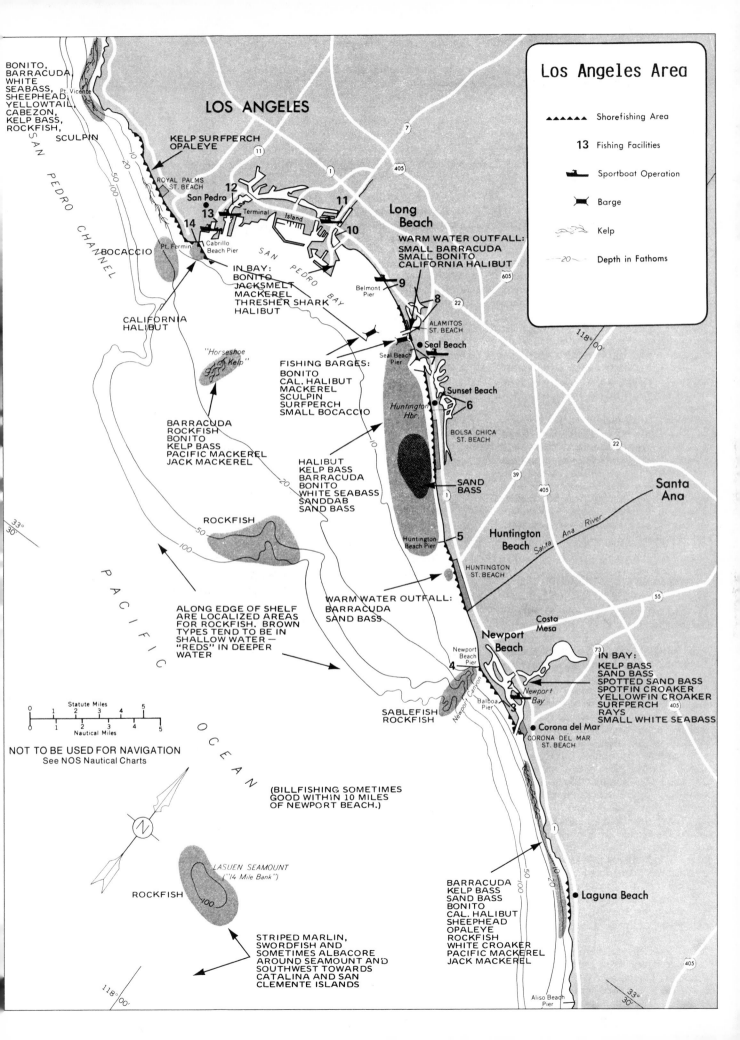

BONITO,
BARRACUDA,
WHITE
SEABASS,
SHEEPHEAD,
YELLOWTAIL,
CABEZON,
KELP BASS,
ROCKFISH,
SCULPIN

Pt. Vicente

LOS ANGELES

KELP SURFPERCH
OPALEYE

ROYAL PALMS
ST. BEACH

12
San Pedro
13
14

Terminal
Island

11

10

Long
Beach

WARM WATER OUTFALL:
SMALL BARRACUDA
SMALL BONITO
CALIFORNIA HALIBUT

Los Angeles Area

▲▲▲▲▲▲▲ Shorefishing Area

**13** Fishing Facilities

⛴ Sportboat Operation

🐟 Barge

〰 Kelp

‒20‒ Depth in Fathoms

118° 00'

BOCACCIO
Pt. Fermin

Cabrillo
Beach Pier

SAN
PEDRO
BAY

605

CALIFORNIA
HALIBUT

IN BAY:
BONITO
JACKSMELT
MACKEREL
THRESHER SHARK
HALIBUT

Belmont
Pier

9

8

22

ALAMITOS
ST. BEACH

"Horseshoe
Kelp"

Seal Beach

7

Seal Beach
Pier

FISHING BARGES:
BONITO
CAL. HALIBUT
MACKEREL
SCULPIN
SURFPERCH
SMALL BOCACCIO

Sunset Beach

6

BARRACUDA
ROCKFISH
BONITO
KELP BASS
PACIFIC MACKEREL
JACK MACKEREL

Huntington
Hbr.

BOLSA CHICA
ST. BEACH

22

HALIBUT
KELP BASS
BARRACUDA
BONITO
WHITE SEABASS
SANDDAB
SAND BASS

10

SAND
BASS

39

405

Santa
Ana

ROCKFISH

50

100

5

Huntington
Beach Pier

Huntington
Beach

Santa Ana River

HUNTINGTON
ST. BEACH

Santa Ana River

55

33°
30'

ALONG EDGE OF SHELF
ARE LOCALIZED AREAS
FOR ROCKFISH. BROWN
TYPES TEND TO BE IN
SHALLOW WATER —
"REDS" IN DEEPER
WATER

WARM WATER OUTFALL:
BARRACUDA
SAND BASS

Costa
Mesa

Newport
Beach Pier

Newport
Beach

73

IN BAY:
KELP BASS
SAND BASS
SPOTTED SAND BASS
SPOTFIN CROAKER
YELLOWFIN CROAKER
SURFPERCH
RAYS
SMALL WHITE SEABASS

4

Newport
Bay

405

PACIFIC

Balboa
Pier

3

Corona del Mar

SABLEFISH
ROCKFISH

CORONA DEL MAR
ST. BEACH

Statute Miles
0  1  2  3  4  5

Nautical Miles
0  1  2  3  4  5

NOT TO BE USED FOR NAVIGATION
See NOS Nautical Charts

OCEAN

(BILLFISHING SOMETIMES
GOOD WITHIN 10 MILES
OF NEWPORT BEACH.)

N

1

BARRACUDA
KELP BASS
SAND BASS
BONITO
CAL. HALIBUT
SHEEPHEAD
OPALEYE
ROCKFISH
WHITE CROAKER
PACIFIC MACKEREL
JACK MACKEREL

50

100

20

10

Laguna Beach

33°
30'

118° 00'

LASUEN SEAMOUNT
("14 Mile Bank")

ROCKFISH

100

STRIPED MARLIN,
SWORDFISH AND
SOMETIMES ALBACORE
AROUND SEAMOUNT AND
SOUTHWEST TOWARDS
CATALINA AND SAN
CLEMENTE ISLANDS

SAN PEDRO CHANNEL

Aliso Beach
Pier

405

to large numbers of people, is a popular place for fishing from shore and small boats. Good locations for catching bay fishes can be found within the harbor itself, along the extensive jetties, or about piers that are on open channels in the outer harbor area. Bay fishing is also popular in Alamitos and Seal Beach bays where jacksmelt, surfperches, skates, sharks, rays, sargo and turbot are taken by anglers along with an occasional small mackerel or Pacific bonito.

Numerous fishing piers(public and commercial) and open bulkhead areas provide many thousands of recreational fishing hours each month for only the cost of bait and tackle. In addition to the many commercial piers and marina floats available for fishing in Los Angeles Harbor, there are piers built specifically for fishing at Cabrillo Beach(near Point Fermin), Belmont Shore, Seal Beach, Huntington Beach, Newport Beach(two piers) and south of Laguna Beach at Aliso Beach. From these piers, anglers catch California halibut, kingfish(white croaker), sharks, rays, jacksmelt, queenfish, surfperches(barred, black, walleye, pile and shiner) and Pacific and jack mackerels.

Surf fishing takes place along rocky shores from point Fermin to Point Vicente. Southwest from Newport Bay to Dana Point there is fishing from the man-made jetties at Los Alamitos Bay and Newport Bay for opaleye, grass and kelp rock-fishes, halfmoon, cabezon and black perch. The San Pedro Channel entrance is accessible from shore; the rest of the breakwater to the east can be reached by boat. Here there is good fishing for opaleye, halfmoon, kelp bass and rock-fishes(brown types).

Sandy-shore fishing is available from Newport Beach to Long Beach. One of the more popular places for surf fishing is Bolsa Chica State Beach. Species most commonly taken off sandy beaches are surfperches(barred, walleye, shiner, calico and silver), croakers(spotfin, white and yellowfin), California halibut, and corbina. Grunion are also caught during their periodic spawning runs.

## Santa Monica Area

The coast from Point Vicente to Solromar borders one of the most populated areas along the west coast and is intensively fished, particularly from Redondo Beach to Santa Monica. Sandy shore, rocky shore, pier and jetty fishing and excellent facilities for boat fishing are found from Point Vicente to Solromar.

The coastline is rocky from near Point Vicente to Malaga Cove, south of Redondo Beach. Northward from Malaga Cove to northwest of Santa Monica is an extensive stretch of sandy beach. From Santa Monica, the coast swings westward and the coastal shore begins to get rocky once again, with occasional offshore reefs. The first substantial nearshore concentrations of kelp, which are common from here to Point Conception, are found just west of Malibu Point to near Point Dume, and again west of Zuma Beach.

The offshore coastal shelf is very narrow from Point Fermin to Point Vicente,

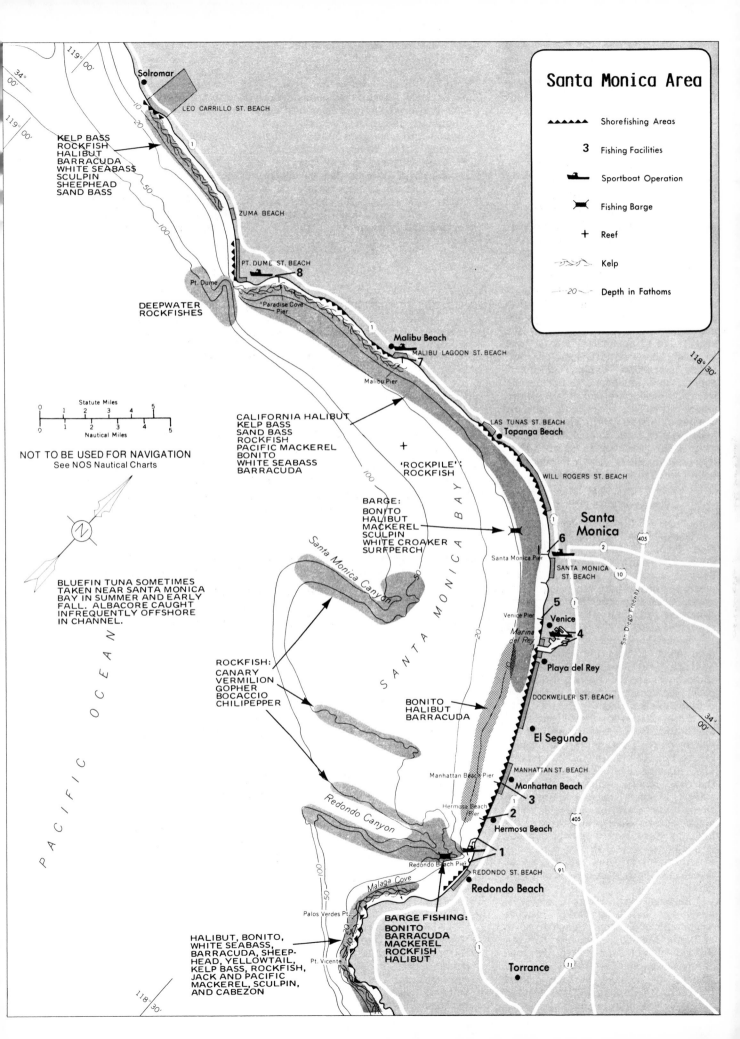

# Santa Monica Area

- ▲▲▲▲▲ Shorefishing Areas
- **3** Fishing Facilities
- Sportboat Operation
- Fishing Barge
- **+** Reef
- Kelp
- ⟿ 20 ⟿ Depth in Fathoms

Solromar

LEO CARRILLO ST. BEACH

KELP BASS
ROCKFISH
HALIBUT
BARRACUDA
WHITE SEABASS
SCULPIN
SHEEPHEAD
SAND BASS

ZUMA BEACH

PT. DUME ST. BEACH

**8**

Pt. Dume

DEEPWATER
ROCKFISHES

'Paradise Cove
Pier

Malibu Beach

MALIBU LAGOON ST. BEACH

**7**

Malibu Pier

CALIFORNIA HALIBUT
KELP BASS
SAND BASS
ROCKFISH
PACIFIC MACKEREL
BONITO
WHITE SEABASS
BARRACUDA

LAS TUNAS ST. BEACH
Topanga Beach

WILL ROGERS ST. BEACH

'ROCKPILE'
ROCKFISH

**+**

Santa
Monica

BARGE:
BONITO
HALIBUT
MACKEREL
SCULPIN
WHITE CROAKER
SURFPERCH

Santa Monica Pier

**6**

SANTA MONICA
ST. BEACH

S A N T A   M O N I C A   B A Y

Santa Monica Canyon

**5**

Venice Pier

Venice

**4**

Marina
del Rey

Playa del Rey

DOCKWEILER ST. BEACH

ROCKFISH:
CANARY
VERMILION
GOPHER
BOCACCIO
CHILIPEPPER

BONITO
HALIBUT
BARRACUDA

El Segundo

Redondo Canyon

MANHATTAN ST. BEACH
Manhattan Beach

**3**

Manhattan Beach Pier

Hermosa Beach Pier

**2**

Hermosa Beach

**1**

Redondo Beach Pier

Malaga Cove

REDONDO ST. BEACH

Redondo Beach

Palos Verdes Pt.

BARGE FISHING:
BONITO
BARRACUDA
MACKEREL
ROCKFISH
HALIBUT

HALIBUT, BONITO,
WHITE SEABASS,
BARRACUDA, SHEEP-
HEAD, YELLOWTAIL,
KELP BASS, ROCKFISH,
JACK AND PACIFIC
MACKEREL, SCULPIN,
AND CABEZON

Pt. Vicente

Torrance

P A C I F I C   O C E A N

BLUEFIN TUNA SOMETIMES
TAKEN NEAR SANTA MONICA
BAY IN SUMMER AND EARLY
FALL. ALBACORE CAUGHT
INFREQUENTLY OFFSHORE
IN CHANNEL.

Statute Miles
0 1 2 3 4 5

Nautical Miles
0 1 2 3 4 5

NOT TO BE USED FOR NAVIGATION
See NOS Nautical Charts

N

34° 00'
119° 00'
118° 30'
34° 00'
118° 30'

10
20
50
100
20
50
100
100
50

and these waters are frequented many times by schools of bait fish such as anchovy and jack and Pacific mackerels. Depths of 200 fathoms or more are found 2 to 3 miles offshore. The bottom then descends to its greatest depth in the San Pedro Channel – over 400 fathoms. Bottom types, aside from rocky areas, are generally green sand; in deeper water, green mud predominates. Along the edge of the shelf are rocky areas that attract sizable concentrations of red rockfishes.

Santa Monica Bay is relatively shallow(less than 50 fathoms deep) and cut by two prominent submarine canyons, the Redondo and Santa Monica canyons. Rocky areas are found near the edges of these canyons as well as along the edge of the coastal shelf, and these places usually provide some of the better rockfishing. A number of shallow reefs are offshore, in lower Santa Monica Bay between Point Vicente and Redondo Beach. The coastal shelf is about 3 miles wide from Santa Monica to near Point Dume and is about 2 miles wide to the west beyond Point Dume. Again the bottom types are usually sand nearshore, grading to mud and sand farther offshore; and green mud at the greater depths.

| Location | Sport Fishing Boats | Pier Fishing | Boat Rental | Launch Ramp | Jetty Fishing |
|---|---|---|---|---|---|
| 1-Redondo Bch | + | + | + | + | + |
| 2-Hermosa Pier | | + | | | |
| 3-Manhatten Pier | | + | | | |
| 4-Marina del Rey | + | | + | + | + |
| 5-Venice Pier | | + | | | |
| 6-Santa Monica P. | + | + | | + | |
| 7-Malibu Pier | + | + | | | |
| 8-Paradise Cove P. | + | + | | | |

Excellent facilities for sport fishing are located at the small-boat harbors of Redondo Beach, Marina del Rey, Santa Monica and to the west at Malibu and Paradise Cove. Sport fishing boats operate locally or travel from these ports to distant waters to fish around Catalina, Santa Barbara, or San Nicolas islands. Special offshore trips for albacore are made during the summer. The boats fish southwest of Redondo Beach along the edges of the Redondo Canyon(the south edge in particular) where there is good deepwater fishing for rockfishes(vermillion, canary, bocaccio, gopher and chilipepper). Rockfishing is also productive off Point Dume where vermillion, olive and bocaccio species enter the catch. Along the kelp beds west of Zuma Beach, olive, grass and kelp rockfishes are taken frequently, along with occasional bonito and yellowtail during summer.

Rocky-shore fishing is popular from Point Vicente to near Malaga Cove, just south of Redondo Beach. Several species of surfperches commonly are taken here along with olive, grass and kelp rockfishes. Opaleye fishing is excellent along this rocky stretch of coast.

Rocky-shore species caught in the area west of Santa Monica are the opaleye, surfperches(black and shiner), rockfishes(grass, kelp and olive), halfmoon,cabezon, sargo and occasionally kelp bass.

From Redondo Beach north to Manhatten Beach are several public fishing piers. These piers are popular for fishing California halibut(spring and summer best) and surfperches(barred, black, walleye, pile and shiner). Mackerel sometimes are taken from these piers as are the usual action-getters-sharks and rays. At the Redondo Piers, excellent bonito fishing is available; these fish are apparently attracted by the warm water discharged by a steam-electric power plant.

Excellent surf fishing is available along the extensive sandy beaches from south of Redondo Beach to north of Santa Monica, especially between Redondo Beach and Playa del Rey. Sandy-shore species taken by surf anglers are barred surfperch(best from January through March), walleye surfperch, California halibut (spring and summer best), jacksmelt and shovelnose guitarfish. In some years fishing is good for corbina, spotfin croaker and yellowfin croaker, particularly along the sandy shore from Playa del Rey to Venice and from Manhatten Beach to Redondo Beach. Grunion are sometimes gathered along Malibu, Santa Monica, Venice and Hermosa beaches during periods of evening high tides in the spring and summer. Zuma Beach's sandy shores offer good fishing for barred surfperch, with occasional catches of corbina and croakers.

## Ventura Area

The principal sport fishing ports in the Ventura area are Port Hueneme, Channel Islands Harbor and Ventura Harbor. These are the principal ports that specialize in fishing about the Santa Barbara Channel Islands and offshore south of the islands for albacore during the summer fishing season. On isolated occasions, catches of coho salmon are made in late winter and early spring by party boats fishing southeast of Point Mugu and south and west of Ventura. The catches during this time are not large, but represent the southern extension of salmon sport fishing.

About 11 miles offshore from Port Hueneme and the Channel Islands Harbor is Anacapa Island, one of the more important islands for marine sport fishing. The island is the eastward extension of the chain of Santa Barbara Channel Islands and is less than one-half mile wide in most places, rising to an elevation of 930 feet above sea level. There is excellent fishing around Anacapa for kelp bass and black sea bass, as well as for bocaccio and canary rockfishes. Occasional catches of Pacific barracuda and yellowtail are made here in summer. Broadbill swordfish and striped marlin are taken south of Anacapa Island during summer and early fall.

The coastal shelf east of Port Hueneme is very narrow; from Point Mugu eastward it is no more than 1 mile wide. Immediately west of Point Mugu, the Mugu Submarine Canyon cuts through the coastal shelf, and water depths plunge to 250 to 300 fathoms. The coastal shelf widens slightly between Point Mugu and Port Hueneme before being interrupted by another submarine canyon, Hueneme Canyon. Northwest of Hueneme the shelf becomes several miles wide, an area commonly known as the Ventura Flats. The shelf narrows slightly west of Ventura, and the more offshore rocky reefs provide good rockfishing.

| Location | Sport Fishing Boats | Pier Fishing | Boat Rental | Launch Ramp | Jetty Fishing |
|---|---|---|---|---|---|
| 1-Port Hueneme | + | | | | + |
| 2-Hueneme Pier | | + | | | |
| 3-Channel I.Hbr | + | + | | + | + |
| 4-Ventura Hbr | + | | | + | + |
| 5-Ventura Pier | | + | | | |

The bottom types range from rock to sand and shells in the southeast to mud, sand, and shells in the Mugu-Hueneme area. Sand and mud predominate on the Ventura Flats, which has good fishing for flatfish such as California halibut. In deeper water the typical mud and green mud bottom predominates. The offshore bottom becomes shallower west of Hueneme Canyon, and adjacent to Ventura Flats the depth at mid-Santa Barbara Channel is only about 130 fathoms.

Immediately offshore of the area from Solromar to Point Mugu, anglers fish along the edge of the kelp beds for rockfishes(grass, olive and kelp) and occasionally bonito. About 4 miles offshore of Solromar there is a shallow area approximately 45 fathoms deep. This is a good fishing spot for chilipepper rockfish and sometimes yellowtail and Pacific barracuda. Limited catches of coho salmon are made occasionally in the early spring.

The coast is rocky from Leo Carrillo State Beach to Point Mugu. The shore borders the coast highway and is readily accessible to the fishing public. This rocky coast offers good fishing for opaleye, kelp bass, surfperches and rockfishes(grass, kelp and olive). From about Point Mugu to near Port Hueneme, access is restricted since it is part of the Point Mugu Naval Air Station and Pacific Missile Range. The sandy shore starts at Point Mugu and extends up along the coast all the way to Ventura; from Ventura west to Rincon Point, sandy beaches are interspersed with rocky points of land. Along the sandy beaches extending from Point Mugu northwestward, the following species are taken from shore; walleye and barred surfperches excellent fishing area for barred; January to March best), California halibut(spring and summer best), jacksmelt, sharks(several species), corbina, spotfin croaker, yellowfin croaker and occasionally kelp bass.

Anglers fish about the jetties and docks at Port Hueneme and from the sport fishing pier(actually a fishing float) in the Channel Islands Harbor. About the

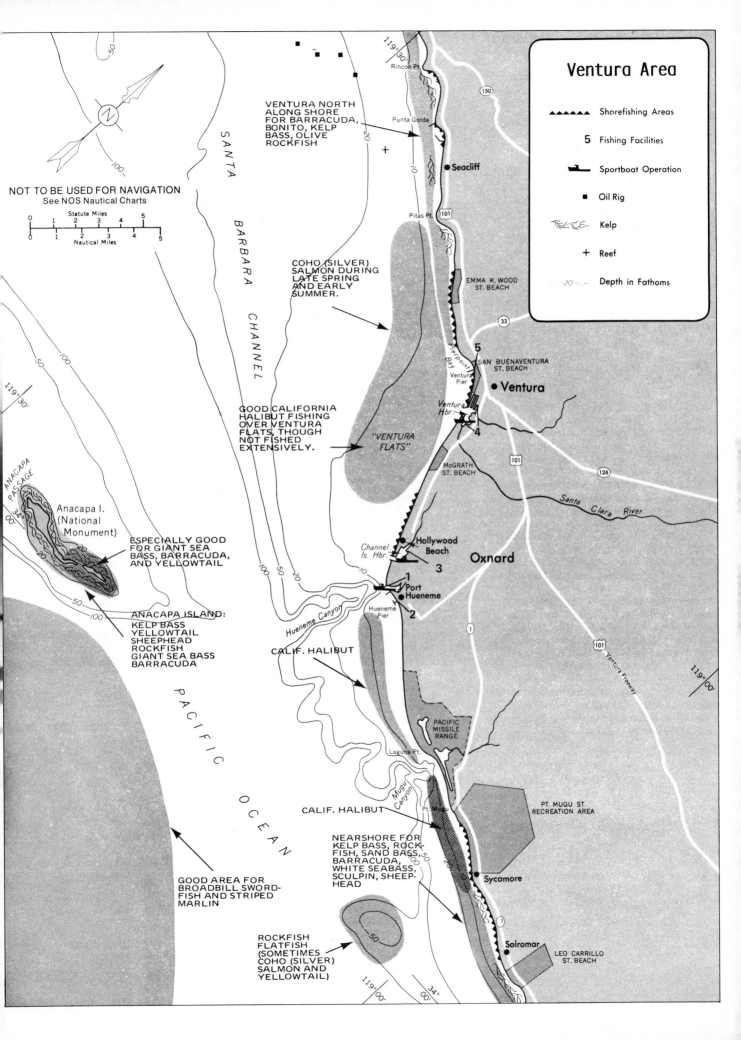

NOT TO BE USED FOR NAVIGATION
See NOS Nautical Charts

Statute Miles
0 1 2 3 4 5
Nautical Miles
0 1 2 3 4 5

SANTA BARBARA CHANNEL

SANTA BARBARA

Anacapa I.
(National Monument)

Anacapa Passage

ESPECIALLY GOOD
FOR GIANT SEA
BASS, BARRACUDA,
AND YELLOWTAIL

ANACAPA ISLAND:
KELP BASS
YELLOWTAIL
SHEEPHEAD
ROCKFISH
GIANT SEA BASS
BARRACUDA

PACIFIC OCEAN

GOOD AREA FOR
BROADBILL SWORD-
FISH AND STRIPED
MARLIN

ROCKFISH
FLATFISH
(SOMETIMES
COHO (SILVER)
SALMON AND
YELLOWTAIL)

VENTURA NORTH
ALONG SHORE
FOR BARRACUDA,
BONITO, KELP
BASS, OLIVE
ROCKFISH

COHO (SILVER)
SALMON DURING
LATE SPRING
AND EARLY
SUMMER.

GOOD CALIFORNIA
HALIBUT FISHING
OVER VENTURA
FLATS, THOUGH
NOT FISHED
EXTENSIVELY.

"VENTURA FLATS"

CALIF. HALIBUT

CALIF. HALIBUT

NEARSHORE FOR
KELP BASS, ROCK-
FISH, SAND BASS,
BARRACUDA,
WHITE SEABASS,
SCULPIN, SHEEP-
HEAD

Rincon Pt.

Punta Gorda

Seacliff

Pitas Pt.

Pierpoint Bay

Ventura Pier

EMMA K. WOOD
ST. BEACH

SAN BUENAVENTURA
ST. BEACH

Ventura

Ventura Hbr.

McGRATH
ST. BEACH

Channel Is. Hbr.

Hollywood Beach

Oxnard

Port Hueneme

Hueneme Pier

Hueneme Canyon

Mugu Canyon

Laguna Pt.

Pt. Mugu

PACIFIC
MISSILE
RANGE

PT. MUGU ST.
RECREATION AREA

Sycamore

Solromar

LEO CARRILLO
ST. BEACH

Santa Clara River

Ventura Freeway

119°30'

119°00'

34°00'

## Ventura Area

▲▲▲ Shorefishing Areas

5 Fishing Facilities

⛴ Sportboat Operation

■ Oil Rig

Kelp

+ Reef

20 Depth in Fathoms

Port Hueneme jetties, anglers will likely find opaleye, surfperches(black and shiner), rockfishes(grass, kelp and olive), halfmoon and cabezon. Some of the fishes caught from the public fishing float at Channel Islands Harbor are walleye and barred surfperches, staghorn sculpin, California halibut(spring and summer), lingcod(winter), kelp bass, several species of sharks and rays and occasionally croakers.

## Santa Barbara Area

This coastline which encompasses the major Southern California sport fishing port of Santa Barbara, is oriented in an east-west direction. This is the only sizable coastal segment of the U.S. Pacific coast to have this orientation other than the south side of the Strait of Juan de Fuca in Washington. The area is distinguished by the most extensive and best-developed kelp beds along the California coast. Lush kelp beds are present throughout the region, but are best developed from about Goleta Point to Point Conception.

At the west end of this area is one of the most notable of coastal geographical features, Point Conception. This is often called the "Cape of Good Hope of the West Coast" because of the wide variation in winds and weather found about the point. Many times the waters south and east of Point Conception may be relatively smooth and have low wind speeds over them. Immediately north and west of the point and offshore only a short distance, however, the seas may be rough and the wind near gale force. The coastline south of Point Conception is protected by a coastal mountain range that parallels the shore and provides a dampening influence on the prevailing northwest winds, which are most intense from spring to early fall.

Point Conception is often described as an ecological dividing point for marine life. South of the Point is the subtropical zone; north of it is the temperate zone. Many coastal open-ocean fishes, such as Pacific barracuda and yellowtail that are common to the waters off Southern California and Baja California, Mexico, are taken only rarely north of Point Conception. Conversely, some northern marine and anadromous species, such as coho salmon, are taken only in small numbers southeast of Point Conception in late winter and early spring.

The shoreline from Carpenteria to Point Conception and Point Arguello is predominantly a sandy one, broken occasionally by a few prominent points with shallow reefs close to shore. Along most of the coast, the shore is backed by cliffs 50 to 150 feet high.

Offshore the coastal shelf is quite broad when compared to the coastal areas to the south. The shelf is about 5 miles wide south of Santa Barbara, narrowing westward to about 2 to 3 miles wide off Point Conception. The depths in the center of the Santa Barbara Channel range from about 200 fathoms off Santa Barbara to 250 fathoms south of Point Conception.

From Santa Barbara, sport fishing boats travel to grounds along the coast to the

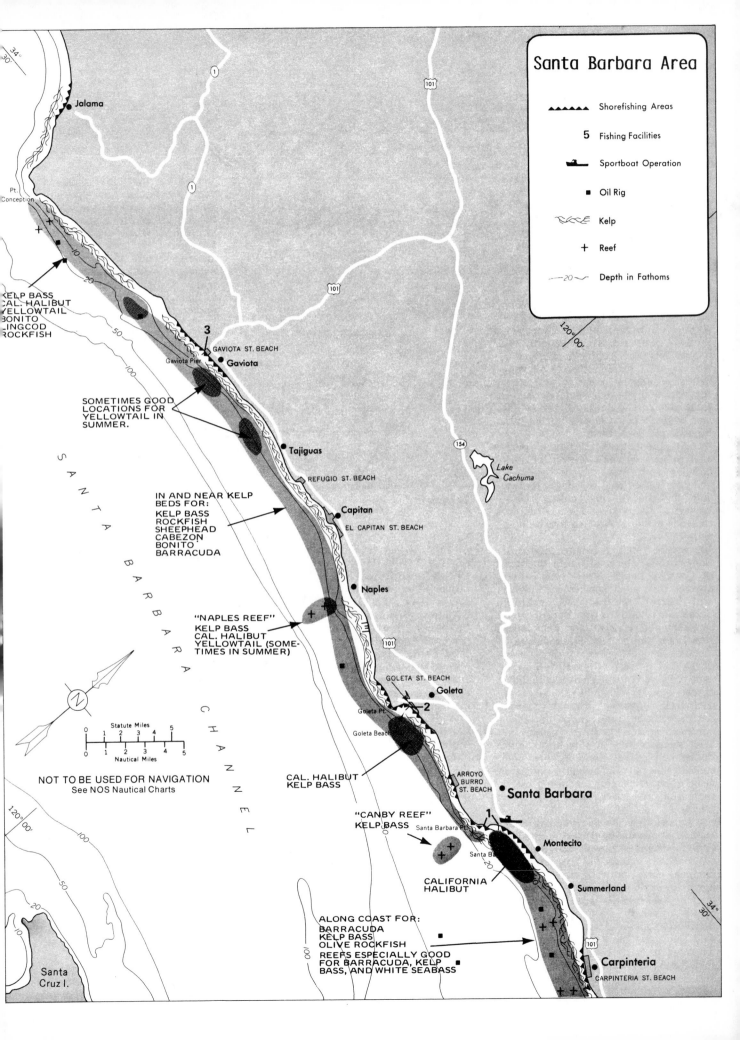

# Santa Barbara Area

Shorefishing Areas
5 Fishing Facilities
Sportboat Operation
■ Oil Rig
Kelp
+ Reef
—20— Depth in Fathoms

Jalama

Pt. Conception

KELP BASS
CAL. HALIBUT
YELLOWTAIL
BONITO
LINGCOD
ROCKFISH

SOMETIMES GOOD
LOCATIONS FOR
YELLOWTAIL IN
SUMMER.

GAVIOTA ST. BEACH
Gaviota Pier
Gaviota
3

Tajiguas

REFUGIO ST. BEACH

IN AND NEAR KELP
BEDS FOR:
KELP BASS
ROCKFISH
SHEEPHEAD
CABEZON
BONITO
BARRACUDA

Capitan
EL CAPITAN ST. BEACH

Lake Cachuma
154

Naples

"NAPLES REEF"
KELP BASS
CAL. HALIBUT
YELLOWTAIL (SOME-
TIMES IN SUMMER)

S A N T A   B A R B A R A   C H A N N E L

N

Statute Miles
0  1  2  3  4  5
0  1  2  3  4  5
Nautical Miles

NOT TO BE USED FOR NAVIGATION
See NOS Nautical Charts

GOLETA ST. BEACH
Goleta
Goleta Pt.
2
Goleta Beach

CAL. HALIBUT
KELP BASS

ARROYO
BURRO
ST. BEACH

Santa Barbara

"CANBY REEF"
KELP BASS
Santa Barbara Pt.
1
Montecito

CALIFORNIA
HALIBUT

Summerland

ALONG COAST FOR:
BARRACUDA
KELP BASS
OLIVE ROCKFISH
REEFS ESPECIALLY GOOD
FOR BARRACUDA, KELP
BASS, AND WHITE SEABASS

Santa Cruz I.

Carpinteria
CARPINTERIA ST. BEACH

west and east and offshore to the Santa Barbara Channel Islands.

A number of reefs along the coast are excellent fishing spots, as are the extensive kelp beds. West of Santa Barbara, near and amid the kelp, are resident populations of kelp bass, rockfishes(olive, grass and vermillion), sheephead, and cabezon. During summer, anglers also catch Pacific barracuda and an occasional yellowtail or white seabass. Pacific barracuda generally work up the coast toward Point Conception from September to November and down the coast from January to April. Pacific bonito sometimes show along the coast in summer and fall.

Good drift-fishing locations for California halibut and kelp bass are found off the the Goleta Beach pier; other good halibut grounds are just east of Point Conception, where fishing is best in spring and summer. This area also yields occasional summer catches of bonito and yellowtail.

| Location | Sport Fishing Boats | Pier Fishing | Boat Rental | Launch Ramp | Jetty Fishing |
|---|---|---|---|---|---|
| 1-Santa Barbara Harbor | + | + | + | + | + |
| 2-Goleta Beach | | + | + | + | |
| 3-Gaviota Bch Pier | | + | | + | |

Pier fishing is available at Santa Barbara(Sterns Wharf) and at the Goleta Beach and Gaviota public piers. The Goleta Beach pier is noted for sizable catches of surfperches. Walleye surfperch are abundant, and barred surfperch fishing is excellent in winter and spring. Best California halibut fishing is in spring and early summer, and tomcod, spotfin croaker, sand shark and jacksmelt enter the pier angler's catch mostly during July, August and September.

At the Santa Barbara pier, anglers also catch a variety of surfperches(rubberlip, shiner, walleye and barred surfperches, sharks, California halibut(in spring and summer), lingcod(winter), kelp bass, rockfishes and occasionally croakers.

The beaches west of Capitan to north of Point Conception are especially good for surf fishing. Sandy-shore species include the barred surfperch(January through March best), walleye and rubberlip surfperches, spotfin croaker(usually a brief summer run in this area) and California halibut(late spring and summer best). Rocky-shore anglers most often encounter cabezon, black surfperch and olive, kelp and grass rockfishes.

Immediately north of Point conception at Jalama, anglers cast into the surf for barred, silver and walleye surfperches and kelp greenling. Farther north, from Point Arguello north to Point Sal, the coastal area is usually closed to civilian use due to Navy and Air Force missile-launching facilities, with the exception of a small beach at the town of Surf. Here there is good surf fishing for barred, silver, calico and walleye surfperches and California halibut.

## Santa Barbara Channel Islands

Sport fishing boats visit all these islands from Port Hueneme, Channel Islands Harbor, Ventura Harbor and Santa Barbara. During the summer, albacore boats occasionally travel farther offshore near the edge of the continental shelf, southwest of Santa Rosa and San Miguel Islands and below San Nicolas Island.

The climate about the Santa Barbara Channel Islands is usually influenced by northwest winds from spring through summer, though the wind intensity is moderated slightly owing to their distance south and east of Point Conception. Fog and low stratus clouds are common about the westernmost islands during late spring and summer.

The westernmost island, San Miguel, is 7 miles long, 3 miles wide, and rises to a height of 831 feet. The island coastline is predominately rocky with many shoal areas along the west and north sides. Sandy beaches are scattered about the island; the beach at the west end contains one of the largest seal and sea lion rookeries in Southern California. About the island are several good places for fishing lingcod and rockfishes.

Santa Rosa Island has a rocky shore along the northwest and southwest sides; however, the east end has a number of sandy beaches. Good fishing for rockfishes and lingcod can be found nearshore about the northern and western ends of the island.

The western islands(Santa Rosa and San Miguel) have not been fished as extensively as the islands closer to the ports in the Ventura and Santa Barbara areas. The distance that sport fishing boats are required to travel is an important factor. Additionally, wind, weather and sea conditions about these islands are usually more severe than at the islands to the east.

Santa Cruz is the largest of the Channel Islands. It and Anacapa Island have the most sport fishing pressure. Rock fishing is good all about the island; fishing is usually best on the southeast side, which is protected from the westerly winds. Sometimes this lee side of the island has excellent fishing for yellowtail and bonito. Bluefin tuna have been taken off the southwest end commercially during the summer, so this area has a potential for a sport fish catch of this species.

## San Nicolas Island

San Nicolas is 25 miles southwest of Santa Barbara Island. The nearest point on the mainland is Point Vicente, 55 miles to the northeast.

The island is 8½ miles long, and the highest point is 907 feet above sea level. A sizable shoal area extends around it, principally on the northwest and north sides. The bottom types are scattered rocky areas on the north and west ends, with shallow areas of sand and white and green shells. The shore is rocky, except for

ROCKFISH
KELP BASS
HALIBUT

LINGCOD

Harris Pt.

ROCKFISH
LINGCOD
WHITE SEABASS
SHEEPHEAD

CAL. HALIBUT

San Miguel I.

SAN MIGUEL PASSAGE

West Pt.

Fraser Pt.

KELP BASS
ROCKFISH

BARRACUDA

20

Brock Pt.

Harrington Pt.

Bechers

BARRACUDA

Chinese Hbr.

San Pedro Pt.

ANACAPA PASSAGE

34°
00'

Sandy Pt.

ROCKFISH

Santa Cruz I.
YELLOWTAIL

34°
00'

LINGCOD
OLIVE ROCKFISH
BLUE ROCKFISH

GIANT SEA BASS

Santa Rosa I.

SANTA CRUZ CHANNEL

Smugglers Cove

BONITO

East Point

GOOD HALIBUT
AREAS

Bowen Pt.

BEST ROCKFISHING
AREA — ALSO GOOD
FOR KELP BASS

South Pt.

20

BLUEFIN
TUNA

KELP BASS AND
BLUEFIN TUNA
(WHEN RUNS
DEVELOP).

50

ALBACORE

BROADBILL SWORDFISH
(OCCASIONALLY STRIPED MARLIN)

120° 00'
122° 00'

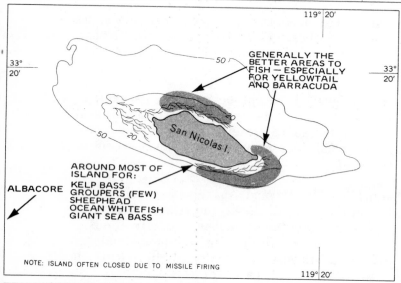

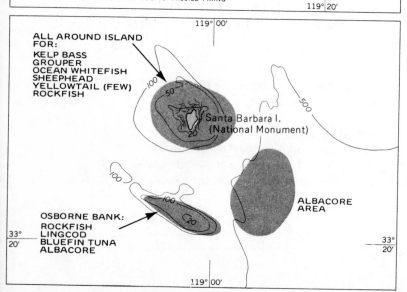

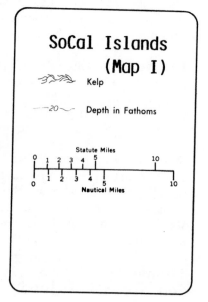

isloated sandy beaches, and the east end has the greatest predominance of sand.

Fishing is good about the entire island, but only a small amount of fishing effort is expended in the area. Sport fishing boats from Port Hueneme and Channel Islands Harbor and from the Los Angeles area sometimes fish here. No one section is noted for being distinctively better than the others.

## Santa Barbara Island

The small island of Santa Barbara is 20 miles west of the "west end" of Catalina Island. It is about 1 mile long and ½ mile wide and rises abruptly to a peak of 635 feet above sea level. The shore is rocky, and kelp areas are common about the entire island; the heaviest kelp growth is along the north side.

Fishing boats from the Los Angeles area and from Port Hueneme and Channel Islands Harbor frequent Santa Barbara Island. Anglers fish all about the island, and no one area is noted for having better fishing than another. Albacore are sometimes taken about 5 miles southeast of the island. To the south about 6 miles is Osborne Bank, a good fishing area for rockfishes, lingcod and occasionally bluefin tuna and albacore.

## Santa Catalina Island

Because of its proximity to metropolitan Los Angeles, Santa Catalina Island has been fished intensively by marine game fish anglers for a great number of years. Santa Catalina Island is one of the largest of the eight Southern California islands. Although the island points in a northwest-southeast direction, common terminology results in the northwest end being called the "west end" and the southeast end, near Avalon, being called the "east end." The island is about 6 miles wide and 18 miles long. The northwest third is constricted, and the narrowest point is called the "isthmus." Here the island is only about one-third of a mile wide with Isthmus Cove on the northeast side and Catalina Harbor on the southwest side. The island rises to an altitude of about 2,000 feet; much of it is over 1,000 feet high.

| Location | Sport Fishing Boats | Pier Fishing | Boat Rental | Launch Ramp | Jetty Fishing |
|---|---|---|---|---|---|
| 1-Avalon, Catalina I. | + | + | + | | |

The coastline about Catalina is rocky in most places, and patches of kelp frequently are found nearshore. Sizable kelp areas occur near the west end and near the entrance to Catalina Harbor. Some patchy areas occur south of the isthmus toward the east end. The south side(southwest) has good fishing for a number of species and white seabass are frequently caught while nightfishing.

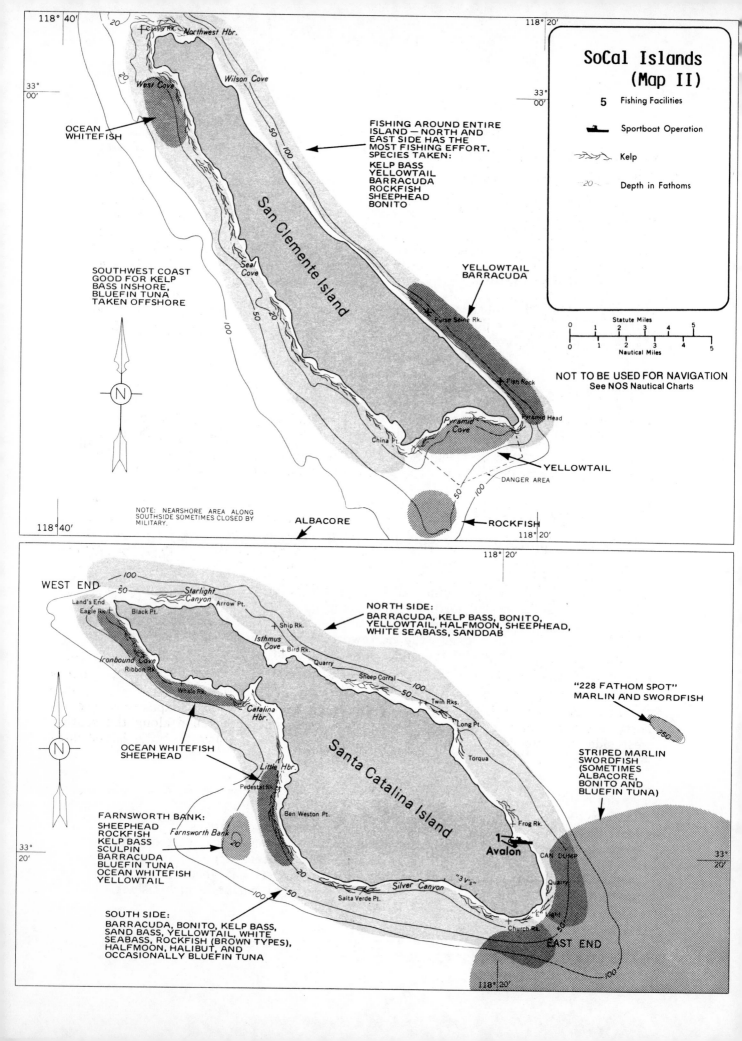

SoCal Islands
(Map II)

5    Fishing Facilities

Sportboat Operation

Kelp

20    Depth in Fathoms

Statute Miles
0 1 2 3 4 5
0 1 2 3 4 5
Nautical Miles

NOT TO BE USED FOR NAVIGATION
See NOS Nautical Charts

**San Clemente Island (top map)**

118° 40'  118° 20'

33° 00'

Castle Rk.  Northwest Hbr.

Wilson Cove

West Cove

OCEAN WHITEFISH

San Clemente Island

FISHING AROUND ENTIRE ISLAND — NORTH AND EAST SIDE HAS THE MOST FISHING EFFORT. SPECIES TAKEN:
KELP BASS
YELLOWTAIL
BARRACUDA
ROCKFISH
SHEEPHEAD
BONITO

YELLOWTAIL BARRACUDA

SOUTHWEST COAST GOOD FOR KELP BASS INSHORE, BLUEFIN TUNA TAKEN OFFSHORE

Seal Cove

N

Purse Seine Rk.

Fish Rock

Pyramid Cove

Pyramid Head

China Pt.

YELLOWTAIL

DANGER AREA

NOTE: NEARSHORE AREA ALONG SOUTHSIDE SOMETIMES CLOSED BY MILITARY.

ALBACORE

ROCKFISH

118° 40'  118° 20'

**Santa Catalina Island (bottom map)**

118° 20'

WEST END

100
50

Starlight Canyon

Arrow Pt.

Land's End
Eagle Rk.

Black Pt.

Ship Rk.

Isthmus Cove  Bird Rk.

Quarry

NORTH SIDE:
BARRACUDA, KELP BASS, BONITO, YELLOWTAIL, HALFMOON, SHEEPHEAD, WHITE SEABASS, SANDDAB

Ironbound Cove
Ribbon Rk.

Whale Rk.

Catalina Hbr.

Sheep Corral

Twin Rks.

Long Pt.

"228 FATHOM SPOT"
MARLIN AND SWORDFISH

N

OCEAN WHITEFISH SHEEPHEAD

Little Hbr.

Pedestal Rk.

Santa Catalina Island

Torqua

STRIPED MARLIN SWORDFISH (SOMETIMES ALBACORE, BONITO AND BLUEFIN TUNA)

FARNSWORTH BANK:
SHEEPHEAD
ROCKFISH
KELP BASS
SCULPIN
BARRACUDA
BLUEFIN TUNA
OCEAN WHITEFISH
YELLOWTAIL

Ben Weston Pt.

Farnsworth Bank

20

Frog Rk.

1
Avalon

CAN DUMP

33° 20'

33° 20'

100
50

Salta Verde Pt.

Silver Canyon

"3 V's"

"E" Light

Quarry

Church Rk.

EAST END

SOUTH SIDE:
BARRACUDA, BONITO, KELP BASS, SAND BASS, YELLOWTAIL, WHITE SEABASS, ROCKFISH (BROWN TYPES), HALFMOON, HALIBUT, AND OCCASIONALLY BLUEFIN TUNA

100

118° 20'

Kelp bass are fished inshore, and the sandy coves offer good fishing for Califonia halibut and ocean whitefish.

Excellent billfishing for striped marlin and broadbill swordfish can be found off the east end during the summer. Bluefin tuna are sometimes taken south and west of the island, between Santa Catalina and San Clemente Islands. The "228-fathom spot," 5 miles northeast of Avalon Harbor, is good during late summer for marlin and swordfish. The "58-fathom spot"(also known as "14-mile bank" and Lasuen Seamount), about midway between Avalon Harbor and Dana Point on the mainland, is good for striped marlin, swordfish and albacore(July through September). This bank also provides good fishing for rockfishes. Southwest of the 58-fathom spot, toward Catalina and San Clemente Islands, is another good fishing area for striped marlin and swordfish.

## San Clemente Island

The large island of San Clemente is about 70 miles west of the mainland off Oceanside and about 45 miles south of Long Beach. The entire island is the property of the U.S. Navy and there are no civilian marinas or public access. Portions of the surrounding waters are restricted because of naval operations.

The island is about 18 miles long and from $2\frac{1}{2}$ to $3\frac{1}{2}$ miles wide; its highest elevation is about 1,900 feet. The coastal shelf is narrow, particularly on the northeast side. The shore is rocky, and the bottom types nearshore are a mixture of rock, mud and sand. This type of substrate allows kelp to attach, and kelp patches are common with the most prominent growths at the north end. Kelp also is found along the west side with concentrations around China Point and just west of Pyramid Head at the southern end. Along the northeast side, to about 20 fathoms in depth, there is kelp. The kelp growth is close to shore owing to the sharp slope of the bottom.

Sport fishing boats from the Los Angeles area frequent the island, and most of the fishing is at about the north end and along the east side. Three well-known grounds are "Slide Area," "Purse Seine Rock," and "Fish Hook" - all on the east side. Good fishing is also found along the southwest side, although it is more exposed to the northwest winds and rough seas. Bluefin tuna sometimes are found along the southwest side, and albacore are frequently caught south and southwest of the island during the summer.

# Baja Fishing

Fishing in Southern California ocean waters is great. Inland regions would be thrilled to have it. But as it turns out, we've got it and even more. That's because there's Baja fishing too. Baja fishing is world class fishing at its best. The fish are exotic, big and abundant. And the accomodations, whether they be on a long range boat out of San Diego or at a seaside resort, are first class all the way.

It's impossible to cover everything about Baja fishing in the limited space of this section, so by necessity, only highlights and a few basics are treated. More information is available in other books and magazines, from tackle stores, long-range trip operators and from conversations with people who've fished Baja. Since planning and preparation are important to making this type of an adventure a success, do explore all these sources of Baja fishing insight before heading south.

## Baja Trip Alternatives

There are several ways to enjoy Baja fishing. Some people cruise their ocean going fishing boats down the Baja Peninsula. But this is a small minority of anglers. By far a much more popular alternative, is to fly down to one of the outstanding resorts in Baja and fish in waters near that locale. Many of these resorts are

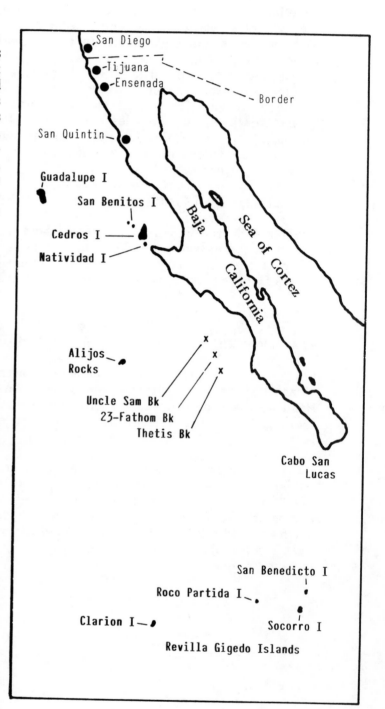

relatively new and built to American standards, offering air conditioned rooms, swimming pools, tennis and many other amenities. Anglers who like to combine a plush resort vacation with some fine fishing will enjoy Baja resorts.

A third Baja alternative, one that is especially suited to dedicated anglers, is the long range sport fishing boat trip. These trips are offered by several operators located in San Diego and are very popular. Part of the reason is the accomodations on the 90-115 foot aluminum-constructed boats. They feature air-conditioned staterooms, sundecks, large galleys and lounges complete with interior carpeting and video cassette T.V.

There is a great deal of variability in the duration of these trips. They can extend from 5 days to over 2 weeks. Of course, the length of the trip dictates the fishing grounds and the likely catch. Shorter 5-6 day trips mostly concentrate on larger fish of the same species as taken in Southern California waters. 8-10 day trips are needed to reach the truly exotic species(wohoo, dorado, etc.) and two week trips to Clarion and other islands in the Revilla Gigedo chain improve both the chance and size of these catches. Cost is another variable. A 7-day trip costs about $700-900, while a 16-day trip may go for about $2,000.

| Miles | Trip Days | Fishing Grounds |
|-------|-----------|-----------------|
| 250–300 | 5–6 | Guadalupe |
| | | San Benitos |
| | | Cedros |
| 500–600 | 7–8 | Alijos |
| | | Uncle Sam Banks |
| 600–700 | 10–12 | Alijos |
| | | Cape San Lucas |
| 900–1000 | 14–16 | Clarion |
| | | Roca Partida |
| | | Socorro |
| | | San Benedicto |

# Fish Cleaning

There's a syndrome among some anglers that I like to call, "The Fear of Filleting." It's not unlike "The Fear of Flying." But, fortunately, it's a lot easier to overcome. It just takes a little knowledge, a little willingness and an extra sharp filleting knife.

But, don't be mislead, filleting is not the end-all, or be-all of fish cleaning. It's only one of several basic approaches(all are presented here, in detail), and filleting is not even desirable or appropriate for some fish.

## Field Dressing

Actually, the word dressing is not accurate, but we're stuck with it, so here goes. Field dressing means removing the entrails and gills of a fish just after catching. This process is generally reserved for large fish(several pounds or more). It's purpose is to preserve the fish at its height of freshness. Field dressing, for example, is quite common among ocean salmon anglers. It's the kind of thing that's desirable but not absolutely necessary. Especially if your catch is kept cold.

Here's how it's done. With the fish pointing away from you, put the tip of your knife in the anal vent and cut through the belly(leaving the intestines as undisturbed as possible) up to where the gills come together under the chin of the fish.

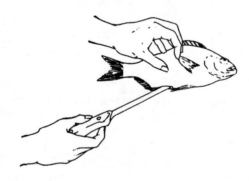

Next, with short cuts, free the bottom of the gills from the chin flesh and from the belly flesh, as illustrated on the top of the next page.

Now, pull open the gill cover on each side of the fish and cut the top of the gills free from the head. The gills and entrails can now be lifted or slid out of the fish in one unit. Now, finally, remove the strip of reddish tissue near the backbone in the intestinal cavity(these are the fishes kidneys). You may have to cut through a thin layer of tissue covering this area. As a last step, rinse off the fish. It is now ready for icing down.

## Traditional Fish Cleaning

This approach is basically an extension of field dressing. As a young boy my earliest memory of fish cleaning was the assembly line my Dad set up with my brother and myself to clean a stringer of well over 100 Lake Michigan perch (about ½-1 pound each). Here are the steps;

1) Scaling - Using a knife(not necessarily real sharp) or a fish scaler, scrape from the tail towards the head. This is best done out-of-doors, since the scales fly around. Actually some fish(like salmon and sanddabs) can be scaled with the spray from a garden hose nozzle. It's quick and easy.

2) Gutting - This is actually the same as the beginnings of field dressing. Open the belly from anal vent to gills.

3) Be-Heading - The entrails are slid forward and out of the body cavity, and then with a sharp knife, cut perpendicular to the backbone at the top of the gill cover, cut off the entrails, gills and head.

4) Rinsing - Rinse inside and outside of fish after removing red flesh in body cavity(see Field Dressing above).

5) Fish is now ready for cooking and preserving.

## Filleting

Filleting is simple and has many advantages. For example, scaling is not necessary since the skin(and scales) will be removed. It can and often is done without even gutting or field dressing the fish first. It produces boneless or almost bone-free slabs of meat. And filleting works great on fish of all sizes and both round bodied and flat bodied fish.

Here are the steps in filleting;

1) Make the first cut just behind the gills. Cut down to the backbone, then turn the knife toward the tail of the fish and slice above the spine(feeling for it as you proceed) all the way to the tail. One flank of the fish will now be removed. Flip the fish over and repeat the process. This step is illustrated below.

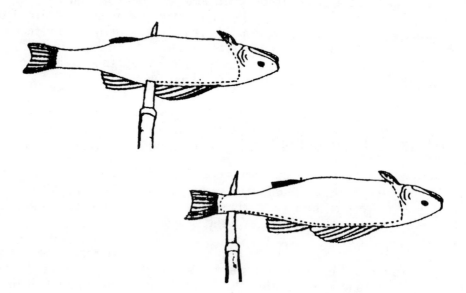

2) Now cut away the rib cage from each fillet. Insert the knife at the top of the rib cage and slice down following close to ribs.

3) Lastly, remove the skin. Lay fillet skin side down on cutting board. Insert the knife just about $\frac{1}{4}$" from the tail and cut down to the skin. Now, firmly holding the tail-end, turn the blade forward and work the knife along the skin, "lifting" the meat from the skin all the way to the large end of the fillet.

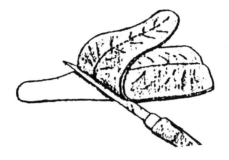

With a little practice, filleting becomes second nature. For a great visual display, watch the pros do it when a party boat docks after a day of fishing. You'll be amazed. Successful filleting depends on two things, once you understand the principles. One: use a good fish fillet knife. Two: keep the knife very sharp.

## Steaking

Steaking simply means cutting a fish into similar-sized parts by making parallel cuts that are all perpendicular to the spine! Just joking! I know only math freaks and geometry teachers could understand that definition.

The first step in steaking(which, by the way, is usually reserved only for large fish) is to remove the head(this is done after field dressing), right at the gill cover. Now just lay the fish flat and divide it into about one inch thick pieces. The tail section(where the steaks are small) can be filleted. Some varieties need to be scaled before steaking.

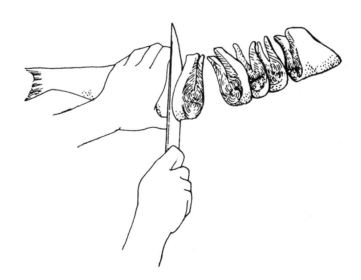

# Keeping Fish Fresh

Fish is delicious. But it is also one of the most perishable of foods. So, from the time a fish is caught until it is served, care must be taken to preserve its freshness.

## Freshness on the Water

If possible, the best way to keep a fish fresh, while continuing to fish, is to keep your catch alive. This can be done in several ways;

- For pan fish, use a collapsible basket. A fully submerged burlap bag also will serve the purpose.

- The best stringers are those that have large safety pin type clasps, and some type of swivel mechanism so fish are less likely to get twisted up.

- The proper stringing technique is to run the stringer through both the upper and lower lip. This allows the fish to open and close its mouth, thereby forcing water through its gills to breathe. Never run a stringer through the fishes gills. This prevents it from closing its mouth and therefore starving it of oxygen.

- Let out the full stringer. Even add a rope, if extra length is needed to keep the fish down deep in the water. The water is cooler and more oxygenated down deeper.

- If you move your boat quickly, lift the stringer out of the water during a short trip.

- Surf and river anglers, who use a stringer, move the fish along with them, always placing them back into the deepest water available.

- When using a creel, bed and surround fish in dry grass. Canvas creels or fishing vests should be moist to maintain coolness.

There are some cautions to watch when keeping fish in water;

- Stringered fish have been known to have been eaten by turtles. Never string fish in warm water. Summertime surface water temperatures in some Southern California lakes are in the 80's!

. Stringers are taboo in salt waters. It's just feeding the sharks. Rather, use a cooler or fish-box, preferably with ice in it.

## Freshness During Travel

If you're traveling for any length of time, follow these simple steps to insure freshness;

. Field dress the fish.

. Dry the fish thoroughly.

. Cover each fish with foil or plastic.

. Surround each package of fish, in a cooler, with crushed ice or cubed ice.

## Refrigeration

Fish do not do particularly well under prolonged refrigeration. So it's best to either eat fresh caught fish, or freeze them. Refrigerated fish should be covered with heavy foil, freezer paper or plastic to prevent moisture from escaping.

## Freezing

There are basically two ways to freeze fresh fish. With either approach you can freeze whole-field cleaned fish, fish fillets, steaks or chunks.

The first method is more conventional. Wrap fish in packaging materials with high barriers to moisture and vapor transmission. A good quality freezer wrapping paper or heavy foil is recommended. Wrap tightly and tape securely. This method is adequate. Defrost slowly in a refrigerator. Better flavor and preservation can be achieved by repeatedly dipping and freezing unwrapped fish in water until a layer of ice is formed. Then wrap securely.

Actually, the best and simplest way to freeze fish is to utilize old milk cartons or similar liquid holding containers. Fresh and well-cleaned fish can be placed in the container up to an inch from the top. Now, simply fill the container with water(or a brine solution of 1/3 cup of table salt to one gallon of water) and shake to make sure there are no air bubbles. Seal up container and freeze. Thawing is best done on a drain rack so fish does not sit in cold water.

Date fish packages you put in your freezer. Store it at 0°F or lower and plan to use it within two months, for best flavor.

# Cooking Fish

There are numerous fish cook books jam-packed with recipes. But matching your favorite catch to an unfamiliar or inappropriate recipe often leads to less than enjoyable eating. Rather than special recipes, successful fish cooking depends on adhering to two simple principles;

1) Know when the fish is done - too often fish is over-cooked.

2) Match cooking method to the fish flavor, fish size and fat level.

First, let's address the "when fish is done" issue. Fish, by its very nature is more tender than red meat or poultry. It doesn't contain fibers that need to be broken down by extensive cooking. Some cooking experts say fish should be considered more like egg, than like meat. So, as in cooking egg, just enough heat need be applied to firm-up the protein. Over-cooking makes eggs tough and dry; it does the same for fish.

So how do you tell when fish is cooked for just the right length of time? It's easy. Fish is cooked properly when it flakes when probed with a fork. By flaking, I mean separated into its natural layers or divisions. This test should be done often, at the center, or thickest part of the fish fillet, steak or whole fish.

## Matching Fish to Cooking Method

Now the second key principle of successful fish cooking. That is, matching the specific fish to the specific cooking method. Fish caught in Southern California have a wide variety of flavor levels, fish size and fat level. Typically, all fish is considered a low-fat source of protein. But there are pronounced differences in fat content that do affect taste and texture. Flavor level also varies generally from very mild to quite pronounced. This influences cooking method and seasoning selection. Fortunately, all these fish can be grouped into four cooking categories

**Category One:** Here are the delicate, mild flavored, lean and generally small cuts of fish. Specific examples include sole, flounder and halibut. Cuts of fish in this category are generally thin and oval shaped. The exception is halibut which is thicker and has a heavier texture.

Category One fish are very good sauteed. Sole fillets are so delicate that some only need to be cooked on one side. A flour coating promotes browning. Thicker cuts can have a flour, crumb, cornmeal or egg-wash coating before frying. Oven frying or foil baking also works well, as does poaching.